MANITOBA STUDIES IN NATIVE HISTORY

Manitoba Studies in Native History publishes new scholarly interpretations of the historical experience of native peoples in the western interior of North America. The series is under the editorial direction of a board representative of the scholarly and native communities of Manitoba.

The New Peoples: Being and Becoming Métis in North America

Edited by
Jacqueline Peterson
Jennifer S.H. Brown

 MINNESOTA HISTORICAL SOCIETY PRESS

© The University of Manitoba Press 1985
Winnipeg, Manitoba R3T 2N2

Published in the United States in 2001 by the Minnesota Historical Society Press, St. Paul

10 9 8 7 6 5 4 3 2

www.mhspress.org
The Minnesota Historical Society Press is a member of the Association of
American University Presses.

♾ The paper used in this publication meets the minimum requirements of the American
National Standard for Information Sciences—Permanence for Printed Library Materials,
ANSI Z39.48—1984.

International Standard Book Number
ISBN 13: 978-0-87351-408-8 (paperback)
ISBN 10: 0-87351-408-4 (paperback)

Cover illustration: Horse cruppers with quillworked pattern typical of those used by Red
River Métis (National Museum of Man, Ottawa, No.V-X-290).

Library of Congress Cataloging-in-Publication Data

The new peoples : being and becoming métis in North America /
edited by Jacqueline Peterson, Jennifer S.H. Brown.
      p. cm. — (Manitoba studies in native history ; 1)
    U.S. ed. originally published: Lincoln : University of Nebraska Press, c1985.
    Includes bibliographical references and index.
    ISBN 0-87351-408-4 (pbk. : alk. paper)
  1. Métis.
  2. Indians of North America—Mixed descent.
  I. Peterson, Jacqueline, 1943-.
  II. Brown, Jennifer S. H., 1940-.
  III. Manitoba studies in native history (St. Paul, Minn.) ; 1.

    E99.M47 N48 2001
    971.00497—dc21

                                                              2001032993

This series is published with the financial support of the people of Manitoba, the Honourable Eugene Kostyra, Minister of Culture, Heritage and Recreation.

Research for the volume was supported by the National Endowment for the Humanities
and by the Social Sciences and Humanities Research Council of Canada. Publication was
assisted by a gift from the D'Arcy McNickle Center for the History of the American Indian,
the Newberry Library, Chicago, Illinois, and from the Canada Council.

Manitoba Studies in Native History Board of Directors: J. Burelle, D. Dul, D. Fontaine,
G. Friesen, E. Harper, E. LaRocque, R. McKay, W. Moodie, G. Schultz.

Contents

Continued

Continued

Illustrations

Continued

PLATES

Foreword

To many North Americans it may appear extraordinary that a man coming from a country as remote as France should have focused his attention at the beginning of his career on a general survey of the problems created by the presence of a sizeable halfbreed population in the western prairie provinces of Canada. Having been kindly invited to participate in the scholarly meeting on the métis in North America at the Newberry Library in September, 1981, I found in that friendly and interesting symposium an opportunity to expound on how I had come to feel so much interest in the racial questions concerning western Canada and, by way of comparison, the middle western states.

My interest was awakened at the end of World War I by my first contacts with some American students who were temporarily discharged of their military duties and were studying in a small university in the south of France where I had been enrolled for two years. Since all of those students came from Wisconsin and Minnesota, it occurred to me that this part of America, so completely unknown in France, might provide a possible field of study for someone who was not familiar with its past history and its problems. But my attention was still more attracted, for reasons which I cannot explain, by the seemingly empty spaces, so full of economic possibilities nowadays, which extend north of the international boundary. When I first came to America, in 1934, through the financial help of the Rockefeller Foundation, I was determined to explore whatever possibilities this boundless territory might afford for a scholarly study bearing on a question which had not yet been thoroughly investigated.

Travelling across the western prairie provinces of Canada, I had the opportunity to speak with people of various conditions and origins, and the conversations, added to a considerable amount of reading, made me aware of local problems, the importance of which I had hardly suspected and which were deeply involved in the historical beginnings of the West. I then discovered that these problems were linked to the existence of a large population descended from the early contacts of the whites and natives during the fur trade era. The very hard fate of a considerable number of those mixed breeds, their destitute condition in many cases, and the marginal status to which many were apparently reduced, coupled with the complete lack of sympathy which they encountered among white people, whether French- or English-speaking, struck my imagination and led me to the conclusion that a complete study of their origin and history was necessary to explain their present situation.

The first stage of my work was mainly on-the-spot observation among people whom I had no difficulty approaching and questioning, thanks to the help of the missionaries of the various parishes which I visited. From Manitoba to Alberta I could thus acquire a notable amount of information concerning the living conditions of the métis groups and their relations with the whites. Among other things, I noticed that the métis who had reached a certain social and educational level had a tendency to look down upon the humbler ones and to reject any racial affiliation with them, while denying their own origins in order to avoid any possible confusion. (This was in the 1930s.)

The work of observation which I pursued was associated with a close study of all the documents accessible in those newly born provinces. I did not find much in the libraries, but the "codex historicus" (the daily journals written by the missionaries who in succession took charge of the western missions after their foundation) was an invaluable source of documentation. So was the correspondence of some of their most prominent bishops. And, thus, my visit to the parishes and missions of the West, which I expected would open to me only a field of direct observation, turned out to open as well a remarkable field of scholarly research.

Consequently, when I came back to France, I had gathered a good initial background which enabled me to start building up the general scheme I had in view. Of course this background had to be completed with the Ottawa records and other archival collections in America, but chiefly with the vast reserve of documents which are in Paris – namely the colonial archives and manuscripts, map collections and printed material of the National Library – and above all the rich and varied source materials of the Hudson's Bay Company in London, plus the less important sources of the British Colonial Office. If I were to judge the degree of interest of the various sources which

I have used, I would think that the Hudson's Bay Company records (now in Winnipeg) and the "codices historici" of the numerous missions of the western provinces deserve special mention as being particularly important. These documents are of uneven quality since their worth depends mostly on the capacities and concerns of those who wrote them. But when the author was a careful and perceptive observer, the documents may have an exceptional interest.

The difficulty was finally to have my study accepted by the University of Paris as the subject of my state doctorate. Many of the masters at the Sorbonne objected to it. The subject, le métis canadien et son rôle dans l'histoire des provinces de l'ouest, appeared to them too remote, of too limited a scope, to arouse any interest. The man who supported me and approved of the subject without reserve was a non-university man, but he had great intellectual influence. His name, André Siegfried, used to be well known in the United States and Canada on account of his publications.[1] He is in fact the man who was responsible for the shaping of my whole career. But the greatest reward which I have derived from the ten-year effort devoted to completing this work (begun in 1935 and published in 1945) is the interest which this book, so long out of print, has finally aroused among American and Canadian scholars. I hope that it may contribute to the birth of a growing number of specialized studies which will not only enrich this general field of investigation, but may also suggest satisfactory solutions to the social problems which I found to be so acute years ago in many parts of the western provinces.

Marcel Giraud

NOTE

1 André Siegfried (1875–1959) was a political economist who wrote two books on Canada: *Le Canada, les deux races: problèmes politiques contemporains* (1906), and *Canada* (1937), both later published in English. Frank H. Underhill, in the Carleton Library edition of the former book, retranslated in 1966 under the title, *The Race Question in Canada* (Toronto, McClelland and Stewart), describes him as "the Tocqueville of Canada." The races in question were the French and English; Siegfried did not explore questions concerning the native peoples of Canada. (Editors' note.)

Acknowledgements

We are indebted to a number of individuals and institutions for their help in bringing *The New Peoples* into being. The book's foundation – the 1981 first Conference on the Métis in North America – was securely laid through the assistance of a research grant from the National Endowment for the Humanities. The Newberry Library D'Arcy McNickle Center for the History of the American Indian in Chicago, Illinois, has been a friend and generous contributor to the project from its initial willingness to host the conference to, most recently, preparation of the index. We especially wish to thank Richard H. Brown, academic vice president of the Newberry Library; Francis S. Jennings, former director of the McNickle Center; Raymond D. Fogelson, advisory board member; and the other members of the staff, fellows and advisors for their support.

Jeanne Oyawin Eder, a former McNickle fellow and currently head of American Indian Studies, Eastern Montana College, deserves special credit for sharing her invaluable knowledge and advice as a coordinator of the 1981 conference. Many of the ideas first proposed and discussed at the conference have continued to grow and to influence the development of this volume. We are especially grateful to participants Antoine S. Lussier, Arthur J. Ray, Carol Judd, Jeanne Eder, Dennis Demontigny, Lionel Demontigny, Ronald Bourgeault and David Beaulieu for their suggestions and discussions. We also wish to thank Gerald Friesen for his interest in the book manuscript and his recommendation that it be included in the new Manitoba Studies in Native History series. The skillful weaving of this diverse collection into whole cloth, a task which was accomplished with patience and clarity, belongs to Carol Dahlstrom and the staff of the University of Manitoba Press. To them, to Gerri Balter of the University of Minnesota for typing the manuscript, to

Victor Lytwyn for preparing the maps, to Diane Warner for carefully compiling the index, and to the countless others who gave us their time and spirit, we extend our heartfelt gratitude.

Danny Wanyande, 1919. See *Grande Cache: The Historic Development of an Indigenous Alberta Métis Population* by Trudy Nicks and Kenneth Morgan, pages 163–181. (Photo courtesy of Public Archives Canada.)

James Ross and his wife, Maggy Smith. See *"What if Mama is an Indian?": The Cultural Ambivalence of the Alexander Ross Family* by Sylvia Van Kirk, pages 207–217. (Photo courtesy of Provincial Archives of Manitoba.)

Descendants of Gabriel Azure: Peter Azure and his nephew, Bert Azure (on guitar) play music in Everett Thompson's Saloon in Zortman, Montana. See *Waiting for a Day that Never Comes: The Dispossessed Métis of Montana* by Verne Dusenberry, pages 119–136. (Photo by Verne Dusenberry.)

The Hon. James McKay of Deer Lodge (with whip in his hand). See *The Métis and Mixed-Bloods of Rupert's Land Before 1870* by Irene Spry, pages 95–118. (Photo courtesy of Provincial Archives of Manitoba.)

Petitioner William Moore. See *Treaty No. 9 and Fur Trade Company Families: Northeastern Ontario's Halfbreeds, Indians, Petitioners and Métis* by John S. Long, pages 137–162. (Photo courtesy of Mr. Harry Moore.)

The Cadotte homes at Biddle Point, Mackinac Island, showing early style of building, made of logs and covered with cedar bark. See *Many Roads to Red River: Métis Genesis in the Great Lakes Region, 1680–1815* by Jacqueline Peterson, pages 37–71. (Taken from Edwin Orin Wood, *Historic Mackinac*, 2 vols. [New York: The MacMillan Company, 1918] 2:408, facing page.)

St. Gabriel Street Church, Montreal. See *Diverging Identities: The Presbyterian Métis of St. Gabriel Street, Montreal* by Jennifer S.H. Brown, pages 195–206. (Photo courtesy of the Archives of The United Church of Canada, Victoria University, Toronto, Ontario.)

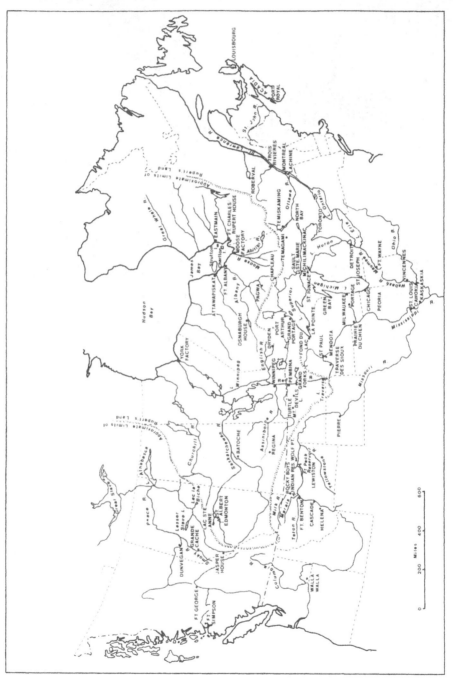

The métis landscape. (Map by Victor Lytwyn.)

The New Peoples

Introduction

Jacqueline Peterson and Jennifer S.H. Brown

At what historic moment and by what means does a "people" spring into being? This is an especially pertinent question for the western hemisphere, and one of great significance and sensitivity for those peoples who would be "nations." One North American mythmaker, Frederick Jackson Turner, found the autochthonous origins of the American people on the frontier, where detached from European parentage and nourished by a vast and unspoiled land, an American national identity grew from the soil, as transplanted immigrants were "fused . . . into a mixed race."[1]

This is a compelling image of national genesis precisely because of its mythic quality. However, a much older and more fundamental process was at work in the western hemisphere which the Turnerian myth and its variants have been loath to glorify. The New World was neither new nor uninhabited and what fusion occurred involved far more than the mixing of European immigrants upon the soil of North and South America. Rather, following the invasion and colonization of the American Indian worlds by various European nation states, nearly four centuries of inter-mingling and intermarriage between Indian and European produced ample opportunity for the genesis of composite "mestizo" populations and the creation of bold and startlingly original ethnic and national identities throughout the two continents.

In Latin America, such hybrid groups are now the dominant popula-tions, a fact which has somehow been lost on most English-speaking North Americans who are accustomed to thinking in terms of "Spanish- and Portuguese-speaking" peoples to the south. It is nonetheless true that the rise of the "new peoples," as Brazilian anthropologist Darcy Ribeiro has so appropriately named them, is the most significant historical consequence of the wrenching collision and entanglement of the Old World with the New.[2] It also appears certain that despite Latin America's continued domination by Euro-American financial interests and ethnic minorities, the future identity and direction of many of its post-colonial and post-revolutionary nations belong to the "new peoples."

In North America, by contrast, both the historical process of mixing and the resultant peoples themselves have been obscured. Persons of mixed Indian and European ancestry who, for whatever reasons, are not regarded as either Indian or white are referred to, often pejoratively, as "halfbreeds," "breeds," "mixed-bloods," "métis," "michif" or "non-status Indian." Collectively, they are characterized by an almost universal land-lessness and an oppressive poverty, conditions which historically have inhibited political combination or action. Until the 1982 passage of Canada's Constitution Act, they lacked the potential benefits or even the hope of legal recognition as a separate native people everywhere except in the province of Alberta.[3] As late as 1980, one such group in Canada could refer to themselves, not without irony, as North America's "non-people."

It was not always so. A century ago, in 1885, at a fording place called Batoche on the Saskatchewan River, the local métis inhabitants under the leadership of Louis Riel and Gabriel Dumont took up arms against the Dominion of Canada in defence of their rights to the soil and to self-government. In what has become known as the North West Rebellion, they were defeated, just as an earlier nationalistic resistance by the métis at Red River was put down in 1869–70. Thus did the dream of "la nation métisse" – "the new nation" – die on the gallows with Riel in 1885, ensuring the orderly sweep of Anglo-American settlement across the western prairies.

These events are familiar to students of the history of Canada and the northwestern United States.[4] However, as the twelve essays in this volume demonstrate, the history of the métis peoples runs deeper and more broadly across the North American landscape than has previously been acknowledged. In the aftermath of the Red River and North West Rebellions, several thousand métis suffered widespread demoralization, loss of lands and status and dispersal to marginal rural areas and the peripheries of Indian reserves on both sides of the international border. Yet, in many locales, community life and métis collective identity persisted. By 1909, former associates and contemporaries of Louis Riel had helped to found the Union Nationale Métisse St.-Joseph de Manitoba, whose efforts to collect and record métis recollections of the important events of

1869–70 and 1885 were rewarded by the publication of A.-H. de Trémaudan's *History of the Métis Nation in Western Canada*.[5] A decade later, provincial métis associations had been established in Alberta and Saskatchewan, and in 1945 the first full-scale scholarly history of the métis appeared: Marcel Giraud's monumental *Le Métis canadien: son rôle dans l'histoire des provinces de l'Ouest*.[6]

At the time of Giraud's study, *métis* (meaning *mixed*) was a term which, when used by French speakers, applied broadly to the offspring of Indian and white parentage, but more specifically to the French- and Cree-speaking descendants of the Red River métis. The word *métis* was rarely applied, on an individual basis, to persons of English-Indian or non-French and Indian ancestry, nor was it generally extended in its collective usage to mixed populations outside western Canada or to those with no historical connection with the Red River group. Even in its Manitoba heartland, the term was rarely used by English speakers before the 1960s.[7] In the United States, the word itself was virtually unknown.

Twenty years later, *métis* had burst its linguistic and geographical confines. By the 1970s, it had come to signify, in certain parts of Canada and in the northern border states of the United States, any person of mixed Indian-white ancestry who identified him- or herself and was identified by others as neither Indian nor white, even though he or she might have no provable link to the historic Red River métis. Such an enlarged usage poses certain problems. It differs from the racial classifications of the United States government, and from those of Canada on the federal level until 1982, which have insisted that anyone of native ancestry who is not an enrolled Indian is legally white, no allowances being made for natives "in between." Perhaps more seriously, the substitution of the French-language "métis" for its English language counterparts, "halfbreed" and "mixed-blood," while semantically more accurate because it does not carry the freight of a phony and damning folk biology, would seem to confuse or muddle an historically based political and ethnic identity with the genetic attributes of individuals, regardless of their ethnic or cultural identities.

On the other hand, the broader usage recalls Marcel Giraud's suggestion that the processes and conditions which caused the métis to coalesce at Red River as a self-conscious ethnic group were rooted in both an historic past and a wider geographical frame, just as the processes of ethnic formation or "métisation" continued after 1885, often independent of the Red River métis. The Alberta Métis Association gave recognition to this larger phenomenon at its founding in 1932, by offering membership to anyone of native ancestry.[8] Similarly, Richard Slobodin, in his 1966 publication,

Métis of the Mackenzie District, enlarged the scholarly focus on métis culture and identity by applying the term *métis* both to those with Red River roots and to the more northerly first- and second-generation subarctic mixed-bloods with part-British, Hawaiian and other ancestries who shared a collective identity.[9]

Discussions about whether to capitalize "métis" as in the English-language usage for national identities ("Canadian," "German" or the etymologically falsified "Indian" for native North Americans) or to retain the lower-case usage of the original French term as an inclusive category reflect continuing debates and difficulties over terminology and definition. The Métis National Council, in its opening statement to the United Nations Working Group on Indigenous Populations in August 1984 in Geneva, pinpointed semantic differences between "Métis" and "métis": "Written with a small 'm,' metis is a racial term for anyone of mixed Indian and European ancestry. Written with a capital 'M,' Metis is a socio-cultural or political term for those originally of mixed ancestry who evolved into a distinct indigenous people during a certain historical period in a certain region in Canada."[10] In this book, for the sake of editorial consistency, the term is lower-cased throughout, on the French model, since, in many or indeed most instances, authors are using the term for people whose inclusion in the Métis Nation would be problematic. To attempt a dual usage (Métis/métis) would be to take it upon ourselves to decide who belongs to socio-political categories that are still subject to redefinition and evolution. For the Métis National Council, the "Métis" people form "a distinct indigenous nation with a history, culture and homeland in western Canada," consisting specifically of the descendants of those who were dispossessed by Canadian government actions from 1870 on.[11] The Native Council of Canada, however, formed in 1971 "to represent the interests of the Métis and Non-Status Indian people across Canada," uses "Métis" more inclusively, arguing that those people "who base their claims on national rights rather than aboriginal rights . . . undermine the aboriginal rights of all Metis people."[12] On these issues, we can only warn that history is still being made.

The increasing tendency of groups and writers in the United States and Canada to use "métis" to describe mixed Indian/white communities or populations which share a collective identity accordingly should not be allowed to obscure the fact that disagreement continues over whether the term is appropriate for mixed peoples outside western Canada, or, for that matter, English-speaking groups within the prairie provinces. Such disagreement may itself be taken as an indicator of genuine historical complexities. Contrast and disjunction indeed appear to mark the histories, cultures and ethnic formulations of numerous regionally and ethnically diverse biracial groups, some of which have only recently begun to identify themselves as "métis." But the existence and numerical significance of these peoples are undeniable on both sides of the border. Their numbers, if non-status Indians are included, may approach 750,000 persons in Canada and 250,000 in the Great Lakes and northern plains regions of the United States. Since 1965, métis associations and federations, some of them also representing non-status Indians, have been founded in every Canadian province and in the states of Michigan, Minnesota, North Dakota, Montana and Washington. In Canada on the national level, the Native Council of Canada has spoken for métis aboriginal rights since 1971, as noted before, while the Métis National Council, formed in 1983, has espoused the concept of métis nationhood.[13]

Aside from the political motives for these resurgences – what Joe Sawchuk has called the "political reformulation" of métis identity[14] – many heretofore invisible and submerged groups are also rediscovering and expressing a shared past with deep roots. Between August 31 and September 3, 1979, for instance, the métis people of Montana gathered in Lewistown, Montana, to celebrate the centennial of the town's founding by métis settlers in 1879 and to reaffirm their cultural and ethnic identity along with others from Idaho, the Dakotas and Canada. At Belcourt, North Dakota, two "michif" women of the Turtle Mountain Chippewa Reservation have recently compiled a dictionary of their own language which is spoken widely there and elsewhere.[15]

These are compelling signs of a people, or perhaps several peoples, each with a history and cultural identity. Yet their history, particularly in the United States, remains for the most part unwritten. In Canada, research and writing on the métis has tended to be regionally based and particularistic, focusing largely on the Red River métis and their descendants.[16] Left to their own devices, historians might well have missed the changing dimensions of métis identity over the last several decades. However, the activities of métis groups and individuals in the United States and Canada since the mid 1970s have roused the scholarly community to probe more deeply.[17]

The realization in 1980 that significant work was underway on both sides of the border, but that few of the researchers involved were familiar with one another's work, led to the call for a first conference on the métis in North America to be held at the Newberry Library in Chicago. With the assistance of the National Endowment for the Humanities and the Social

Sciences and Humanities Research Council of Canada, twenty-six Canadian and American scholars representing the disciplines of history, anthropology, linguistics, economics, geography, literature and education gathered in early September, 1981 to honour the pathbreaking work of Marcel Giraud and to attempt to synthesize the research accomplishments of the previous decade. It was hoped that in a preliminary way, the exchange of ideas among conference participants – some of them métis themselves – might illuminate the process of ethnogenesis in North America, of how new ethnicities and new nationalities come into being. *The New Peoples* is a product of that memorable meeting and dialogue.

The papers contained in this volume are organized into four parts, representing the broad historical, comparative and cultural themes that emerged during the 1981 Newberry Library conference as central to current métis studies. Questions of origins come first. In Part I, Olive Dickason, Jacqueline Peterson and John Foster address, from varied perspectives, issues of métis roots and emergence in the contexts of New France, early Great Lakes history and the westward-moving Canadian fur trade.

Dickason relates early French efforts "to use racial intermixing as an instrument of empire" to the invisibility of eastern métis in the traditional historiography of eastern Canada. Church-sanctioned unions between French men and native women were accompanied by baptismal renamings obscuring the wives' origins; children were similarly baptized with French names, hence being unidentifiable as métis. Children of unsanctioned mixed unions, on the other hand, received no official recognition in the records, leading again to a dearth of written evidence for métissage in New France. Yet contemporary observations on the extent of intermarriage, both sanctioned and unsanctioned, and, in particular, the thunderings of the clergy against the *libertinage* of their French charges among the Indians, indicate extensive racial mixing, even though sociocultural means of acknowledging its human consequences as a new category – métis – were absent. Official opposition to interracial marriages of all kinds became prevalent in New France in the early eighteenth century, and this attitude tended to reinforce pressures against the recognition of a distinctive intermediate racial group.

Dickason observes that conditions were different in the Old Northwest, around and beyond the Great Lakes, however, and at this point Jacqueline Peterson takes up the story. Drawing on her studies of early fur-trade-based communities around the Great Lakes – Detroit, Chicago, Green Bay, Michilimackinac and others – Peterson demonstrates that their real founders were biracial families that grew and flourished as traders, suppliers to the trade and intercultural brokers and buffers between European and Indian societies. They combined wilderness skills with small-scale gardening on waterfront lots, the use of moccasins and feathers with pantaloons, capot and woven sash, and the consumption of crepes with the harvesting of maple sugar. Their intersecting lineages and growing endogamy, their rapidly increasing numbers, their relative isolation from New France and their distinctive lifestyle all justify Peterson's description of them as a new people, and as a vivid example of ethnogenesis – the birth of a new ethnic group – the ramifications of which we are just beginning to understand.

John Foster concludes Part I by broadening our perspectives on the problems of tracing métis roots in all their complexity and diversity. Métis origins, both around the Great Lakes and in more westerly and northerly regions in later years, may uniformly be traced to the fur trade. Yet métis history, like Indian history, is beset by problems of reconstruction. Few métis generated their own documents. Most records before the late nineteenth century come from outside observers, and have in turn been used and interpreted by outsiders whose inter-cultural perspectives have often been deficient. Foster urges the increased application of new techniques being developed in quantitative and oral history, and the utilization of anthropological frameworks, notably the conceptualizations of Fredrik Barth, as aids to overcoming these problems. He goes on to raise questions about the localized emergence of distinct métis groups, not just around the Great Lakes but on the northern plains, in the Great Slave Lake and Mackenzie regions, and also (although denoted by different terms) in the Hudson Bay lowlands.

Foster notes that the roles of the *gens libres* ("free men" or ex-employees of the Montreal trade) merit special attention in the search for sources of a métis sense of separateness. And he suggests that much may be learned from examining and defining the mores, values and shared experiences that characterized three interacting fur trade social spheres or subsocieties: the worlds of adult men, of adult women and of families as units – building on the studies of fur trade women and families already accomplished by Sylvia Van Kirk and Jennifer Brown (who are also contributors to this volume).

The three papers in Part II bear out Foster's point that métis peoples have had diverse origins and histories, forming a variety of distinctive communities in widely separated areas of the north. John S. Long presents a detailed discussion of the history of a forgotten people, the James Bay descendants of Hudson's Bay Company [HBC] men and the Cree or "homeguard" women with whom they founded families in the decades after the coming of HBC traders to Hudson Bay in the 1670s. Male descendants of these families were by the early 1800s a notable category among HBC employees and, after 1840, some also found roles as native clergy and catechists. Yet in both church and fur trade, they tended to be confined to the lower echelons.

Between 1900 and 1910, the coming of fur trade opposition (Revillon Frères) to James Bay, the building of and projections for new rail lines to the south, and HBC retrenchments brought a more diversified and precarious economy to this corner of northeastern Ontario. Treaty Number 9, negotiated in 1905–06, entailed the surrender of northern Indian lands in consideration of the railroad's arrival, and the government assumption of treaty and relief obligations. The "halfbreeds" of Moose Factory, however, were excluded from treaty rights on "grounds that they were not living the Indian mode of life." Some of them petitioned the Ontario government for compensation, but no settlement of their claims or of the broader question of their status was reached. The case shows in microcosm the complexity of the question, who are the native people?, and illustrates the inadequacy of arbitrary government decisions about who was eligible and ineligible for treaty status. Some James Bay natives now cast their lot with the Ontario Métis and Non-Status Indian Association, adopting on the basis of their mixed ancestry a political identity that is new to this northeastern region.

Irene M. Spry focuses her attention on the community that in its genesis and history was most critical to the coalescence of a collective and conspicuous métis political and cultural identity – Red River (present-day Winnipeg) before 1870. In contradistinction to some other scholars, she emphasizes the solidarity and communal spirit that linked the various mixed-blood sectors of that community – the Protestant English and Scotch "halfbreeds" and the French Catholic métis – as expressed in intermarriages, linguistic and cultural blendings, friendships, and involvement in shared businesses and occupations, whether freighting or the buffalo hunt. In the free trade campaigns of the 1840s and 1850s, Anglophone and French métis cooperated in petitioning the HBC and the British Colonial Office for extensions of their economic rights.

Instead of cleavages among the mixed-bloods of Red River, Spry finds two other deep divisions, non-racially based. The first is that between the educated wealthy gentry, professionals, and retired HBC officers, and the group comprised of "unlettered, unpropertied natives of the country." The second separated the sedentary, professional farmer from the mobile plains hunter and trader. These basic splits were greatly deepened after 1870 when the arrival of surveyors, Ontario settlers and new modes of governance disrupted forever the equilibrium and consensus of the old Red River community. Its history is unique. Yet its changing configuration and eventual fragmentation under external pressures – themes that recur in Sylvia Van Kirk's analysis of the Ross family in this volume – had vast implications for western Canadian history.

Verne Dusenberry's article, "Waiting for a Day that Never Comes," is reprinted here for its poignant portrayal of the dispossessed métis of Montana. A pioneering statement when it first appeared (in 1958, in *Montana, the Magazine of Western History* 8(2), pp. 26-39), the essay remains of special value for its synthesis of oral and documentary data on Montana's "Landless Indians" – people of French and Cree or Chippewa descent with roots in the early Great Lakes fur trade and in the Red River region. By the time of Louis Riel's provisional government in 1869–70, many of these métis were already traders and buffalo hunters ranging from Pembina to Turtle Mountain (North Dakota) and along the tributaries of the Missouri River into Montana where they formed several new settlements. It was no mere chance that both Riel and Gabriel Dumont later found a welcome in Montana during their periods of exile.

From the 1880s on, the Montana métis were increasingly people in between – neither white nor enrolled as Indians – while suffering the destitution that followed upon the loss of the buffalo and other wild resources, as white settlement advanced. Dusenberry's record of his conversations with Joseph Dussome, president of "The Landless Indians of Montana," affords a portrait of an outcaste community of American métis that persisted despite great odds. Having long sought a land settlement with the United States government, they are still, as a sympathetic Indian agent wrote in 1903, "waiting for a day that never comes."

The final community study in Part II is Trudy Nicks's and Kenneth Morgan's analysis of the Grande Cache métis in western Alberta. This population originated with independent trappers or "freemen," including a number of Iroquois and métis, who began to occupy the area in the early nineteenth century. They formed scattered regional bands of 150 to 500 people, who during each fall and winter were dispersed in small, extended families, and assembled in larger groups in spring and summer. Their flexible residence patterns and relative isolation gave them a certain invisibility and has meant that their numbers, like those of similar groups elsewhere, have tended to be underestimated. Statistical analyses of available data document the endogenous growth of this population which, although dispersed, was generally characterized by endogamy, multiple kinship linkages, and common occupations and lifestyle.

For many years, the Grande Cache people had intermittent and optional contacts with the outside world, cultivating as their patrons traders, missionaries, forestry officials and others who mediated between them and Euro-Canadian society. The twentieth century, however, brought great changes – the creation of Jasper National Park in 1907 and the concomitant eviction of native "squatters" inside its boundaries, the coming of the Grand Trunk Pacific Railroad in 1911, legislation to register traplines in the 1930s, subsequent problems concerning métis land titles in the Grande Cache area, and the advent of construction and mining activities that disrupted hunting and trapping. Confronted with these accumulated pressures, the people of Grande Cache, later than many less isolated groups, began in the 1970s to associate themselves with the Métis Association of Alberta as their patron, and with the identity that this affiliation implies. Nicks and Morgan point out that this identity best fits "the perceptions which outsiders have historically had of the group" and affirms its longstanding distinctiveness from Indian groups, as well as providing a useful political affiliation.

The four papers in Part III have as a common theme the options, tensions and dilemmas that people of mixed ancestry could find themselves confronted with in those varied social, cultural and political contexts where a secure community base was either threatened or absent. Jennifer Brown notes that while modern ethnically based movements show strong centripetal tendencies, drawing people together by emphasizing some shared aspect of their ancestry, strong centrifugal forces often characterized the lives of potentially "métis" individuals in the fur trade past. The registers of the St. Gabriel Street Presbyterian Church in Montreal for the years between 1796 and 1835 contain the baptisms and/or burials of eighty-eight children of Montreal-based white fur traders and women "of the Indian Country." The traders named here, mostly Anglophone officers, were making highly selective decisions about which family members to bring or send to Montreal – decisions that typically resulted in familial fragmentation, as children, at an average age of six, were separated from one or both parents and from siblings for the long trip to eastern Canada. By a two-to-one margin, sons outnumbered daughters in these entries, a ratio that indicates these traders' preferences for granting opportunities for Euro-Canadian assimilation and education to males. Many of these boys must have remained in Montreal, judging by the disappearance of their names from fur trade records. Others eventually returned to the west, contributing in some instances (notably the example of Cuthbert Grant) to early métis nationalism. Daughters too followed divergent paths. The relatively few who travelled to Montreal seem to have remained in the east; many others remained with their native maternal kin as members of Indian and biracial communities. The St. Gabriel Street Church registers, in sum, tell of the centrifugal forces exercised on fur trade familial life, as individuals, subjected to paternal decision making and to other constraints involving particularly gender and familial economic resources, were drawn into widely varying adult roles and identities, despite their similar biracial heritage.

R. David Edmunds, in his study of attitudes toward métis groups in the old American Northwest, pursues the nineteenth-century fate of the communities whose origins Jacqueline Peterson traced earlier in this volume. In the United States, in contrast to western Canada, no rallying points developed around which métis nationalism and ethnic consciousness could persist. Rather, the pattern was again centrifugal – dispersal and submergence as American settlers and governmental structures overwhelmed their fur-trade-based predecessors. Edmunds documents the ethnocentrism of the intruders – their complaints that neither the Great Lakes Indians nor the métis had become farmers, and that both were culturally stagnant. Often the métis were severely criticized as quasi-Europeans who had yet failed to advance in accord with white Anglo-American values. The trouble was, Edmunds concludes, that the Great Lakes métis accepted the *wrong* European culture, that of the creole French. They were judged and set aside as failed Europeans. Their descendants either disappeared among growing local populations or migrated north and west to more remote areas.

Sylvia Van Kirk tells the story of one Red River biracial family as it experienced the changes, pressures, and prejudices that beset the nineteenth-century Canadian Northwest. The twelve children of retired fur trader Alexander Ross and Sally, his Okanagan Indian wife, grew up mainly in Red River where the family settled in 1825. Ross emphasized his family's religious instruction and education, and saw several of his children attain seeming assimilation into the Briticized upper levels of society. Four daughters married white men, and some of the sons did well as scholars, university students and holders of public office in Red River. Yet in the climate of the times, the children were sensitive and insecure about their standing, while devoted to their Indian mother. James, the most brilliant of the sons, early proved himself academically and professionally as lawyer and journalist, and advocated the amalgamation of Red River and the West into Canada. Yet the rise of métis activism under Louis Riel and escalating conflict with Canadian governmental authorities in 1869 presented hard choices. Ultimately James Ross became chief justice in Riel's provisional government, affirming the bonds of his native ancestry, yet unable fully to support Riel's actions. He died in 1871, after a stressful period in which his hopes for a role in the new Canadian regime, and then for recognition of the merits of the métis cause, were successively dashed. What Van Kirk calls the "cultural ambivalence" of the Ross family was fully and poignantly epitomized in the tormented course of James Ross's life.

Part IV addresses important but often neglected aspects of métis cultural heritage. John C. Crawford examines the question of métis linguistic distinctiveness on the basis of his studies of the language known as Michif at the Turtle Mountain Reservation in North Dakota. He argues that Michif merits study as both a product of language contact (notably French/Cree) and as a language or dialect (definitions vary) in its own right, exhibiting, as it does, a striking consistency and regularity. His paper makes it clear that linguistic distinctiveness is an important marker of métis ethnic identity, and one that seems to exhibit a fair time depth.

Ted J. Brasser takes up the subject of métis art and its cultural significance. For many years, the existence of such an art went unrecognized because museums classified its products under various tribal names. But Brasser has carefully traced the linkages of these materials with métis communities and especially with their Roman Catholic missions. He identifies the special characteristics of this art: primarily, quillworked and beaded floral and abstract decoration of leather garments, horse-gear and gun cases. Métis artisans and traders distributed these wares widely; and as suppliers of goods, they also disseminated a unique art style that is finally, thanks to Brasser and a few other scholars, achieving recognition.

In his afterword, Robert K. Thomas reviews the basic questions about "métis peoplehood" that underlie the papers in this volume. He notes, as we all must, the tremendous variability in métis historical experience, and in the very definitions of peoplehood that must be framed in dealing with the complexities of the past. Historical variability is reflected in the variability of scholarly points of view regarding, in particular, métis roots and origins. There is no consensus on this matter; nor, perhaps, can there be, given the "many histories" represented in this volume. Thomas urges the need for extensive further study to discover whether a broader consensus on origins may emerge, and to elucidate questions about how new peoples arise. He adds that the results of research done on the métis should be placed in a broader comparative framework, so that ethnogenesis in northern North America is not narrowly viewed as unique but is juxtaposed to experiences known from elsewhere in the hemisphere. We, as editors of this volume, hope that its publication begins to afford the materials needed to attain such broader perspectives, as well as enhance specific knowledge of a complicated and still-continuing aspect of the social history of northern North America.

NOTES

1 Frederick Jackson Turner, *The Frontier in American History* (New York: Henry Holt and Company, 1920, 1924), 22–23.
2 Darcy Ribeiro, *The Americas and Civilization,* trans. Linton Lomas Barrett and Marie McDavid Barrett (New York: E.P. Dutton and Co., 1972), 173–344.
3 The Constitution Act (section 35) defines Canada's aboriginal peoples as Indian, Inuit and métis.
4 See, for example: George F.G. Stanley, *The Birth of Western Canada: A History of the Riel Rebellions* (London: Longmans, Green and Co., 1936, reprint ed., Toronto: University of Toronto Press, 1960); Arthur S. Morton, *A History of the Canadian West to 1870–71* (Toronto: Thomas Nelson and Sons, 1939); and Joseph Kinsey Howard, *Strange Empire* (New York: Morrow, 1952).
5 A.-H. de Trémaudan, *History of the Métis Nation in Western Canada* (1936), translated by Elizabeth Maguet as *Hold High Your Heads* (Winnipeg: Pemmican Publications, 1982).
6 Marcel Giraud, *Le Métis canadien: son rôle dans l'histoire des provinces de l'Ouest* (Paris: Institut d'ethnologie, 1945). Les éditions du Blé (Winnipeg) has recently reissued the French text, and an English translation is in press at the University of Alberta Press (Edmonton).
7 Jean H. Lagassé, *The People of Indian Ancestry in Manitoba: a Social and Economic Study* (Winnipeg: Dept. of Agriculture and Immigration, 1959), vol. 1, pp. 54–56.
8 Murray Dobbin, *The One-and-a-Half Men: The Story of Jim Brady and Malcolm Norris* (Vancouver: New Star Books, 1981), 61.
9 Richard Slobodin, *Metis of the Mackenzie District* (Ottawa: Canadian Research Centre for Anthropology, 1966).
10 *The Metis Nation* (Ottawa: Metis National Council, fall 1984)1:6.
11 Ibid.
12 R.E. Gaffney, G.P. Gould and A.J. Semple, *Broken Promises: The Aboriginal Constitutional Conferences* (New Brunswick Association of Metis and Non-Status Indians, 1984), 3, 19. The NCC has expressed concern about the Canadian government being "able to exploit the differences between those Metis with a strong national rights outlook and those Metis with [a] strong aboriginal rights outlook" (ibid., p. 20). Antoine S. Lussier, in his paper, "The Question of Identity and the Constitution: The Métis of Canada in 1984" (prepared for the Treaties and Historical Research Centre, Department of Indian and Northern Affairs, Ottawa, March, 1984) provides a useful discussion of these issues.
13 See notes 10, 12.
14 Joe Sawchuk, *The Metis of Manitoba: Reformulation of an Ethnic Identity* (Toronto: Peter Martin Associates Ltd., 1978).
15 Patline Laverdure and Ida Rose Allard, *The Michif Dictionary: Turtle Mountain Chippewa Cree,* ed. John C. Crawford (Winnipeg: Pemmican Publications, 1983).
16 See, for instance: Antoine S. Lussier and D. Bruce Sealey, eds., *The Other Natives: The Metis,* 3 vols. (Winnipeg: Manitoba Metis Federation Press/Editions Bois-Brulés, 1978); and, D.N.

Sprague and R.P. Frye, *The Genealogy of the First Metis Nation: The Development and Dispersal of the Red River Settlement, 1820–1900* (Winnipeg: Pemmican Publications 1983). For an important exception suggestive of future directions in métis studies, see Antoine S. Lussier, ed., "The Metis Since 1870," special issue, *Canadian Journal of Native Studies* 3 (1983)1. The essays in this issue were presented at a Métis Symposium sponsored by the Native Studies Department, Brandon University, in Winnipeg in November, 1982.

17 Publications by writers of mixed ancestry have been especially instructive. See particularly the pioneering scholarship of Antoine Lussier, cited above, and the personal statements of: Maria Campbell, *Halfbreed* (Toronto: McClelland and Stewart, Ltd., 1973); Howard Adams, *Prison of Grass: Canada from the Native Point of View* (Toronto: New Press, 1975); Duke Redbird, *We Are Metis: A Metis View of the Development of a Native Canadian People* (Willowdale, Ontario: OMNSIA, 1980); and Gerald Vizenor, *Earthdivers: Tribal Narratives on Mixed Descent* (Minneapolis: University of Minnesota Press, 1981).

Métis Origins: Discovery and Interpretation

I

From "One Nation" in the Northeast to "New Nation" in the Northwest: A look at the emergence of the métis

Olive Patricia Dickason

The mixing of the races, as the cliché would have it, began in North America as soon as Europeans and Amerindians met; it was another manifestation of a universal phenomenon that was re-experienced under the particular conditions of the New World. But the universality of the event in its biological sense was not matched by a corresponding generality in its social and political aspects. In this regard, racial intermixing was as individual as the societies experiencing it. In the New World, such powers as Portugal and Spain accepted it as an inevitable consequence of colonization and sought to deal with it by integration and assimilation. France also sought to assimilate Amerindians, but added a new dimension by trying to use racial intermixing as an instrument of empire. In so doing, France unwittingly helped to prepare the way for a phenomenon which the French not only did not want, but would have disapproved of thoroughly: that is, the development, among the métis of the Canadian Northwest, of the sense of a separate identity, the spirit of the "New Nation."

Although in Canada today the métis are identified with the West, specifically with the three prairie provinces (Manitoba, Saskatchewan and Alberta), it is doubtful that there was any more mixing of the races, in a biological sense, in those regions then there was in the East or on the West Coast. In fact, the reverse may well be true, at least as far as the East is concerned; Jacques Rousseau, eminent Quebec biologist, claimed in 1970 that forty percent of French Canadians could find at least one Amerindian in their family trees.[1] What did not occur on either coast or in the St. Lawrence Valley was the emergence of a clearly defined sense of separate identity, of a "New Nation." In comparing the métis of the Northeast with those of the Northwest (principally Red River, but also Hudson Bay and the Great Lakes), the question immediately presents itself: why did a "New Nation" arise in the latter region but not in the former? And why do we rarely hear of the métis on the West Coast? For that matter, why do we practically never hear of métis in the Northeast?

The invisibility of the eastern métis has been abetted by historians who write as though they never existed.[2] Until recently, this has been particularly true of Quebec historians, culminating with Lionel Groulx, who denied the existence of Amerindian ancestry within the contemporary French-Canadian community.[3] Although such attitudes are now changing,[4] old ideas die hard. For instance, such an eminent historian as Marcel Trudel, while acknowledging that some *métissage* (racial mixing) did occur, based his estimate of its extent in 1663 on what he could find explicitly stated in the official record;[5] in his opinion, intermarriage fell into disfavour in New France because of the bad quality of the offspring.[6]

Some nineteenth-century historians found even less evidence of intermixing. Emile Salone, using Cyprien Tanguay's genealogy[7] as his guide, uncovered only four French-Amerindian marriages in the St. Lawrence colony during the seventeenth century. Generally, he wrote, such marriages were not tolerated as the influence of the missionaries was against them: "This did not mean that there were no infractions of the rule, but that they were without consequence. Métis children were left to the tribe, and so lost to the colony."[8] This was the prevalent belief; another expression of it was Abbé Joseph-A. Maurault's theory that the Malecite of St. John's River were the mixed-blood descendants of fishermen from St. Malo, who had left behind their children by native women. It is an argument that has recently been picked up by Lucien Campeau.[9]

The major exception to such cogitations among nineteenth-century French-language historians was expressed by Rameau de Saint-Père, who published in Paris. In his study of the French in Acadia, he attempted to assess the role of racial mixing.[10] It was not a line of thought that has been continued by Naomi Griffiths, a contemporary English-language historian of Acadia. Even though she concedes that Amerindian skills were passed on to European settlers and that "occasionally an Indian woman would be absorbed into an Acadian village through marriage," she produces only two documented cases of this.[11] She does not even mention Jean-Vincent d'Abbadie, Baron de Saint-Castin (1652–1707), the best-known of the "Indianized" Frenchmen of Acadia, whose half-Abenaki son, Bernard-Anselme, became a celebrated forest fighter in the French cause.[12] This reluctance on the part of Canadian historians to acknowledge mingling of the races in the Northeast becomes all the more anomalous in the face of their ready acceptance of this phenomenon in the Northwest. Thus they reduce to irrelevance the fact that in Canada, France officially supported "one race" throughout the seventeenth century.

What the historians are reflecting, even at this late date, is the profound dichotomy between official policy and popular myth. This was particularly striking during the period of official encouragement of intermarriage;[13] even then social attitudes toward crossing racial barriers were at best ambivalent. There were always strong feelings against métissage in certain sections of society, on the grounds that it adulterated the purity of the blood, leading to deterioration. Europeans brought such attitudes with them across the Atlantic as part of the cultural baggage which they had inherited from the days of the Renaissance and earlier. It was an aspect of the prevalent belief in absolutes: the pure, white and good were seen as being at the top of the world hierarchy, while the impure, black and evil were at the bottom.[14] In practice, this was at least partially countered by the natural interest of some fathers in their children, even though mixed-blood, and their desire to have them carry on family farms and enterprises.

All of this, of course, raises questions about the nature of early contacts between Europeans and Amerindians in the Northeast, Northwest and on the West Coast; about how they compare with each other; and why they appear to have developed along different lines. The focus of this article is on the first two regions, since it was in the Northeast that contacts first occurred in Canada, in large measure establishing the pattern for what was to happen in the Northwest. The West Coast presents a separate picture, because contact there occurred much later and because the French element, which was so important in the other regions, was severely reduced and had no political importance.

"Our young men will marry your daughters, and we shall be one people," Samuel de Champlain (about 1570–1635, "Father of New France"), is reported to have said on two occasions.[15] This much-quoted remark, which seems to fly in the face of European devotion to hierarchy based on "purity of blood," has been cited frequently as an example of Champlain's enterprise and tolerance in dealing with Amerindians as he set about establishing France as a colonial presence in North America. Without diminishing Champlain's achievements, it can still be pointed out that such an approach was neither original with him nor particular to him. It was a general French colonial policy at the time,[16] a logical position in view of the fact that in the early seventeenth century, France, as well as Europe generally, still had all-too-vivid memories of the demographic disasters of the Black Death during the fourteenth century. In the seventeenth century, a direct relationship was perceived between a nation-state's power and the size of its population; France, aspiring to continental pre-eminence in Europe, needed its people at home. Thus, the French were suspicious of sending out citizens to colonize distant lands, for fear of depopulating the homeland. The alternative would be to send out a small corps of people who would intermarry with indigenous populations, producing, as it were, on-the-spot French nationals overseas. It was with such a goal in mind that the charter for the Company of New France included, in its Article 17, provision that "the Savages who will be led to the faith and to profess it will be considered natural Frenchmen, and like them, will be able to come and live in France when they wish to, and there acquire property, with rights of inheritance and bequest, just as if they had been born Frenchmen, without being required to make any declaration or to become naturalized."[17]

Such a policy indicates that when a compromise with the prevailing hierarchical view was necessary, spiritual conformity was given priority over race. In the case of New France, this compromise was eased by the widespread and persistent belief that Amerindians were really white, turning brown because of certain practices.[18] Consequently, France saw its immediate problem with Amerindians as one of evangelization, to pave the way for assimilation, which contributed considerably to the great missionary drive in the seventeenth century.

During France's first decades in North America, whether in Acadia or along the St. Lawrence River, few Frenchwomen hazarded the dangers of the Atlantic crossing.[19] There was no alternative to at least some intermarriage for the colony to have struggled through those first years.[20] Such a course would have been dictated as much by problems of survival in an unfamiliar and difficult climate as by the shortage of French women. An Amerindian wife or, later, a métis wife, had obvious advantages over her European counterpart. The taking of native wives was a pattern that was repeated by the English when they established themselves on Hudson Bay later in the same century, despite determined efforts from London to prevent it.[21] It was also a pattern that the French had already developed in another context in Brazil, where they had established interpreters among Amerindian peoples, who had intermarried with them and thus confirmed the trading alliances by which the French were challenging the Portuguese claim to the territory. However, this had been achieved at the cost of French citizens "going native," which officials now sought to avoid in New France.[22] Viewed in this light, the position of Sulte and Salone, not to mention Groulx, is more indicative of nineteenth-century attitudes than it is of seventeenth-century facts.

The silence as well as the ambiguity of the record presents a problem for the historian. If, on the one hand, it is unrealistic to deny that racial mixing occurred within French communities (particularly in Acadia) on the grounds that it was so seldom recorded as such, on the other hand it is extremely difficult, if not impossible, to determine just how prevalent it was.[23] The rarity of recognizably recorded intermarriages could be related to the probability that many of them took place *à la façon du pays* – that is, according to the Amerindian way; apparently this sometimes happened even among those who more or less lived within the French colony.[24]

Such unions would have incurred disapproval at official levels whatever their acceptance (or non-acceptance) at others, not so much because they involved Amerindians but because they had happened outside Christian practice. The truly shocking aspect of the situation during the seventeenth century, particularly for a France in the throes of the Counter Reformation, was the fact that Frenchmen, raised in the true Christian faith, "became Savage simply because they lived with them."[25] It was a phenomenon which drew considerable enunciation from authorities; the very prevalence of such thunderings suggests the extent of the problem.[26] Missionaries worked hard to counteract it, not so much by opposing intermarriages as such, as Salone wrote, but by baptizing native brides of Frenchmen, preferably before marriage, and, by regularizing unions in accordance with Christian ritual and seeing that the children were baptized and raised within the colonial community. The overriding need was for a workforce, which would have led to many such children becoming French as far as the record was concerned. "Children are the wealth of the country," a visiting French surgeon observed in 1700.[27] There was also adoption. Particularly in the seventeenth century, colonial policy encouraged French families to take in Amerindian children and raise them as their own; as with the mixed-bloods, there is almost no way of detecting this in the documentation, unless explicitly acknowledged.

The dearth of direct record is to some extent counterbalanced by indirect evidence. This is especially true for Acadia. For example, an eighteenth-century memoir on Acadia refers casually to Amerindians and "children of the country accustomed to going with the savages."[28] Colonel Samuel Vetch, second English governor of Port Royal, noted in 1714 that as the Acadians had contracted marriages with Amerindians who had been converted, they had a strong influence over them.[29] An anonymous letter published in London in 1758 purporting to be from a "Mons. de la Varenne," claimed: "We employ besides a much more effectual method of uniting them to us, and that is, by the intermarriage of our people with the savage women, which is a circumstance which draws the ties of alliance closer. The children produced by these are generally hardy, inured to the fatigues of the chace [sic] and war, and turn out very serviceable subjects in their way."[30] Later in the same letter there is a description of Acadians, who had recently been dispersed by the

English: "They were a mixed breed, that is to say, most of them proceeded from marriages or concubinage of the savage women with the first settlers, who were of various nations, but chiefly French."[31] That point had already been made by Pierre-Antoine-Simon Maillard (1709–1762, "Apostle to the Micmacs") who had written in 1753 that he did not expect more than fifty years would elapse before the French colonists were so mixed with the Micmacs and Malecites that it would be impossible to distinguish them.[32] Acadians appear to have been well on the way toward realizing the official goal of "one race."

Such mixing would have been reinforced by the exigencies of the fur trade, which was the economic reason that the colony had been established in the first place. The trade, which remained the principal economic activity for the colony throughout the French regime, functioned best when certain formalities were observed. Not the least of these was intermarriage; Amerindian society, with its stress on kinship, much preferred such a relationship as a basis for its trading alliances. A contemporary description of such an arrangement tells us that

when a Frenchman trades with them [Amerindians – in this case, Ottawa], he takes into his services one of their Daughters, the one, presumably, who is most to his taste; he asks the Father for her, & under certain conditions, it is arranged; he promises to give the father some blankets, a few shirts, a Musket, Powder & Shot, Tobacco & Tools; they come to an agreement at last, & the exchange is made. The Girl, who is familiar with the Country, undertakes, on her part, to serve the Frenchman in every way, to dress his pelts, to sell his Merchandise for a specified length of time; the bargain is faithfully carried out on both sides.[33]

Historians of the fur trade in the Northwest will recognize this description because it so closely parallels what happened in that region at a later date. In the eastern trade, no less than in that of the Northwest, women played a vital role because of their family connections and because of their particular skills. Only recently have historians begun to pay attention to this fundamental aspect of our early history, and then mainly in connection with the much better documented Northwest.[34]

Such an arrangement for accommodating fur traders was facilitated by attitudes of Amerindians toward marriage. While kinship was all-important to them, they did not consider marriage to be necessarily permanent, particularly if no children were involved. Besides, *polygyny* (the taking of more than one wife) was an integral part of their social and economic framework. As far as they were concerned, it was perfectly acceptable for a European trader to marry one of their women even if he were known to have another wife back in his own community. Inevitably, such arrangements developed, not only within the framework of the fur trade, but also within that of military alliances: two outstanding French envoys who had concurrent French and Amerindian wives were Paul Le Moyne de Maricourt (1663–1704) with the Onondaga and Louis-Thomas Chabert de Joncaire (about 1670–1739) with the Seneca.[35]

This was one of the principal aspects of the "disorderliness" and "libertinage" which aroused the concern of missionaries, rather than intermarriages as such, which they generally supported as long as their rules were obeyed. Jesuit Paul Le Jeune's relation for 1673 tells of a delegation to Huronia to ascertain "whether it would be acceptable to them that some of our Frenchmen should marry in their country as soon as possible." This drew the response from the Huron, ". . . those Frenchmen who had resolved to marry were free to take wives where it seemed good to them; that those who had married in the past had not demanded a general council for the purpose but that they had taken them in whatever way they had desired."[36] This is precisely what was worrying the French:

The Father replied to this that it was very true that the Frenchmen who had hitherto married in the country had not made such a stir about it, but also that their intentions were far removed from ours, – that their purpose had been to become barbarians, and to render themselves exactly like them. He said that we, on the contrary, aimed by this alliance to make them like us, to give them knowledge of the true God, and to teach them to keep his holy commandments, and that the marriages of which we were speaking were to be stable and perpetual; and he laid before them all the other advantages they would derive therefrom.[37]

In other words, the French were not fully in control of the situation. Something of their feelings in this connection can be seen in their reaction to the Mohawk chief known as the Flemish Bastard, whom they described as "the monstrous offspring of a Dutch Heretic Father and a Pagan woman,"[38] and in their difficulties in controlling their own coureurs de bois. In this cultural context, Amerindian societies displayed an unexpected strength, which in the eighteenth century caused French officialdom (as distinct from the missionaries) to turn against intermarriage.

Despite the apparent appeal of native societies, to assume that mixed marriages always resulted in assimilation to the Amerindian side is to fly in the face of what little evidence has survived. The best known case is that of the Baron de Saint-Castin, who came to New France as an ensign with the Carignan-Salières Regiment in 1665 and stayed to marry Marie-Mathilde Madokawando (whose Amerindian name was Pidianske, unless sisters were involved). She was the daughter of an Abenaki chief, apparently a beautiful and accomplished woman. The baron elected to live in the land of his in-laws;

in spite of that fact, however, he not only never lost his French connection but became extremely valuable to it, a tradition that was carried on by his sons, most prominently by Bernard-Anselme, but also by Joseph.[39] Several of Jean-Vincent's children (he had at least eleven) married into well-established French families, some of whom, such as the Mius d'Entremonts and the Damours, had other connections with Amerindians.[40] In fact, a granddaughter (Marie Anselme, oldest daughter of Bernard-Anselme) married into lesser nobility in France.[41] In 1709, Jeanne Mius d'Entremont married Louis Du Pont Duchambon, who was acting governor of Louisbourg during its siege by New England troops in 1744–1745. For a while she acted as official interpreter for the Micmac, until the chiefs objected to the presence of a woman during their deliberations.[42] Charles Saint-Etienne de La Tour (1593–1666), another leading French settler in Acadia, had three daughters by an unnamed Micmac woman, whom he had married in 1626. Two of them became nuns, but the third, Jeanne, married Martin Aprendestiguy, Sieur de Martignon, who later became the proprietor of Fort Latour on the Saint-John River. In 1686 their daughter Marianne married Guillaume Bourgeois, a Port Royal merchant who was the son of Jacques, a surgeon and the founder of Beaubassin.

Still another example is that of Richard Denys, Sieur de Fronsac (about 1654–1691), son of the pioneering Nicolas Denys. Richard married Anne Parabego, by whom he had a son, Nicolas, and a daughter, Marie-Anne. The son, who became Sieur de Fronsac in 1682, in his turn married an Amerindian woman who presented him with three children; however, they died in a fire in 1732. The family continued through Marie-Anne, who married a Quebecker.

A family that became noted for its interpreters was launched by schooner captain Claude Petitpas (about 1663–1731), son of the Sieur de Lafleur, when he married Marie-Thérèse, a Micmac, in 1686. They had seven children. Their son Barthélemy established himself at Port Toulouse, a convenient location for his work as official interpreter at Louisbourg. Another member of the family, Louis-Benjamin, worked with Father Maillard.[43]

Such evidence speaks for itself. The Quebec church declared the Micmac to be all Christianized by the end of the seventeenth century, although the quality of their Catholicism was not beyond doubt.[44] But the fact that they were considered to be at least officially Christian would have meant one less barrier to intermarriage. The colony's perennial need for a workforce would also have ensured official efforts to keep the resultant children within the French community. This was particularly the case after the establishment of royal government in 1663. Jean Talon (intendant 1665 to 1668 and 1670 to 1672), even considered the feasibility of police action to prevent Amerindian women from nursing their children for extended periods. He saw this practice as inhibiting reproduction, an "obstacle to the prompt formation of the Colony."[45] There is no evidence that this suggestion was acted upon.

Official support for "one nation" also produced results in the St. Lawrence Valley. In 1638, Jesuits gave four arpents of cleared land to two Amerindian girls about to marry Christians; the next year, "a worthy and pious person" gave a hundred *écus* (crowns) for the wedding of a "young Savage girl sought in marriage by a young Frenchman of very good character."[46] However, the earliest such marriage at Quebec for which we have an actual record is that of Martin Prévost (about 1611–1691), a settler who married Marie-Olivier Sylvestre Manitouabeouich in 1644. They had nine children. Probably the most prominent of such marriages was that of Pierre Boucher, Sieur de Grosbois, captain and later governor of Trois Rivières (1651–1667), who married Huron Marie Ouebadinskoue (also referred to as Marie-Madeleine Chrestienne) in 1649. She was one of the small group who had been educated by the Ursulines. However, she died in her first childbirth, and her baby did not survive. Boucher then married Jeanne Crevier, of the family that was deeply involved in the fur trade.

Another product of the Ursulines, Catherine Annennoutauk, "Creature de Dieu," was provided with a dowry of 260 *livres* (pounds) on the occasion of her wedding in 1662 to Jean Durand. This union proved more fruitful, producing three children. In fact, Catherine survived her husband to marry another Frenchman, Jacques Couturier, in 1672, by whom she had five children.[47] Also recorded in 1662 was another wedding involving a dowry, that of Huron Marie-Felix Arontio to Laurent Dubocq. The bride's dowry was for five hundred livres, and had been provided by her mother, "an excellent Christian."[48] This union was blessed with seven children.

Official encouragement became more systematic in 1680, when three thousand livres were budgeted to provide dowries of fifty livres each for French and Amerindian girls who married Frenchmen. Officialdom had apparently acceded to persistent pressure from the Jesuits, who had been lobbying for such a measure for something like half a century. One of the benefits they had seen resulting from official support was greater marriage stability.[49] But support, even when official, did not produce the results the Jesuits had so confidently forecast. Few claimed the money, and officials were soon complaining that Amerindian girls were not marrying into the colony.[50] The dowries remained in the budget until 1702; His Most Christian Majesty also provided one thousand livres annually to pay women to teach Amerindian girls French household skills with a view to making "marriages customary between these girls and the French."[51]

In spite of disclaimers concerning Amerindian marital preferences, not to mention those unclaimed dowries, mixed marriages were recorded more frequently toward the end of the century than they were at its beginning. Not, as those officials who still supported "one race" had hoped, within the settled areas where French civility more or less prevailed, but on the frontier of the "Old Northwest" – the area of the Great Lakes and the Ohio Valley. Most of the Frenchmen established in this region by 1700 were reported to have taken Amerindian wives. The much-publicized irregularities of frontier life to the contrary, missionaries did find something to approve of in this situation, which after all represented a measure of success for the "one race" they had been working for ever since their first days in Acadia. Father Julien Binneteau wrote from the Illinois country in 1669: "There are also some women married to some of our Frenchmen who would be a good example to the best regulated households in France. Some of those who are married to Savages manifest extraordinary care in maintaining piety in their families."[52]

However, by the early eighteenth century, opposition to intermarriage was growing. On the official level, this opposition reflected the difficulties the French were having in maintaining alliances in the Old Northwest; in that region at least, "one race" was proving to be of doubtful value as a political instrument.[53] Socially, a certain ambivalence had always been present, as we have seen. For instance, when the elder Baron de Saint-Castin died in 1707, a lawsuit was launched by relatives in France who claimed family lands and titles on the grounds that his marriage had not been legitimate, despite abundant evidence to the contrary produced by colonial authorities. Bernard-Anselme was only partially successful in maintaining his claim. In Quebec on military service in 1718, Claude-Michel Bégon de La Cour permanently damaged whatever career potentialities he would have had in France by marrying Marie-Elizabeth de La Morandière, known as "la iroquoise."[54] He did well in Canada, however, first as an officer, and finally, in 1743, becoming governor of Trois Rivières. Another scandal erupted in 1754 when an ensign serving at Louisbourg married a métis girl without his commanding officer's consent. Part of the objection in this case was that the girl's mother, Irene Muis d'Entremont, had issued from a union that had not been sanctified by Christian ritual.[55] Thus, in spite of individual exceptions, neither official encouragement nor economic necessity ensured social acceptance. One can reasonably assume that such acceptance was probably greatest during the seventeenth century, particularly when the colony was first being established. As for the intensifying climate of official opposition, it manifested itself in the Old Northwest in a regulation restricting the right of Amerindian women to inherit their French husbands' property. This was followed in 1735 by an edict requiring the consent of the governor or commanding officer for all mixed marriages.[56] Thus foundered the ideal of "one nation."

The establishment of the French in the Americas had been a long and difficult process, involving much trial and error. The first French attempt to colonize on the St. Lawrence – that of Cartier-Roberval between 1541 and 1543 – had ended in failure. Subsequent attempts to establish in Brazil and "Florida" – including part of the Carolinas – had met with a no better fate.[57] In analyzing these disasters, the French had concluded that, among other things, there had not been proper cooperation with Amerindians. This was particularly true in Canada, where an unfamiliar and intimidating climate and separation from the parent country by a difficult ocean crossing[58] put a premium on native survival skills. By the time the French settled permanently in Acadia, they had a lively appreciation of the advisability of keeping on good terms with the natives, and that they lived up to this is attested by their record with the Micmac, Malecite and Abenaki. Their bonds of friendship with these peoples lasted as long as the French maintained a presence in North America. For a century and a half French and Amerindians lived and fought side by side in a symbiotic relationship that is without parallel in the colonial history of North America.[59]

The relationship appears to have been encouraged by the fact that the French and Amerindians developed mutually reinforcing lifestyles in Acadia. The fur trade, of course, called for cooperation between the two peoples wherever it was carried on. Farming, which usually had the opposite effect, in Acadia developed harmoniously because French farmers utilized tidal flats, lands of little interest to Amerindians.[60] The result was that the French agricultural settlement did not infringe upon the Amerindian way of life; until the dispersal of the Acadians by the British, friction between the two groups rarely reached the point of violence.[61] Another factor strongly encouraging this happy state of affairs was the position of Amerindians and French on the "frontier" in the midst of the prolonged confrontation between English and French. A common enemy in dangerously close proximity did much to encourage good relations between allies and blood relatives.

It also did much to discourage the emergence of the métis as a separate group. The tensions of protracted frontier warfare, lasting until the final defeat of the French in 1760, polarized the racial situation in Acadia even as it encouraged good relations. In other words, the children of mixed unions tended to identify with either the French or the Amerindians rather than considering themselves as a separate entity. This would have been particularly true for the men.[62] The two areas where a biracial heritage as such would have given them an advantage, the fur trade and diplomatic relations with Amerindians, provided only limited opportunities in the East during the latter part of the seventeenth and first half of the eighteenth centuries. Other occupational fields, particularly prestigious ones such as the missionary and military, demanded identification with the French.[63] The alternative would have been to join allied Amerindian guerrillas in their "petite guerre" against the English, which would have meant identification as Amerindian. If they stayed within the colony in any other occupation, children of mixed unions would have been considered French. The British takeover of Acadia in 1710, which became official with the Treaty of Utrecht of 1713, did not alter this. Thus the Acadians, even as they cited their blood ties with the Amerindians as one of their reasons for not taking the oath of loyalty insisted upon by the British, never thought of themselves as anything other than French. French official-dom worked hard to encourage this, with the aid of missionaries. It was not a conviction that was wholeheartedly shared by the British, who profoundly distrusted Acadian-Amerindian connections.[64]

The situation was somewhat different in the Old Northwest, and much more so in the Far Northwest. To begin with the former: while the Ohio Valley, like Acadia, was a disputed frontier area, it was even farther removed from the centres of colonial government. On the face of it, such a state of affairs should have encouraged French–Amerindian alliances, as it had done in Acadia. However, the English by this time had become more knowledge-able in dealing with Amerindians, and were able to prevent the French from consolidating their position with the peoples of the region; what alliances the French succeeded in establishing were never as firm as their earlier partner-ships had been in Acadia.[65] Consequently, the forces influencing the métis to identify with either French or Amerindian were much weaker; instead, they began to look upon themselves as representing a distinctive blend of two cultures. This was encouraged by the overriding importance of the fur trade, more so than it had ever been in Acadia. It put a premium on the services of the métis, who had grown up in the trade and who were uniquely qualified to carry it on.

There was also the fact that Anglo-French rivalries placed them in a good bargaining position. A feeling of economic and cultural value expressed itself in dress, which became a distinctive blend of Amerindian and French. The métis of the "Old Northwest" were a short step from the "New Nation." But it was a step that was never taken, as it was forestalled by the rush of settlement.

Instead, it was in the Far Northwest that a sense of separate identity finally crystallized.[66] It was only there that appropriate conditions were found: isolation, slowness of settlement and the enduring importance of the fur trade.[67] In this context, French-English rivalries encouraged the new spirit, contrary to what their effect had been in the East. The fur trade allowed it to be born; the isolation, far from the pull-and-haul of intercolonial warfare (except, perhaps, for the period between 1670 and 1713 on Hudson Bay, which did not involve Amerindians), allowed it to develop. When settlers finally arrived at Red River in 1812, they were too few to overwhelm this spirit; instead, their presence was the catalyst which transformed mild awareness into conviction. From that point, the métis knew they were a distinct people with a way of life that was worth defending. Although some Canadian historians have attributed this phenomenon to the machinations of the North West Company,[68] the process was actually much more profound and complex. There is no doubt, however, that the North West Company encouraged the situation for its own ends.[69]

On the Northwest Coast, Amerindians and Europeans met and interacted from the latter part of the eighteenth century onwards. However, the particular conditions required to create a separate métis identity either were nonexistent or not in place long enough to produce such a result. To begin with, the climate was such that special survival skills did not need to be learned; secondly, the fur trade (at least on the coast) was dominant for less than a century, soon giving way to agricultural settlement, to be augmented later by gold rushes. On the Northwest Coast, European and Amerindian never developed the kind of symbiotic relationships they had achieved in other areas, which meant that there was never any question, officially or otherwise, of encouraging mixing of the races. This is not to say that intermarriage did not occur, or even that mixed-blood settlements did not appear – witness the métis migration from Red River during the mid-nineteenth century – but only that it was without official support. Neither did colonial rivalries produce alliances with Amerindians, as they had on the East Coast and in the Old Northwest; indeed, the very suggestion of such a possibility by that former fur trader, Governor Sir James Douglas, aroused considerable unease on the part of the settlers.[70] There never was any fighting side by side against a common enemy. Rather, what fighting there was occurred between Amerindians and the white community, with colonial authorities applying heavy-handed "justice." It is not surprising that under such circumstances there was very little noticeable Amerindian influence on colonial society, despite the fact that Douglas's wife, Lady Amelia, was half Cree. The only area where such influence was destined to become appreciable at a later period was in the visual arts.

France's initial policy of creating one race in New France may have very largely failed, but what it did do was to set in motion a train of developments which eventually culminated in the emergence of the "New Nation" in the Far Northwest. In Acadia and Quebec, the tendency was for métis to identify with one side or the other; if it did not eliminate Amerindian cultures as the French had hoped, at least it kept their peoples in alliance. In the Old Northwest, a sense of separate identity began to manifest itself on the part of the mixed-blood inhabitants, but became submerged in the sweep of events following the establishment of the United States. It was in the Canadian Far Northwest that conditions allowed for the development of a "New Nation," destined to collide with the new confederation, Canada. This was not at all what central-ist French authorities had envisioned when they had declared in 1627 that Christianized Amerindians were to be considered fully French. The original concept of "one people" had, through the course of time and the pressures of unforeseen circumstances, produced instead a "New Nation."

NOTES

This article was published previously, in slightly altered form, in *American Indian Culture and Research Journal* 6 (1982)2. The author would like to acknowledge the helpful comments on this article by Dr. Lewis H. Thomas, University of Alberta.

1 Cited by Donald B. Smith, *Le Sauvage* (Ottawa: National Museums of Canada, 1974), 88.

2 An example of this approach is Jacques Henripin, *La population canadienne au début du XVIIIe siècle* (Paris: Presses Universitaires de France, 1954). Jacqueline Peterson made some cogent observations in this regard in "Prelude to Red River: A Social Portrait of the Great Lakes Métis," *Ethnohistory* 25 (Winter 1978)1:45–46.

3 Lionel Groulx, *La naissance d'une race* (Montreal: Granger Frères, 1938), 24–27. Groulx maintained that ninety-four mixed marriages and four "alliances" were known to have occurred before 1665, but that none of these left descendants who survived after the end of the eighteenth century. See also Georges Langlois, *Histoire de la population Canadienne-française* (Montreal: Albert Lévesque, 1934), 99–100.

4 Smith, *Le Sauvage,* 70–91. See also Isabelle Perrault, "L'Historiographie de la dissolution," *Recherches Amérindiennes au Quebec* 10 (1981)4:273–75. This is an extract drawn from her master's thesis, "Le métissage en Nouvelle-France" (MSc [Sociologie], Université de Mont-real, 1980).

5 Marcel Trudel, *La Population du Canada en 1663* (Montreal: Fides, 1973), 27–28, 149. According to the record, the colony included four French-Amerindian families and one French-métisse, with a total of nine surviving children. However, the surviving official record is far from complete, particularly for the very early period of the colony.

6 Marcel Trudel, *Initiation à la Nouvelle-France* (Montreal: Holt, Rinehart and Winston, 1968), 147. Earlier, in *L'esclavage au Canada français* (Quebec: Les Presses Universitaires Laval, 1960), 290, he had observed that it was not the incidence of intermarriage itself that was important, but rather the number of children.

7 Cyprien Tanguay, *Dictionnaire généalogique des familles canadiennes depuis la fondation de la colonie jusqu'a nos jours,* 7 vols. (Montreal: 1871–1890).

8 Emile Salone, *La colonisation de la Nouvelle-France* (Paris: E. Guilmoto, [1906]; Brown reprint, 1970), 116. "Cela ne signifie pas qu'il n'y ait pas eu quelques infractions à la règle, mais elles n'ont pas eu de conséquences. Les enfants métis sont abandonnés à la tribu, perdus pour la colonie." Benjamin Sulte had already expressed the same idea in "Les Canadiens-français et les Sauvages," *Bulletin des recherches historiques* 4 (1898)12:362. Contemporaries

who see métissage as a phenomenon of Amerindian rather than French society include: Cornelius J. Jaenen, *Friend and Foe* (Toronto: McClelland and Stewart, 1976), 153–89; W.J. Eccles, *The Canadian Frontier, 1534–1760* (New York: Holt, Rinehart and Winston, 1969), 190–91; and Alfred G. Bailey, *The Conflict of European and Eastern Algonkian Cultures, 1504–1700* (Toronto, University of Toronto Press, 1969), 113.

9 Abbé J.-A. Maurault, *Histoire des Abenaki,* (Sorel, Quebec: 1866; Johnson reprint, 1969), 6; Lucien Campeau, *La Première Mission d'Acadie, 1602–1616* (Quebec: Les Presses de l'Université Laval, 1967), 118*; and Bailey, *Conflict,* 113.

10 François-Edme de Rameau de Saint-Père, *Une colonie féodale,* 2 vols. (Paris: Plon, 1889). Marcel Giraud's much acclaimed *Le métis canadien* (Paris: l'Institut d' Ethnologie, 1945), deals exclusively with the West. The best English-language treatment of métissage is that of Bailey, *Conflict.* The University of Manitoba is currently active in métis studies.

11 Naomi Griffiths, *The Acadians: Creation of a People* (Toronto: McGraw-Hill Ryerson, 1973), 5.

12 Biographies of various members of the Saint-Castin family are in the second and third volumes of the *Dictionary of Canadian Biography,* 11 vols. (Toronto: University of Toronto Press, 1966-) (hereinafter referred to as *DCB*). Also, Robert Le Blant, *Une Figure Légendaire de l'Histoire Acadienne – Le Baron de St-Castin* (Dax: 1934).

13 Jean-Baptiste Colbert, Louis XIV's great Minister of the Marine, was particularly keen on such a policy. See, for example, his letter to Talon, dated 1671, cited in Cary F. Goulson, ed., *Seventeenth-Century Canada: Source Studies* (Toronto: Macmillan, 1970), 307.

14 Olive Patricia Dickason, *The Myth of the Savage and the Beginning of French Colonialism in the Americas* (Edmonton: University of Alberta Press, 1984), 44–47, 48–49, 143–44. For some latter-day comments on hybridization, see Bailey, *Conflict,* 115–16.

15 Reuben Gold Thwaites, ed., *Jesuit Relations and Allied Documents,* 73 vols. (Cleveland: Burrows Brothers, 1896–1901), 5:211; 10:26.

16 For instance, the French used such an approach when they attempted to establish a colony at Maragnan in northern Brazil between 1612 and 1614. See Yves (d'Evreux), *Suitte de l'histoire des chose plus memorables advenues en Maragnan, ès annees 1613 & 1614* (Paris: François Huby, 1615), 270. However, Père Yves expressed doubt that such a policy would be workable: "Nous ne verrons pas ces choses." That this was not the case in New France is witnessed by French complaints to the Huron that "you have not allied yourselves up to the present with our French people. Your daughters have married with all neighbouring nations but not with ours, . . . not that we have need of your daughters, . . . but we would like to see only one people in all the land" (Thwaites, ed., *Jesuit Relations,* 9:219).

17 *Edits, ordonnances royaux, déclarations et arrêts du Conseil d'état du roi concernant le Canada,* 3 vols. (Quebec, Frechette, 1854–1856), 1:10. My own translation.

18 Dickason, *Myth of the Savage,* 144–47; Samuel de Champlain, *Works,* ed. Henry P. Biggar, 6 vols. (Toronto: Champlain Society, 1922–1936; reprint, 1971), 2:48. The persistence of this belief may also have been the result of physical resemblances between Amerindians and Europeans. Today, anthropologists explain this by theorizing that Amerindians represent an early form of *Homo sapiens sapiens,* before differentiation between Caucasoids and Mongoloids.

19 An outstanding exception was Marguerite, who accompanied the colonizing expedition of Jean François de La Rocque de Roberval in 1542, and who, because of an affair, was abandoned with her lover on an island in the Gulf of St. Lawrence. See Marguerite of Navarre's *Heptameron* (Paris: 1559). A different version of the story is found in André Thevet, *Cosmographie* (Paris: L'Huillier, 1575), 1019–1020v.

20 Rameau de Saint-Père, *Une Colonie feodale,* 1:152–53; Bailey, *Conflict,* 111–13; Andrew Hill Clark, *Acadia: The Geography of Nova Scotia to 1760* (Madison, The University of Wisconsin Press, 1968), 377.

21 See Jennifer S.H. Brown, *Strangers in Blood: Fur Trade Company Families in Indian Country* (Vancouver: University of British Columbia Press, 1980), and Sylvia Van Kirk, *"Many Tender Ties": Women in Fur-Trade Society, 1670–1870* (Winnipeg: Watson and Dwyer, 1980).

22 This point was also made by Benjamin Sulte, *Histoire des Canadiens-français, 1608–1880,* 8 vols. (Montreal: Wilson, 1882–1884), 1:154. The brazilwood trade, like the fur trade, provided an economic basis for the métis. See Darcy Ribeiro, *The Americas and Civilization* (New York: Dutton, 1972), 190–91.

23 For some comments by Rameau de Saint-Père on this subject, see *Collection de documents inédits sur le Canada et l'Amerique publiées par le Canada-Français,* 3 vols. (Quebec: Demers, 1888–1890), 3:134–138. Later he illustrates these difficulties as presented by the Martin and Lejeune families (pp. 141–51). See also Bailey, *Conflict,* 111–13.

24 An example of this was Philippe Enault, Sieur de Barbaucannes, a physician who established himself on his seigneury at Nipisquit, N.B. (today's Bathurst), in 1676. After his death, his children apparently opted for the Amerindian way of life. See: *DCB* 2; Chrestien Le Clercq, *New Relation of Gaspesia,* ed. William F. Ganong (Toronto: Champlain Society, 1910), 160–161, n2. In spite of this, Le Clercq had a high opinion of Enault (pp. 177–85).

25 Gabriel Sagard-Théodat, *Histoire du Canada et Voyages que les frères Mineurs Recollects y ont faicts pour la Conversion des Infidèlles depuis l'an 1615* (Paris: Sonnius, 1636), 166.

26 For some examples, see the writings of Marie de l'Incarnation in *Word From New France,* ed. Joyce Marshall (Toronto: Oxford University Press, 1967).

27 Sieur de Diéreville, *Relation of the Voyage to Port Royal in Acadia or New France,* ed. John C. Webster (Toronto: Champlain Society, 1933), 94. Interestingly enough, the word *métis* does not appear to have been used in early seventeenth-century documentation connected with New France.

28 Public Archives of Canada (hereinafter referred to as PAC), Preconquest Papers, J3:39, Memoir of Gregoire (or Robert) Challe, 1716.

29 Abbé H.R. Casgrain, "Coup d'oeil sur l'Acadie," *Le Canada Français* 1(1888):116–17.

30 *An Account of the Customs and Manners of the Micmakis and Maricheets Savage Nations* (London: Hooper and Morley, 1758), 89–90. The letter has been attributed to Father Pierre Maillard.

31 Ibid., 101–02.

32 Michel Le Courtois de Surlaville, *Les derniers jours de l'Acadie (1748–1758),* ed. Gaston du Boscq de Beaumont (Paris: Lechevalier, 1899), 85.

33 Diéreville, *Voyage to Port Royal,* 187.

34 The two principal works in this connection are cited in footnote 21.

35 Robert-Lionel Seguin, *La vie libertine en Nouvelle-France au XVIIe siècle,* 2 vols. (Montreal: Lemeac, 1972), 1:47. Several members of the Chabert de Joncaire family followed this path (PAC, C11A 18:82; Giraud, *Le métis canadien,* 321–22). Biographies of members of the Chabert de Joncaire family are in *DCB* 2, 3 and 4; for Le Moyne de Maricourt, *DCB,* 2. See also E.B. O'Callaghan and J.R. Brodhead, eds., *Documents Relative to the Colonial History of the State of New York,* 15 vols. (Albany: 1853–1887), 9:580 (hereinafter referred to as *NYCD*). Its index lists Philippe-Thomas Chabert de Joncaire (1707 to about 1766) as a French Amerindian. See also PAC C11A 18:147–48.

36 Thwaites, ed., *Jesuit Relations,* 14:17–19. Similar assurances were made by an Iroquois delegation to the French at Trois Rivières in 1645 (Thwaites, ed., *Jesuit Relations,* 27:283).

37 Ibid., 14:19.

38 Ibid., 35:213.

39 Pierre Daviault, *Le Baron de Saint-Castin* (Montreal: Editions de L'A.C.F., n. d.), 185; Clarence J. d'Entremont, "The Children of the Baron de St. Castin," *French-Canadian and Acadian Genealogical Review* 3 (Spring 1971), 1:9–28.

40 For some official observations on the Damours brothers, see Beamish Murdoch, *A History of Nova Scotia or Acadie,* 3 vols. (Halifax: Barnes, 1865–1867)1:216. The Amerindian connections of the Mius family are touched on by Rameau de Saint-Père in *Collection de documents inédits,* 3:165.

41 John Clarence Webster, *Acadia at the End of the Seventeenth Century* (Saint John: The New Brunswick Museum, 1934), 196.

42 PAC, C11B 5:398–99, de Mézy to Council, November 20, 1722.

43 As this family was engaged in coastal trade, including smuggling to the English, it attracted official attention. In one official's view, the fact that the family was "allied by blood" with Amerindians made it advisable to keep on good terms with them (PAC C11B 2:38–39, Soubras to Council, April 10, 1717). See also Rameau de Saint-Père, *Collection de documents inédits,* 3:165–68.

44 Olive Patricia Dickason, "Louisbourg and the Indians: A Study in Imperial Race Relations," *History and Archaeology* 6 (1976):60–61.

45 PAC, Archives des Colonies, C11A 2:355, "Memoire sur l'estat present du Canada," 1667. See also *Rapport de l'Archiviste de la Province de Quebec pour 1930–1931,* 63. In the words of Talon, "Cest obstacle à la prompte formation de la Colonie peut estre surmonté par quelque réglement de Police aisé à introduir, et faire valoir, si on n'empesche pas les sauvages de s'y sousmettre."

46 Thwaites, ed., *Jesuit Relations,* 14:263; 16:35.

47 Ibid., 47:289.

48 Ibid.

49 Ibid., 14:261–63; 16:151–53; and 21:137ff.

50 *NYCD* 9:207, La Barre to Seignelay, November 4, 1683. The budgets are in PAC FIA, Fonds des Colonies, 1–10.

51 *NYCD* 9:269–71.

52 Thwaites, ed., *Jesuit Relations,* 65:69, 263. See also: the table of marriages at Michilimackinac, 1698–1765, in Peterson, p. 50 this volume; Marcel Giraud, *Histoire de la Louisiane française,* 2 vols. (Paris: Presses Universitaires de France, 1953–1958), 1:315–16; Louise Phelps Kellogg, *The French Régime in Wisconsin and the Northwest* (New York: Cooper Square, 1968), 386–405; and Natalie Maree Belting, *Kaskaskia under the French Regime* (New Orleans: Polyanthos, 1975), 13–16.

53 PAC C13A 3:819–24, Duclos to minister, December 25, 1715.

54 It is tempting to speculate that Marie-Elizabeth was an Amerindian who had been adopted by Rocbert de la Morandière.

55 PAC, F3 50:504v–524, Superior Council, February 17, 1755; PAC, G2 189:270–360, Greffes des Colonies, 1754–1755. See also Rameau de Saint-Père, *Collection de documents inédits,* 3:170; and *Une colonie féodale,* 2:376.

56 Belting, *Kaskaskia,* 74–75; Jaenen, *Friend and Foe,* 164–65.

57 The principal attempts were those of Nicholas Durand de Villegaignon, at Rio de Janeiro, 1555–1560; Jean Ribault and René de Gouloine de Laudonnière, in the Carolinas, 1562–1564; and François de Razilly and Daniel de La Touche de La Ravadière at Maragnan, northern Brazil, 1612–1614.

58 The generally easiest route from Europe to America with the sailing and navigational techniques of the time was that taken by Columbus, which had brought him to the West Indies.

59 Clark, *Acadia,* 376–77.

60 Ibid.

61 One case where Micmac dispersed a French village was the 1692 attack by Halion on a settlement near Bathurst, N.B. (Abraham Gesner, *New Brunswick; with notes for emigrants* [London: Simmonds and Ward, 1847], 29). There was also forbearance on the part of the French when Amerindian hunters did not differentiate between livestock and game (Dickason, "Louisbourg and the Indians," 121). Apparently the Micmac of the Gaspé, after the British conquest, claimed that Acadians were trespassing on their hunting and fishing grounds, and asked for protection. Although this indicates some friction, there is enough evidence to the contrary to suggest the author is assuming too much when he concludes that this means that "bad feeling between Acadians and Micmac dates from very early" (David Lee, "Gaspé, 1767–1867," *Canadian Historic Sites, Occasional Papers in Archaeology and History* 23[1980]:166.)

62 I am indebted to Colleen Glenn, Edmonton, for pointing this out.

63 In the case of the French army, this requires no explanation; as for the missionaries, those born in the colony appear to have been sometimes of mixed blood, although this may not show in the record. For example, Antoine Gaulin (1674–1740), who was particularly troublesome to the British, was referred to by one governor as "that half-breed" (PAC, PRO, Colonial Office Series, 217/4:125–31, Doucett to Lords of Trade, July 2, 1722). At a later period, one of the most effective missionaries in the West was Albert Lacombe, a mixed-blood.

64 The British view of the Acadians as a mixed, and therefore inferior race, may have been a factor in the decision to deport them (Clark, *Acadia,* 316.) On the other hand, the British, in 1729, had issued an offer of ten pounds sterling and fifty acres of free land to any British subject who married an Amerindian woman (PAC, AC, Misc. Docs. 2:196).

65 Giraud, *Louisiane,* 2:318–19.

66 For a discussion of métis identity, see Richard Slobodin, *Métis of the Mackenzie District* (Ottawa: Canadian Research Centre for Anthropology, 1966), 149–68.

67 See D. Bruce Sealey and Antoine S. Lussier, eds., *The Métis: Canada's Forgotten People* (Winnipeg: Manitoba Métis Federation Press, 1975), 9.

68 A.S. Morton, *History of the West to 1870* (Toronto: University of Toronto Press, 1973), 575, 805 passim; "The New Nation," *Proceedings and Transactions, Royal Society of Canada* 33, sect. 2 (1939):137–45; W.L. Morton, "The Canadian Métis," *The Beaver* (1950):3–7; George F.G. Stanley, "The Métis and the Conflict of Cultures in Western Canada," *The Canadian Historical Review* 28 (1947)4:428–33.

69 There are some who see the English conquest of New France as a factor in the emergence of métis nationalism. If the conquest had any influence at all in this regard, it would at most have been tangential, effective only insofar as the métis identified with the French. However, not all of them had French ancestry; some of the most active of métis nationalists were of English or Scottish descent.

70 Robin Fisher, *Contact and Conflict* (Vancouver: University of British Columbia Press, 1977), 64; Margaret Ormsby, *British Columbia: A History* (Vancouver: Macmillan, 1971), 129.

Many roads to Red River:
Métis genesis in the Great Lakes region,
1680–1815

Jacqueline Peterson

I made the acquaintance of a half-breed in the village, who kindly invited me into his house. These men, who have two sorts of blood in their veins, have also generally two names, Indian and French. My good friend's French name was La Fleur, his Indian one Bimashiwin, or as he translated it, "Une chose, ou personne, qui marche avec le vent," as we should say, a sailor. Riviere au Desert, 1855.[1]

The people who are born and grow up at the interstices of two civilizations or nations are almost always in motion, eluding facile identification. They are like weather vanes perpetually testing the winds. If the parent nations happen to be belligerents, then the population at their common frontier is likely to be small, frail, easily dispersed. However, if such nations are peaceable, intermarriages will occur and a relatively stable composite group will develop along their shared geographical or cultural border. Over time, this group may begin to serve as a conduit for goods, services, and information and to see its function as a broker. It will not usually recognize, in the process of acquiring a group history and identity, that it is, to a large degree, a dependency of the nations or societies it links or separates, to be snuffed out when there is no longer a need for its services.

Just such a people – calling themselves métis – burst upon the historical stage in 1815, its leaders stridently declaring themselves (rather than the Hudson's Bay Company [HBC]) the rightful owners of the heartland of North America, that part of the greater Northwest where the woodland prairies dissolve into plains. So sudden was the birth of métis consciousness that it seemed almost autochthonous, an unpredicted welling up from the soil of nationalistic aspirations. Or it might have been the result of intellectual air currents, drifting across the Atlantic, which carried the seeds of the Age of Nationalism to so remote a locale.

Scholars generally have searched in more accessible quarters, and have attributed the first wave of métis nationalism and the armed effort to prevent the establishment of a HBC colony at Red River to the self-interested intrigues of the rival North West Company (NWC). Marcel Giraud has been particularly persuasive in linking métis territorial claims to company rather than ethnic or racial affiliation. While Cuthbert Grant gathered in both Anglophone and Francophone métis, suggesting, as does Irene Spry's analysis elsewhere in this volume, that language and culture were not the critical divide, the métis opposition did not attract the sympathy of the "Hudson's Bay Company Half-breeds." Instead, as Factor James Bird at Edmonton reported in 1816, these men were rallying to challenge the claims of the North West Company métis.[2]

Because the members of the first métis movement were overwhelmingly partisans or employees of the NWC does not mean that métis nationalism was a NWC invention, however. Rather the debate over the role of the NWC and the connection between métis political consciousness and the HBC and NWC war for control over the interior fur trade begs the question of métis group identity. The métis "nation" may have been *une idée nouvelle*. Nonetheless, its wide and persistent appeal throughout the nineteenth century suggests that it stood for a type of social cohesion which was much older. Rather than imputing métis nationalism to the designs of outsiders, it may be more fruitful to treat it as a paradigmatic reformulation of a set of symbols, however inchoate and unarticulated, which had formerly joined those who, after 1815, wore the new identity.[3]

This process was not unique to Red River, or to the métis. Nationhood, wrung from revolution, was, in fact, the new paradigm for the age, on both sides of the Atlantic. The heroic nationalism of Napoleon Bonaparte touched even the northwestern prairies, as it did Mexico and much of the western hemisphere. However, nations do not, except metaphorically, spring from the soil. Group identities are not mere fabrications. They must have a beginning and they must depend upon a core of experiences and characteristics held even if not yet fully recognized in common.[4]

One of the beginning points – and there were several regional populations which converged at Red River after 1815 to become métis – occurred during the eighteenth century a thousand miles to the east in the Great Lakes region. Here, in the heart of the North American fur-trade arena, in response to the desire of diverse Algonkian-, Iroquoian- and Siouan-speaking tribes and successive waves of French, British and American traders to forge a commercial alliance, a new society came into being. At first it was a tiny society. Always, it was a society in flux, connecting and continually forced to absorb disparate cultural and ethnic representatives whose mutual interest in the traffic in furs and metal utensils and weapons barely masked their ethnocentric antagonisms. Yet, it was also a society whose members – if not self-consciously métis before 1815 – were a people in the process of becoming. We know this because their distinctiveness was fully apparent to outsiders, if not to themselves.

During the 1820s, Englishmen and Americans travelling into the Great Lakes fur-trade universe discovered to their surprise that they had entered a foreign land. Such travellers generally wrote disparagingly, but their comments are provocative. Whereas eighteenth-century observers had been apt to refer to members of Great Lakes fur-trade settlements as "Canadien," "French," or "Indian," depending upon cultural attributes such as dress, demeanour or social rank, by the early decades of the nineteenth century, this cultural classification system was being challenged and supplanted by a system based upon pseudoscientific ideas about race. Following the War of 1812, terms such as *half-breed, métis* and *métif* began to appear with increasingly frequency in the travel literature, carrying with them the pejorative baggage of social inferiority or degeneracy. William S. Keating's description of the mixed inhabitants of Fort Wayne, Indiana, and Chicago was typical: "They were a miserable race of men." Caleb Atwater similarly derided the society at Prairie du Chien in 1829 as a "mixed breed," "as motley a group of creatures (I can scarcely call them human beings) as the world ever beheld." It was as if Jean Hector de Crèvecoeur's prophetic vision of a half-savage new American race had been fulfilled![5]

Such negative labels reveal a good deal more about the observers than the observed, and confirm that the decades of the 1820s and 1830s were marked by an intensifying race prejudice in the United States and Canada. Yet, ironically, while travellers' accounts tell us nothing about how residents of Great Lakes trading communities perceived themselves, they illuminate the distinctive contours of a new society. They point directly, in fact, to the emergence of a unique hybridization of native and Euro-American cultures, to a highly fluid, although bounded, geographical domain, and an occupational identity which was recognizable to outsiders at such distant points as Sault Ste. Marie (Michigan); Vincennes (Indiana); and Prairie du Chien (Wisconsin). They affirm George Croghan's observation of a half century earlier, that Indians and French men and women were being "bred up together like Children in that Country."[6]

The roots of such communities and the boundaries of "that Country" are easily traceable to fur-trade expansion under the French regime and to the particular attributes of that commercial system as it evolved in the Great Lakes region. By the early decades of the eighteenth century the French in Canada had constructed a framework for trade with the native inhabitants of the interior which was to survive, with minor modifications by the British and Americans, until overexploitation and subsequent scarcity of wildlife rendered the fur trade unprofitable and Indian land cessions opened the region to agricultural settlement. The hallmarks of the Great Lakes trade included the following: (a) a licensing program which, while far less restrictive under British and American auspices than under the French, attempted to regulate the flow of furs to market and the dimensions and quality of Indian-white contact; (b) a recognition of the fur-gathering tribes as necessary, if unequal partners, with whom economic and diplomatic alliances were maintained through fair dealing and gift exchange; (c) a willingness to trade with Indian hunters at their residential source, which necessitated the erection of a string of trading posts and the garrisoning of military forts for protection; (d) the employment of an occupational class – the voyageur-trader – in the middle- and lower-rung trade positions requiring travel to and contact with Indian hunters; and (e) widespread intermarriage between these employees and native women.

The imperial and commercial designs of the French did not include a commitment to settle large numbers of non-Indian agriculturalists upon lands wealthy in fur-bearing animals. With the exception of Detroit, Kaskaskia and Cahokia, the French colonial administration established no farming communities in the Great Lakes region. After 1763, only partly in response to the regionwide resistance movement known as Pontiac's Rebellion, the British likewise discouraged settlement west of Lake Ontario. Desire to keep the peace and to monopolize the profits of the Great Lakes Indian trade were the overriding considerations favouring this policy. To have simultaneously encouraged an influx of white farmers would have upset both the diplomatic alliance with the native inhabitants inherited from the French and the ratio between humans and animals on the ground, straining the fur-bearing capacities of the region.[7]

Thus, in contrast to the rapid growth of a white agricultural population along the eastern seaboard after 1680, actually a repopulation of native lands "widowed" by epidemic diseases, the Great Lakes region remained under tribal domination. Prior to 1815, there were few non-Indians in the present states of Michigan, Wisconsin, and Minnesota and in northern Indiana and Illinois, and almost none of them were farmers, stock keepers or tradespeople inhabiting commercial towns tied to an agricultural hinterland. Yet, despite administrative restrictions and almost no inducements in the form of land titles, numerous Canadians did cast their fate, and the future of their progeny, with the Great Lakes country after 1700.[8]

These people were neither adjunct relative-members of tribal villages nor the standard bearers of European civilization in the wilderness. Increasingly, they stood apart or, more precisely, in between. By the end of the last struggle for empire in 1815, their towns, which were visually, ethnically and culturally distinct from neighbouring Indian villages and "white towns" along the eastern seaboard, stretched from Detroit and Michilimackinac at the east to the Red River at the northwest.

The establishment of permanent settlements and the concomitant weaving of a social fabric or community ethos in the Great Lakes region appear to have been unique developments in the early history of the fur trade in North America. More durable and complex than the factories of the HBC or the forts and posts of the NWC, these settlements deserve close scrutiny for the clues they may provide to the origin of institutions and nexuses subsequently linking members of a far-flung "fur trade society."

All Great Lakes trading communities founded between 1702 and 1815 shared two characteristics. First, such towns were occupationally monolithic, their residents dependent almost exclusively upon a single industry – the fur trade. Occupational and material homogeneity marked these towns as well. Wealth was fairly evenly distributed, status distinctions were few, and residents – voyageurs and merchants alike – drew upon a local subsistence base rather than on European imports, not only in terms of foodstuffs, but in terms of clothing, tools, utensils and building materials, all of which, if not manufactured to suit Indian tastes and sold as trade goods, were borrowed or adapted from neighbouring tribal populations. Second, such towns grew as a result of and were increasingly dominated by the offspring of Canadian trade employees and Indian women who, having reached their majority, were intermarrying among themselves and rearing successive generations of métis. In both instances, these communities did not represent an extension of French, and later British colonial culture, but were rather "adaptation[s] to the Upper Great Lakes environment."[9]

Several qualifications of these generalizations are in order. Lyle Stone's archaeological analysis of the remains at Fort Michilimackinac, the commercial hub of the Great Lakes fur trade, confirms that even during the French period the community at the straits joining Lakes Huron and Michigan was growing increasingly heterogeneous, its population more stratified and dependent upon a wider range of imported materials. Other Great Lakes trading communities, even those most isolated, experienced the same trend although at a somewhat later date.[10]

On the other hand, Stone's conclusion that the British takeover in 1763 spawned a transformation of the homogeneous, subsistence-based, trade-oriented community at Michilimackinac into an economically and socially diverse military outpost whose orientation and artifact source was the eastern seaboard cannot easily be extended to most of the other Great Lakes trading towns. Important distinctions must be drawn between the French and Anglo-American occupations of the Great Lakes region, particularly after 1790 when the growth of powerful monopoly companies ended the rise of French-speaking men to positions of influence in the trade, creating both a caste system based on ethnicity and sharp divisions of status and wealth. However, the social and occupational composition and the material bases of communities such as Green Bay and Chicago suggest that despite increasing complexity the early French period model was the rule rather than the exception until American agriculturalists, land speculators and logging interests swept across the region after the American Revolution in the south and after the end of the War of 1812 in the north.[11]

The foundations for settlement of the Great Lakes region by Canadian men of the trade were laid between 1702 and 1714 at Detroit and Kaskaskia and at French trading sites which had been formally abandoned when the interior fur trade was closed in 1698. Such settlement by the trading fraternity was not inspired by the Crown. On the contrary, the inability of the Canadian governor-general to control the growing numbers of illegal voyageurs (or *coureurs de bois*) drawn from the widely dispersed *habitant* (original settlers, largely peasant farmers) population along the St. Lawrence, as well as Jesuit complaints that Canadians were debauching the natives of the interior were at least partly responsible for the decision to close the Great Lakes posts and to call all traders home to the St. Lawrence. Only Kaskaskia and Detroit remained as formal concentration points – military-mission centres – where Jesuits and Récollets and a small number of civilians relocated from the St. Lawrence worked to purify Great Lakes tribesmen of the traders' earlier contamination.

Instead, as the missionaries discovered, Indian villages located adjacent to former trading stations were sheltering Canadian outlaws, some of whom, by 1702, had taken Indian wives. At St. Ignace (Fort Buade) on the north shore of the Straits of Michilimackinac, for instance, an unknown number of "dissolute" coureurs de bois still plagued the Huron and Ottawa villages in 1702, despite the recall. The remaining Jesuit missionary, Etienne Carheil, thought that the traders resident among the Indians had been "supported" by a succession of "unchaste commandants" (notably

Antoine de LaMothe Cadillac) whose lax leadership had encouraged movement away from the men's barracks and the building of "separate houses for themselves alone," and their Indian consorts. The result was that "one of them [had] more than one child in the village."[12]

Even after the post was abandoned, the illegal traders continued to leave the French houses within the fort and "to go to live with the women in their Cabins." Initially the cabins of the Canadians which were "separated from one another," were probably within one of the adjacent Indian villages. Eventually, however, these single-family dwellings at St. Ignace clustered, distinguishing themselves by 1712 from the old French fort and the pallisaded Huron and Ottawa villages.[13]

Illegal traders were also settling in the Illinois Country, at Peoria and, after 1700, at the new mission villages of Kaskaskia and Cahokia on the Mississippi River. Cahokia, in particular, seemed to attract the criminals of the trade. In 1715, Acting Governor Ramezay and Intendant of Canada Michel Bégon reported that "about 100 coureurs escaped to Cahokia where they joined forty-seven others who had previously settled there." The town, they declared, was "a retreat for the lawless men both of this colony and of Louisiana." The wives of these men were by and large Kaskaskias and Peorias, judging from the Jesuit complaints.[14]

A similar pattern of intermarriage and illegal trade was discernable at Detroit, to which Cadillac brought fifty soldiers, fifty traders and artisans, and Jesuit and Récollet priests in 1701. A year later, some six thousand Indians were gathered about the new fort in four or five villages. Among them were Potawatomi and Miami drawn eastward from the St. Joseph's River valley in search of trade goods, as well as Ottawa, Huron and Ojibwa from the straits of Michilimackinac.[15]

Such concentration provided abundant opportunity for Detroit's primarily male Canadian population. Although Cadillac held a personal trade monopoly, many of his men surreptitiously bartered with their Indian neighbours. Personal relations were intimate and friendly, as they had been at St. Ignace under Cadillac's management. The commandant did not discourage commingling with Indians, particularly on the part of single men. And, while he personally brought a wife from the St. Lawrence, "it was no uncommon thing for a citizen to have left behind him a lawful wife and to have selected another in Detroit from some savage tribe."[16]

The failure of the Crown's concentration policy was evident as early as 1710. The illegal fur traffic and debauchery of Indian women persisted; French tribal allies did not all gravitate to the centres; and many of those

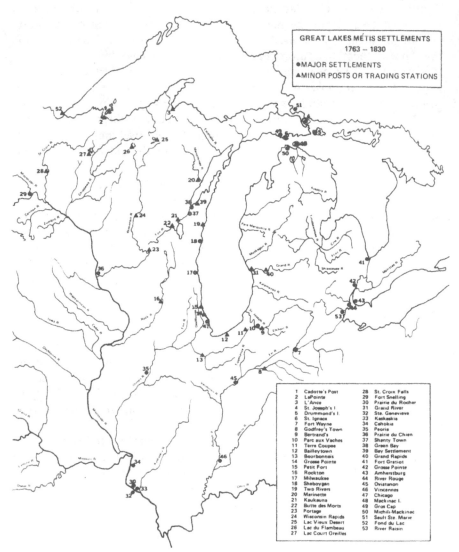

GREAT LAKES MÉTIS SETTLEMENTS
1763 – 1830
● MAJOR SETTLEMENTS
▲ MINOR POSTS OR TRADING STATIONS

1	Cadotte's Post	28	St. Croix Falls
2	LaPointe	29	Fort Snelling
3	L'Anse	30	Prairie du Rocher
4	St. Joseph's I.	31	Grand River
5	Drummond's I.	32	Sta. Genevieve
6	St. Ignace	33	Kaskaskia
7	Fort Wayne	34	Cahokia
8	Godfrey's Town	35	Peoria
9	Bertrand's	36	Prairie du Chien
10	Parc aux Vaches	37	Shanty Town
11	Terre Coupee	38	Green Bay
12	Bailleytown	39	Bay Settlement
13	Bourbonnais	40	Grand Rapids
14	Grosse Pointe	41	Fort Gratiot
15	Petit Fort	42	Grosse Pointe
16	Rockton	43	Amherstburg
17	Milwaukee	44	River Rouge
18	Sheboygan	45	Ouiatanon
19	Two Rivers	46	Vincennes
20	Marinette	47	Chicago
21	Kaukauna	48	Mackinac I.
22	Butte des Morts	49	Gros Cap
23	Portage	50	Michili-Mackinac
24	Wisconsin Rapids	51	Sault Ste. Marie
25	Lac Vieux Desert	52	Fond du Lac
26	Lac du Flambeau	53	River Raisin
27	Lac Court Oreilles		

Map 1
Great Lakes métis settlements, 1763–1830. (Map by Connie Peterson.)

who did, did so only temporarily. By 1716, Louis de la Porte Sieur de Louvigny had left Quebec with a force of 425 men, plus farmers, carpenters and an armourer, destined for the straits of Michilimackinac.[17]

The decision to reoccupy this strategic military site was accompanied by the reopening of the licenced trade, limited as before to twenty-five congés and the extension of amnesty to all coureurs de bois who would return to the St. Lawrence. Few went home. In fact, their numbers multiplied as licence holders inflated the number of canoes allowed, sneaking unknown hundreds of anonymous men into the field. Some of these men trafficked in places where no licences had been granted, but by and large they tended to congregate about the cordon of wilderness posts garrisoned after 1714: at Fort Miamis (now Fort Wayne) on the Maumee River in northeast Indiana (1715); Fort St. Joseph at Niles, Michigan (1715); Fort St. Louis at Peoria (1715); Fort St. François at La Baye or Green Bay (1717); at Madeleine Island (LaPointe) in Chequamegon Bay (1718); at Kaministiquia on the northwest shore of Lake Superior (1717); and between 1727 and 1750 at Fort Beauharnois on the western shore of Lake Pepin, near Frontenac, Minnesota; at Sault Ste. Marie; at Ouiatanon (Lafayette) and Vincennes, Indiana; at Fort Nipigon on the north shore of the lake of the same name; and at nearly a dozen other forts stretching to Lake Winnipeg and beyond called, jointly, "Posts of the Sea of the West." Many of the early trading posts, particularly those north of forty-four degrees latitude, were located near sites already exploited by large numbers of Indians for their mild, lake-warmed climate and relatively long growing season. At nearly all of these places, self-contained métis communities were to develop during the eighteenth century[18] (see map 1).

Michilimackinac ranked as the most important of all the advance posts of Canada. The name, later shortened to Mackinac, which the French used to designate the shore on both sides of the straits between Lakes Michigan and Huron as well as the island itself, referred in Indian oral tradition only to the island. Although the first French mission and trading post in the upper lakes was temporarily located upon the island itself, nearly a century of contact was to pass before the Ojibwa were persuaded to deed their "mother" to the British who then raised a fort upon it in 1779. Rather, it was upon the north shore, or at St. Ignace, where Father Jacques Marquette founded a mission in 1671 and the stockade and barracks of Fort Buade were raised in 1689. It was here that an advance party of several hundred men sent to quell the Fox under Monsieur de Lignery in 1712 discovered the log and bark cabins of the coureurs de bois and their families. The exact population of this early settlement is unknown, although among the odd one hundred coureurs de bois were certainly men by the names of L'Esperance, DuRivage, Vieux, Menard and Villeneuve. These voyageurs were living with Indian women.[19]

Anticipating the arrival of a large force, Lignery's men raised, between 1715 and 1717, a rectangular fort with corner bastions on the south side of the straits close by the Ottawa village. Soon thereafter, the mission and at least some of the St. Ignace traders moved across the six-mile expanse of water into the fort and its shadow. The caption on an anonymous map of the straits dating from about 1717 demonstrates to what purpose the new "fort" was immediately put: "The fort on the south side of the Straits has a commandant, a few settlers, and even some French women, and . . . in 1716 about 600 coureurs-de-bois were gathered there during trading time."[20]

Although the garrison at the straits was the largest in the region during the French regime, its commandant outranking all his counterparts, the military force rarely numbered more than thirty-five men. The garrisons at other posts were considerably smaller and generally, after 1742, were employees of commandant-traders who had leased or were licenced to engross the profits of a given area. At Michilimackinac, as elsewhere, the garrison engaged in little military activity; it "served primarily to protect traders" and the free flow of goods and furs across the straits.[21]

Trade was the preoccupation of all residents, civilians and soldiers alike. Michilimackinac was the inland seat of the Montreal merchants who, if they did not personally visit there, sent agents to supervise the unpacking of trade-good laden canoes shipped from Montreal and Lachine late each summer. Once inside the post, goods were sorted and outfits organized for voyages to Lakes Michigan and Superior. Then, in the spring, the water gate saw the last of the voyageurs heading east with their furs weighed, baled and marked.

The population of Michilimackinac rose and fell with the mercury. In the summer months, the narrow beach stretching west to the Ottawa villages was crowded with the canoes and portable mat- and bark-covered wigwams of thousands of visiting natives who came to barter furs, corn, maple sugar, dried fish and bear's grease for ammunition, traps, stroud (coarse woollen cloth), thimbles, glass beads and trinkets, and brandy, as well as to receive their annual present, a reward for a good hunt and fidelity to the Crown. Several hundred voyageurs, clerks and their *bourgeois* (wintering traders) came in to tally up the year's receipts, to revive family ties and obligations or, if single, to spend their meagre wages on riotous amusements for a few months, and, if not returning to Montreal, to catch their breath before indebting and indenturing themselves for the next winter's outfit of goods.

When the thousands departed in the fall for the hunting grounds, Michilimackinac battened down for the winter. Those remaining included the garrison and its female camp followers; families of voyageurs and traders gone for the trading season; clerks, apprentices, indentured servants, petty local merchants, representatives of Montreal trading firms; retired voyageurs and traders with their kin and servants; labourers like Joseph Ainse, builder of the rows of one-story dwellings within the fort; and slaves, both Panis (Indian) and black.[22]

Precise descriptions of the community at Michilimackinac during the French regime are relatively rare. Much of what can be pieced together about the permanent residents is gleaned from the incomplete Michilimackinac register of births, marriages, and deaths stretching from 1699 to 1821. Unfortunately, the original register was destroyed and the transcription of the earliest entries up to 1722 is badly fragmented. Nevertheless, the register serves as a useful device for measuring travellers' tallies against a roster of family names persistent at the Straits of Michilimackinac.[23]

An additional source for Michilimackinac in the mid-1700s is the report and map of an officer sent by the governor-general of Canada, M. de La Galissonnière, to survey the route from Montreal to the straits. Michel Chartier de Lotbinière arrived at the fort toward the end of September, 1749. Eight days of wind and rain confined him to quarters, but finally on October 1 he was able to begin his measurements and observations. The human landscape failed to impress him.[24]

Lotbinière counted forty houses within the cedar stockade, but he actually met only "ten French families . . . among whom three are of mixed blood." None of these householders farmed, although the surveyor assumed they had been "born farmers since they all came from rural areas." As far as Lotbinière could tell, the "sole occupation" of the men was "strolling around the fort's parade ground, from morn till night, smoking," and that of the women, putting on "lady-like airs" and "going from house to house for a cup of coffee or chocolate."[25]

The men referred to themselves as "merchants." However, the surveyor insisted they were "only plain *Coureurs de Bois*," who apparently preferred their hewn-log and bark-covered habitations, their "corn and grease," and their leisure to labouring to "give themselves some of the comforts of life." The residents may have appeared lazy, but Lotbinière recorded another explanation of their behaviour: these men would have felt "dishonored if they cultivated the soil."[26]

Lotbinière erred in classifying the residents as mere *"Coureurs de Bois."* Those men whom he met in the stockade as late as October 1, 1749, were not winterers but the petty merchant elite of Michilimackinac. Unlike the summer residents of the abandoned houses, they could afford to pass the winter idly parading and smoking and to supply their wives with imported coffee and tea. What Lotbinière's description confirms, however, is that a relative lack of material status distinctions characterized the Great Lakes communities of the French period. Even "merchants" had adapted themselves to the local environment, wearing the same clothes, eating the same foods, and occupying the same houses as those of common voyageurs. Most of their material goods were either Indian-made or were items designed for the Indian trade.[27]

Lotbinière erred on another count. While the population of Michilimackinac varied seasonally, the summer population was composed less of transients and vagabonds than of half-time residents. The majority of Michilimackinac's inhabitants were forced to migrate in winter in response to the demands of their occupation. These were the non-merchants, men occupying the middle and lower rungs of the trade – the bourgeois, clerks, voyageurs and boatmen – who annually hied themselves into the interior to man distant trading posts or to winter with a native hunting band.

Comparison of the names of house occupants on Lotbinière's map of 1749 and the register of births and marriages at Michilimackinac during the French and British periods confirms that the community at the straits had a stable population from the 1720s onward. Families of many of the householders of 1749, the Langlades, Bertrands, Desrivieres, Amelins, Bourassas, Parents, Amiots, Chaboyers, Ainses, Blondeaus and Chevaliers can be traced over several generations.[28]

Most of Michilimackinac's growth during the French period came from within. While Lyle Stone has estimated the early population at only thirty to fifty souls, 351 baptisms were recorded between 1698 and 1765, of which only 119 were Indian and black slaves or Indian converts. And, while frequent gaps in the register make family reconstitution problematic, those marriages where the wife survived past forty, fulfilling her total childbearing potential, displayed a remarkable fecundity.[29]

Between 1698 and 1765, sixty-two marriages were recorded at Michilimackinac and an additional twenty-five can be inferred from the baptismal register. Of these, twenty-nine, or roughly one-third, were contracted between French-Canadians and only three between Indian men and women. By far the largest number of marriages (forty-eight percent) joined Canadian employees of the fur trade to Indian or métis women. In the French period, métis endogamy and marriage between métis and Indian appear insignificant.

TABLE 1
Marital fertility and family size, Michilimackinac, 1698–1821.

Baptismal date of first child	Families reconstructed	Average number of children	Completed families*	Average number of children
1698–1720	5	5.20	2	9.0
1721–1730	6	7.50	3	10.0
1731–1740	6	5.33	1	9.0
1741–1750	8	4.38	3	8.0
1751–1760	15	3.00	2	4.0
1761–1770	9	2.67	0	
1771–1780	9	3.80	2	8.0
1781–1790	7	4.30	2	8.5
1791–1800	6	4.00	0	

Source: "The Mackinac Register," transcribed and reprinted in *Collections of the State Historical Society of Wisconsin*, 18:469–513, 19:1–149.

*Families where the mother survived to age forty.

Several conclusions can be read from the Michilimackinac register, but at base the register measures only the marital proclivities of previously unmarried, Catholic full- or part-time residents desiring a church ceremony. It does not measure marriages contracted without church sanction, particularly between Canadian males and native women who had no interest in conversion. That number may not have been large given the social pressure generated by close company within the stockade and the keen eye of the curé. However, a steady flow of baptisms of children registered as illegitimate (many of them the offspring of Panis concubines) suggests that unchurched unions frequently occurred.

Not surprisingly, a rising number of residents were métis. During the French period, 38.75 percent of all recorded baptisms were of persons at least one-eighth Indian. If one deducts the large numbers of Indians baptized, often as adults, during this period, the actual percentage of métis births compared to Canadian births is significantly higher. During the British period, between 1765 and 1797, for example, when few Indians received baptism, 71.67 percent of the 131 baptisms recorded were of métis.[30]

The small explosion of children born of mixed marriages revealed in the register explains why the picket walls at Michilimackinac were enlarged at least three times during the French regime. And still quarters were cramped. The average civilian house measured only seventeen feet four

TABLE 2
Ethnic affiliation determined through family reconstruction based on extant records, Michili-mackinac, 1698–1765.

Marriages	Number	Percentage
Between Canadians	20	32.26
Between Canadians and Indians	17	27.42
Between Canadians and métis	13	20.97
Between métis	1	1.61
Between métis and Indians	3	4.85
Between Indians	1	1.61
Uncertain ethnic origin	7	11.29

inches by twenty feet five inches, with two three-foot five-inch doors and a tiny garden attached.[31]

Despite the pressures of limited space, however, Lotbinière's 1749 map and the land-allotment ledger for Detroit for 1749 to 1752 indicate that few residents of either of these posts received title to households and lands outside the forts before 1749. Prior to that time they doubtless held rotating strips in a common field and grazed their few animals on a common pasture, but townsmen like Charles Langlade, the son of Michilimackinac trader Augustin Langlade and a well-connected Ottawa woman, who had built homes beyond the walls did so at their own risk. As late as 1763 the majority of Michilimackinac's inhabitants still made their homes within the walls, although at least one resident, René Bourassa, had by then received more than eight concessions of land.[32]

René Bourassa was a trader, not a farmer, however. And Michili-mackinac grew in response to the demands of the fur trade rather than the granary. Its residents tended to eschew farming except for family garden patches. Foodstuffs, particularly corn, squash, beans and maple sugar, were acquired from the neighbouring Ottawa who, until their fields gave out in about 1741, were situated a few miles distant. After that date, residents purchased corn and bear's grease from the new Ottawa villages stretching southward from Arbre Croche along Little Traverse Bay and at Cheboygan, Michigan.[33]

If the Ottawa crop failed, the town turned to the Potawatomi and Menominee at Green Bay. Fish, particularly whitefish, sturgeon and trout, were likewise procured from Indian fishermen who speared their catch through the ice in winter and employed long hemp nets in summer. Although a few European staples and delicacies such as coffee, teas, choco-

TABLE 3
Michilimackinac births, 1698–1765.

Birth	Number	Percentage
Métis	136	38.75
Euro-American	78	22.22
Indian	115	32.76
Black	4	1.14
Uncertain	18	5.13

late, biscuits and white flour were imported from Montreal during the French period, residents relied for the most part upon local resources, catching and drying fish and hunting for game, water fowl and small birds. Enormous numbers of passenger pigeons and squabs, which the Ottawa did not seem to relish, roosted in upper Michigan between March and June, providing a rich source of food in the lean months between corn harvesting and the ice-free spring passage of supply ships from the East.[34]

The disinclination of men of the trade to farm and the rather tight-fisted land policy of both the French and British at Michilimackinac and Detroit meant that growth *in situ* was limited to those who could afford to stay. Thus, despite a high birth rate, the number of year-round residents increased undramatically during the French and British regimes and tended to reflect the ingress of paid affiliates of the military (like the armourer, joiner, blacksmith and carpenter) or official representatives of the colony (for example, the notary and priest). These men, out of all proportion to their actual numbers, lent increasing diversity and complexity to the social structure of the major trading communities as the eighteenth century progressed.

The British takeover seems to have precipitated a major movement of Canadiens and their native families out of the fort at Michilimackinac although in 1767 a traveller, John Portheous, noted that a much-enlarged stockade – nearly 110 yards in length – still enclosed much of the town with its "square, church and several lanes." Residents, if they farmed, were doing so across the straits at the adjunct community of St. Ignace which had never been completely abandoned. The fort itself stood on a "dry barren beach," whose sands, whipped by the winds funneling through the narrow water passage, blew through the "crevices of houses" and into the eyes. The old Indian field, two or three miles distant, was being used as pasture, but the soil was "neither very fit for grain, nor Luxuriant in

TABLE 4
Michilimackinac births, 1765–1797.

Births	Number	Percentage
Métis	94	71.76
Euro-American	8	6.11
Indian	13	9.92
Black	2	1.53
Uncertain	14	10.69

Grass." Maple sugar and dried fish were the staple manufactures of the hundred or so families dwelling at Michilimackinac at that date.[35]

By the early 1770s, Michilimackinac had become a relatively complex and socially differentiated commercial and military centre whose principal British residents imported most of their goods from the East. A suburb of nearly a hundred houses skirted the stockade. Farming was still a minor activity, however, and the persistent wind and thin soil ultimately convinced the British to relocate the town and fort upon the island in 1779.

Mackinac was not destined to grow into a modern agricultural business centre. Under the British aegis, which placed greater emphasis upon military activity, the town lost its simple occupational homogeneity and local orientation but it was not weaned of its attachment to the trade. Although several British and American traders established moderately sized farms and pastures, the majority of residents at the island continued to pursue trade-related occupations, to intermarry (see table 5), and to live in semi-Indianized fashion. In 1797, Mackinac had some seventy-nine log-and-bark houses, two stores and a Catholic church hugging the southern shore of the island which looked out across the narrows to the hardwood groves of Bois Blanc Island.[36]

At Detroit where, in contrast, a salubrious climate, rich soil and government policy encouraged farming, the British ascendancy seems to have slowed an earlier movement of Canadiens onto their own lands. Both Jonathan Carver and John Portheous noted in the late 1760s that the eighty to a hundred houses within the walls were occupied primarily by English traders, whereas the narrow, ribbon farm lots of Canadiens and métis were scattered along the east side of the river north as far as Lake St. Clair.[37]

The titles to most of these "plantations," plus gifts of oxen and seed, were granted by French commandants at the post between 1734 and 1753 to Quebec habitants as inducements to agricultural settlement. By British

TABLE 5
Michilimackinac marriages, 1765–1818.

Marriages	Number	Percentage
Between Euro-Americans*	8	18.60
Between Euro-Americans and Indians	6	13.95
Between Euro-Americans and métis	22	51.16
Between métis	2	4.65
Between métis and Indians	2	4.65
Between Indians	0	0.00
Between blacks	1	2.33
Uncertain ethnic origin	2	4.65

*Includes French and British Canadians, Europeans and Americans.

and American standards the farmers of Detroit were lackadaisical workers, but the point is that they did farm, raising sufficient surplus to feed their kin and to provision the lower Michigan fur trade. During the French regime, therefore, many Detroit residents did not engage primarily in the fur traffic and as a result *métissage* (racial mixing) occurred less frequently there than it did elsewhere, even though the physical appearance of the settlement and the material culture of its households differed little from those of Michilimackinac.[38]

The layout of the community at Detroit was reminiscent of the string settlements along the St. Lawrence, themselves early adaptations to the needs of trade and transportation in an alien environment. Unlike the community within the stockade, with its rectangular grid, orderly rowhouses and avenues, Detroit at large was laid out along the water line. Each man staked out his plot based on the available river shoreline, his cabin hugging the bank and his picketed garden trailing like a streamer into the timber behind. The "estates" were narrow, "only 1, 2 or 3 Square Acres in front," and relatively equal in size. After a generation or two, additional log-and-bark cabins sprang up alongside the original, occupied by sons and grandsons and their families, so that increasingly the straggle on the shore appeared from the water road "like a continued town or village."[39]

Detroit was the largest town in the Great Lakes region after 1765, reflecting the greater commercial and administrative importance attached to it by the British. Significantly, however, while British and later American merchants flocked to the urban core at the stockade, the old Canadian population was forced to cope with its burgeoning population through dispersal and a shift from farming to trade. Governor Henry Hamilton declared at the close of 1778 that he had never granted lands at Detroit despite pressure from settlers "whose farms [were] small and families numerous." The consequences, he admitted, were that "young men growing to age engage as canoe men, go off to distant settlements and in general become vagabonds, so that the settlement does not increase in numbers as may be seen by comparing the *recensement* of 1776 with that of 1766."[40]

Whatever were the motivations behind British restraint, at least a portion of Detroit's French-speaking population met the problem by establishing a new settlement without the benefit of European land titles. During the 1780s, as lands at Detroit moved into the hands of sharp-witted English merchants, several dozen métis families moved south to the River Raisin under the leadership of François Navarre who had acquired a tract from the Potawatomi. More than one hundred families had built cabins on the River Raisin by 1788, recreating both the spatial pattern and lifestyle they had enjoyed at Detroit for two or three generations.[41]

The community at Rivière Raisin (or Frenchtown) was a late example of a second type of Great Lakes métis settlement. Unlike the commercial-military centres of Michilimackinac and Detroit, whose increasingly diversified economies and strategic locations allowed for potentially unlimited growth, corporate trading towns like Frenchtown did not, prior to inundation by American farmers, shrug off their dependence upon the fur trade and the local subsistence base. As a result, few of these towns achieved a population of five or six hundred (see map 1).

Corporate trading towns were marked by a simple social organization, occupational homogeneity, dependence upon either Michilimackinac or Detroit for supplies and recruits, and upon a local "home guard" or Indian band for surplus foods. Less apparent were the clear status and wealth demarcations of a Michilimackinac or Detroit which set apart the intrusive royal officials, commandants and eastern merchants from the lesser locally-based merchants and traders, military officers, master craftsmen and the labouring ranks. The usual presence of a commandant-trader, a small garrison, a militia captain and occasional hired farmers, blacksmith, notary public and missionary, however, provided the outlines of a broader institutional structure which residents struggled to maintain in isolation. The upper class, such as it was, that is, the senior traders and their male métis offspring, assumed when necessary the roles of priest, commandant, judge and notary.

Such towns functioned as corporate entities, laying out relatively equal ribbon-shaped lots, common fields and pastures; regulating trespass and theft; and transferring lands and houses. They did so, with the exception of

Vincennes, Indiana, which was administered from Louisiana and where many of the eighty-eight landholders of 1773 claimed pre-1763 French patents, without the benefit of European or American titles, having purchased or received freely their estates from neighbouring tribal bands.[42]

At Green Bay and Prairie du Chien, for example, prominent traders formally purchased lands of the Menominee and Fox, respectively, but there, as at St. Ignace, Sault Ste. Marie, Fort Wayne, Indiana, and other corporate trading towns, title was not lodged with the inhabitants until after the War of 1812, whereupon American surveyors were forced to take verbal depositions to untangle the métis' customary rights (see map 2). In contrast, claims at Michilimackinac and Detroit carried the weight of French and British documentation.[43]

It was no wonder that the residents of Frenchtown on the River Raisin "had little knowledge of or interest in the exact distance their land extended into the woods," and "gathered their firewood and did their hunting without regard for boundary lines." Preoccupied with the fur trade, they farmed "in the most primitive manner," and "but a short distance back from the river." Métis townsmen cut few land roads; instead, the river served as the year-round highway, a source of food, and as a dumping ground for refuse and accumulated manure.[44]

The growth of the corporate trading towns was accelerated by the British takeover in 1765; however, population pressure and limited opportunities were sufficient catalysts without an expansionistic British policy which encouraged new men to enter the field and which propelled old residents out of Michilimackinac and Detroit. Most of these towns had their beginnings in the French period. All were located along rivers, bays or lakeshores at important breaks in trade or portage points. They were generally sites of Indian agricultural activity and had often been the locations of early French forts and/or missions.

By 1746, for example, on the lower Wabash at Post Vincennes forty male inhabitants and their families and five slaves commingled with a band of 750 Piankeshaw warriors. To the north at Post Ouiatanon (present-day Lafayette, Indiana) twenty householders were living alongside six hundred Wea warriors and their kin. At Fort St. Joseph on the St. Joseph's River near Niles, Michigan, a thriving trade with the neighbouring Potawatomi had gathered forty to fifty Canadian families to its environs by 1750.[45]

The mild climate and rich fur fields of the Green Bay area were attracting traders at least as early as 1720. In 1732, a contract to trade at La Baye was issued to Didace Mouet de Moras, the brother of Michilimackinac trader Augustin Langlade, founder of Green Bay's most illustrious métis family. By

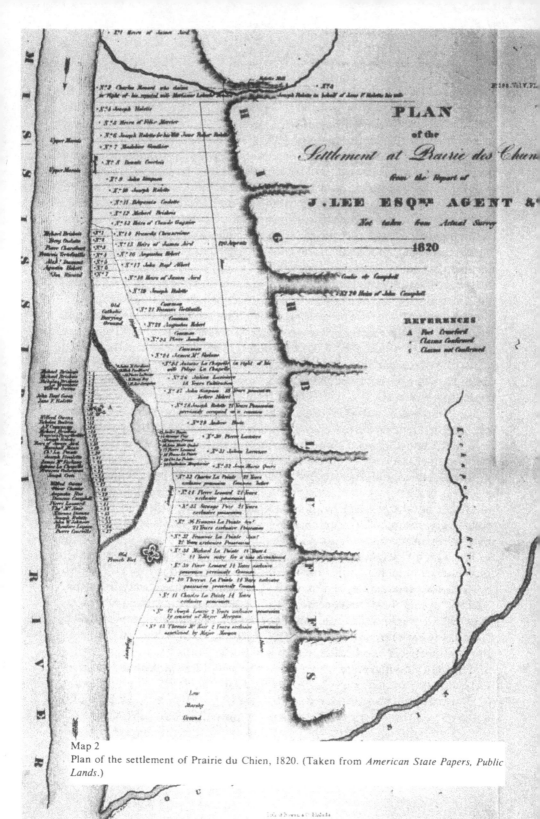

Map 2
Plan of the settlement of Prairie du Chien, 1820. (Taken from *American State Papers, Public Lands*.)

the 1740s, several traders with Indian wives were permanently residing there, among them Pierre Réaume, Claude Caron, LeBeau and Jourdain.[46]

The community at Green Bay was not solidly launched until 1763, however, when following the fall of Michilimackinac to the British, Langlade, his Ottawa wife, and their son Charles abandoned their residences at the straits and engrossed fifteen acres on the east bank of the Fox River opposite the fort. Charles Langlade, whose military career has received less acclaim than it deserves, enjoyed the patronage of both British merchants and the title of Indian superintendent in the Green Bay district. Through Langlade's influence, members of other well-connected Michilimackinac trading families migrated to "La Baye" where they settled upon ribbon plots upriver. By 1785, according to Augustin Grignon, one of Langlade's descendants, the community contained at least fifty-six permanent residents – all traders, voyageurs, hunters and Indian slaves.[47]

Although the residents of Green Bay had marked off common fields and pasture, they, like the inhabitants of Frenchtown and its sister communities, made little effort to keep or raise livestock or to cultivate what they could acquire from the neighbouring Menomini and Winnebago or as easily do without. Travelling through Green Bay in 1793, Scots trader Robert Dickson thought it shameful that "there have long been settled some Canadians [here] who sow but little grain, they have about 100 head of Horned Cattle and a number of Horses which run wild in the woods most part of the year. Altho' every one on his Road to the Mississippi passes LaBaye and would mostly wish to purchase Corn, Flour, Butter, or fresh Provisions, Yet such is the indolence of the People settled there that we pay half a Dollar for a quart of milk and this at all times not to be had."[48]

Twenty years later, the forty or fifty métis heads of household at Green Bay were "generally old worn out voyageurs or boatmen, who having become unfit for the hardships of the Indian trade, had taken wives generally of the Menomonee tribe, and settled down on a piece of land." "Settling down," for men of the trade, generally meant fishing and tinkering in their gardens and orchards, however, for they only "pretended to cultivate the soil."[49]

Similar trading towns were growing at Peoria, St. Ignace, Fort Miamis (Wayne) and Sault Ste. Marie on the eve of the British takeover in 1763 and in that year French and Spanish traders and voyageurs participated in a trade fair at the "Dog Plain." Prairie du Chien had long been a great thoroughfare and market for neighbouring Sioux, Sauk and Mesquakie bands, as well as the site of Perrot's early Fort Nicolas, but it did not attract a permanent mixed population until the British period.[50]

By 1780, John Long affirmed that Prairie du Chien was a "town of considerable note, built after the Indian manner," whose residents were primarily traders who had taken Mesquakie, Sauk or Dakota wives. Some primitive farming was carried on there, but not until the Mesquakie formally ceded nine square miles of prairie in 1781 to a group of British traders did residents take an interest in their lands.[51]

Twenty-five years later, the population of Prairie du Chien had stretched itself along the fertile Mississippi River bottomland for "four miles up and down the river, and nearly a mile wide, from the river to the bluff." They occupied thirty-seven houses, which, according to John Reynolds's generous estimates, held 370 inhabitants, plus several households on the west side of the river at Girard's River. Three years later, Canadiens Dubuque, Antaya, Girard, Brisbois, and Boilvin were still the principal settlers, all of whom had Indian or métis wives. This pattern was true of the less influential settlers as well, so that several decades later Reynolds could claim that "many of the present generation have some Indian blood in their veins." Colonel John Shaw commented similarly in 1815–1816, when the trading village had grown to fifty or sixty houses and counted, in summer, at most six to eight hundred non-Indian inhabitants (see map 2).[52]

Because Prairie de Chien drew some of its residents from the American Bottom in southern Illinois, agriculture appears to have played a more significant role in the life of the settlement than was true of other métis towns, especially after 1812. Nonetheless, when Major Stephen Long visited the community in 1817, he found that the inhabitants, "principally of French and Indian extraction," had been "degenerating . . . instead of improving."[53]

Compared to Green Bay, Peoria, and St. Joseph's, Prairie du Chien had, as Long described it, a sizeable common field. The residents made no effort, however, "to seed the ground with any kind of grain except the summer wheat, which is never so productive as the fall or winter wheat," and the town's continued dependence upon the Sauk and Mesquakie farmers of the Mississippi as corn provisioners suggests that Prairie de Chien raised crops primarily for its own subsistence.[54]

In contrast, far to the north at the rapids of the St. Mary's River which links Lakes Huron and Superior, the métis community of Sault Ste. Marie exhibited almost no occupational diversity. Although this site, which was one of the earliest French missions and posts in the Great Lakes, had attracted a handful of traders and their native spouses during the French regime, Alexander Henry the Elder found in 1761 only four houses; these houses were occupied by the interpreter, Jean Baptiste Cadotte, his Ojibwa wife and their family.

The growing rivalry after the British Conquest between traders out of Hudson Bay, Canadien and métis traders who resided in the Great Lakes region and the independent associations of Scots and Englishmen who joined to form the North West Company after 1774 re-established the strategic importance of the Sault. In 1777, the settlement included "a small picketted fort, built by the Indians, and about ten log houses for the residence of English and French traders." A little more than a decade later, in 1789, Alexander Mackenzie found ten or twelve independent traders and their families living at the Sault. After 1796, when the British were at least theoretically obliged to abandon their posts and interests south of Lake Superior and when Grand Portage on the southwest shore of Lake Superior eclipsed Michilimackinac as the rendezvous of the Nor'Westers, the Montreal-based British North West Company and its short-lived rival, the XY Company, lodged their trading headquarters on the British side of the rapids. A combination of traders from the American side, the Michilimackinac Company, also had a post at the Sault.[55]

Significantly, the highest level of intermarriage for the early corporate towns occurred at the Sault, where, by 1800, a growing number of Canadien, métis, and Scots and Irish traders had fanned out along both sides of the rapids with their native wives and children. Among them were J.B. Nolin, Joseph Piquet, Laurent Barthe and François Comparé. Solely occupied with the greater northwest fur traffic, Sault Ste. Marie imported its corn from the Ottawa at L'Arbre Croche and lived year-round on the whitefish snared by the Ojibwa, maple sugar, waterfowl and game. A limited number of artisans (a blacksmith, cook, tailor and cooper) were employed by the major trading concerns.[56]

Because of its location on the thoroughfare to Lake Superior and the Canadian Northwest, Sault Ste. Marie felt the effect of British institutions and personnel far earlier than did most of the Great Lakes trading towns. Farther south, as late as 1800 the Americans appeared as only a speck on the eastern horizon and even direct British influence was minimal. While the commercial entrepots of Detroit and Michilimackinac, fortified by British troops after 1763, had attracted a few British merchants and adventurers prior to 1776 and a still greater number between 1783 and 1796, the back settlements were surprisingly free of English-speaking people until the 1790s.

In seeming disregard for the era of commercial expansion ushered in by the British ascendancy, the trading towns south of Lake Superior grew from within, and new villages sprang up along the rivers and streams watering native hunting grounds. In addition to fur traders and their employees, such towns usually lured a few independent tradesmen and farmers, plus an

60   Jacqueline Peterson

TABLE 6
Green Bay, 1750–1829.

Years	Heads of household	Estimated * population	Métis heads of household	Métis ** households	Percentage
1740–1796	27	171	4	22	81.48
1796–1816	84	533	22	73	86.90
1816–1829	142	897	40–60	85	59.86

Based upon a reconstitution of families of household heads who appeared as residents in at least two different years.

*Household heads multiplied by a factor of 6.35, the average household size in 1830, according to the Federal Census of Michigan Territory for Brown County.

**Includes all households where one or both parents were at least one-eighth Indian.

occasional miller, in the years prior to 1815. Sporadically, they were blessed with the "protection" of a garrison, "order" imposed by a civil official and the absolution granted by a visiting priest. For the most part, however, these oases of trade thrived in isolation – a mixture of French-Canadian and Indian cultures – depending for their subsistence, household goods and social arrangements upon the materials of the local environment. At Green Bay, the only corporate town for which population estimates have been attempted in the absence of a vital register, of eighty-four households noted between 1796 and 1815, seventy-three (or eighty-seven percent) of them contained at least one métis or Indian parent.[57]

By the last decades of the eighteenth century, a third type of settlement was beginning to punctuate the Great Lakes landscape. Scarcely deserving the name *village*, these new hamlets sprang up around what were known in the vernacular of the American trade as "jack-knife" posts, that is, subsidiary trading outlets run by a single trader and his employees or by one or more trading families related by blood or marriage. Milwaukee, Wisconsin, developed by the Vieau family of Green Bay, was a typical jack-knife post, akin to many of the smaller trading stations established during the British regime in northern Wisconsin and Minnesota as part of the Fond du Lac Department. A very few of these petite trading communities, such as LaPointe, Wisconsin and Chicago, Illinois, had once been occupied as secondary military forts by the French.

The roster of trading hamlets is long, particularly if one includes sites in present-day Minnesota. The more important settlements included Saginaw, Grand Rapids, Baillytown, St. Joseph, L'Anse and Bertrand, Michigan;

South Bend and Peru, Indiana; Chicago, Rockton and Kankakee (Bourbon-nais), Illinois; Lac Vieux Desert, Lac du Flambeau, Lac Court Oreilles, Kaukauna, Butte des Morts, Portage, Milwaukee, Chippewa Falls, Wisconsin; Fond du Lac, Mendota, Traverse des Sioux, Crow Wing and trading stations at Sandy Lake, Lac qui Parle and Lake Traverse, Minnesota.

Villages of this type usually housed as few as one and as many as four or five traders, their native wives and children, plus voyageurs, *engagés* (fur trade employees), and, if the trader was wealthy, slaves or domestic servants. The sites selected most often skirted the wintering ground of a hunting band with whom a marital alliance had been forged. Traders' wives in these intimate encampments were likely to be close relatives – sisters or nieces – of the local band leader rather than outsiders.[58]

Residents of trading hamlets took little delight in farming; instead, they relied upon corn and wild rice gathered by their tribal neighbours, foodstuffs imported from commercial centres, and produce grown by engagés in small garden patches. Occasionally, as was true of Antoine Ouilmette at Chicago prior to 1812, independent traders raised and sold some livestock, primarily horses and pigs. A few, like Ouilmette's predecessor, Jean Baptiste Point du Sable, raised sufficient corn and wheat to warrant a bakehouse. However, few hamlets attracted farmers. In fact, the only tradesmen were blacksmiths imported to care for the metal accoutrements of the trade and a carpenter or sawyer to construct buildings and carts. Most men who contracted to work in the fur trade expected to perform a variety of manual duties in the interior and even blacksmiths like Jean Baptiste Mirandeau, who settled at Milwaukee in about 1798, supplemented their income by trapping or trading when the opportunity presented itself.[59]

Such small communities were often little more than patriarchal fiefdoms. If not related through their Indian or métis wives, the major residents of trading hamlets were predictably brothers, cousins, or fathers and sons, surrounded by their families. After 1790, the extensive Cadotte clan of Sault Ste. Marie ruled at LaPointe, Wisconsin, with subsidiary posts at several of northern Wisconsin's inland lakes; the interrelated Pacquettes, Lecuyers, Fillys and Roys at Portage, Wisconsin; the Vieau and Juneau families at Milwaukee, after the kin-connected LaFramboise and Beaubien familes migrated to Chicago; the Chevaliers, Bertrands and Burnetts on the St. Joseph River in Michigan; the Godfroys and Richardvilles on the Wabash in Indiana; and the Ducharmes and Grignons at Kaukauna and Butte des Morts, Wisconsin. Outsiders settled uneasily at these spots. Whether driven out by group pressure or foul means, most competitors did not stay longer than two or three seasons.[60]

Since the arm of civil government rarely reached these settlements prior to 1815, traders took up, without title, lands according to need and desire. The new posts erected by the North West Company and their competitors in northern Wisconsin and Minnesota usually were fortified by a stockade and provided housing for employees in the form of barracks. Villages settled by a trading family with kin ties to an adjacent Indian village had no need of such defenses. Households at Chicago and Milwaukee, for example, sprawled along the rivers' banks.[61]

Population rarely exceeded one hundred people, most of whom were transient engagés hired for the winter hunting season. Since the purpose of these communities was to engross the traffic of a hunting band occupying a limited region with limited wildlife resources, urban concentration or extensive cultivation was senseless. As it was, depletion of game reserves caused by overhunting fueled a persistent native search for underexploited grounds and the continual migration of traders toward richer fur fields. To the extent that Indian hunters and white traders consciously attemped to "manage" the resources of a particular region, trading posts could be expected to rotate seasonally among several locations. Ultimately, however, the most intense activity shifted to the north and west, and as this occurred new trading hamlets sprang into existence.[62]

By 1815, tangible evidence of a 150-year-long alliance between men of the fur trade and native women was everywhere in abundance. Throughout the upper Great Lakes region, towns and villages populated by a people of mixed heritage illustrated the vitality of the intermarriage compact. The absence of vital records nearly everywhere makes enumeration of the residents of Great Lakes fur trade society difficult; that they were a sizeable and influential population should be obvious, however.

Grace Lee Nute conservatively estimated that, in 1777, five thousand voyageurs plied the waterways of the greater Northwest. Six years later, British merchants, furious at the potential loss to the Americans at the Paris peace table of the fur fields south of Lake Superior, counted ten thousand inhabitants at the chief posts of Niagara, Detroit and Michilimackinac. The figure does not seem unrealistic, despite the obvious benefits of inflation to the British. In 1780, the British at Montreal licensed 3,048 men for the trade west of Niagara. Of course a fair percentage – perhaps as many as one-half to two-thirds – of these men did not remain in the interior, take Indian wives or rear children there. On the other hand, this number does not account for the numbers of métis already resident, many of whom were unlicenced freemen, as well as traders, hunters and voyageurs who hired on at Michilimackinac and the inland posts. Nor does the figure include women and children.[63]

By the late 1820s, a population of ten thousand to fifteen thousand residents of métis communities south and west of Lakes Superior and Huron seems a plausible estimate. Lewis Cass informed John C. Calhoun in 1819 that in Michigan Territory alone (Michigan and Wisconsin) "there are not more than eight thousand Inhabitants." Indiana and Illinois also had sizeable métis concentrations at this date, as did what would become the state of Minnesota. John Johnston, a prominent British trader at Sault Ste. Marie with an Ojibwa wife and a flock of children, was more familiar with the country west of Lake Michigan than was Cass. Both his son George and his son-in-law, Henry Rowe Schoolcraft, served as Indian agents for the combined Sault Ste. Marie-Michilimackinac Indian Agency. Although Johnston made no tallies, he was sufficiently cognizant of the trading class's penchant for native women and the prodigious size of their families to worry about the birth rate. In 1822, he wrote to the senator from Ohio, Colonel Trimble, that "the Canadians and half bloods all over the country are very numerous."[64]

In addition to their numerical strength, which was equal to or even larger than most individual tribal populations in the Great Lakes region by 1822, these people had made a distinctive residential imprint on the Great Lakes region prior to American settlement. By the early nineteenth century, they had established a network of corporate towns and trading villages linked economically and socially to the commercial emporia of Michilimackinac and Detroit. The residents of such towns were not transient vagabonds, although the requirements of their occupation led them on an annual round from town to winter hunting ground, and to the warehouses of Mackinac or Detroit. The commitment to place can be seen in the persistence of family names over several generations in the same location.

On the other hand, because these families did not constitute an agricultural society, they did not develop a keen sense of the value of individual property rights, particularly in the smaller hamlets where houses were easily bartered or swapped among neighbours and even improved lands were sold for a pittance to more sanguine Americans. Trade was the heartbeat of métis growth and vitality, and because success in the occupation demanded an ever-enlarging sphere of contacts, the strongest forces operating on trading towns were centripetal. The eighteenth and early nineteenth centuries saw a host of métis intermarriages linking the dominant lineages of the Great Lakes communities. Intermarriage with distant hunting bands also saw the establishment and expansion of new trading hamlets.

Such intraregional mobility seems to have fostered, by the early decades of the nineteenth century, a personal and group identity which was less place-specific than regionally and occupationally defined. In the 1850s, J.G. Kohl happened upon a métis voyageur in Minnesota who articulated this sense of himself: "Ou je reste? Je ne peux pas te le dire. Je suis Voyageur – je suis Chicot, Monsieur. Je reste partout. Mon grand-père était Voyageur: il est mort on voyage. Mon père était Voyageur: il est mort en voyage. Je mourrai aussi en voyage, et un autre chicot prendra ma place. Such is our course of life."[65]

The geographic mobility of Great Lakes métis was crucial to the spread of the fur trade, but ultimately it was a profound liability. The very diffuseness of fur trade communities, whose members had married among and were related to more than a dozen tribes – Algonkian, Siouan and Iroquoian speakers – made group solidarity and combined action difficult to sustain under pressure. In the end, the identity of the Great Lakes métis, like the transitional economy which gave it life, was to prove a fragile construction.

Between 1815 and 1850, years which witnessed the sudden florescence of a distinctive métis population and culture radiating outward from the junction of the Assiniboine and Red Rivers, present-day Winnipeg, the old fur trade communities of the Great Lakes region collapsed, drowned in the flood of American settlement and capitalistic expansion. But perhaps this was not coincidence. The "new people" of Red River – not merely biracial, multilingual and bicultural, but the proud owners of a new language; of a syncretic cosmology and religious repertoire; of distinctive modes of dress, cuisine, architecture, vehicles of transport, music and dance; and after 1815 of a quasi-military political organization, a flag, a bardic tradition, a rich folklore and a national history – sprang only metaphorically from the soil. Many human roads led to Red River, and several of them stretched from the southeast, from the Great Lakes country.

NOTES

An earlier version of this article appeared in the *American Indian Culture and Research Journal* 6 (1982) 2:23–64, published by the UCLA American Indian Studies Center. Permission to reprint portions of that article is gratefully acknowledged.

1 J.G. Kohl, *Kitchi-Gami, Wanderings Round Lake Superior* (London: Chapman and Hall, 1860; reprint edition, Minneapolis: Ross and Haines, 1956), 314.

2 Marcel Giraud, *Le Métis canadien: son rôle dans l'histoire des provinces de l'Ouest* (Paris: l'Institut d'Ethnologie, 1945), 588, 588n, 617. For the view that métis consciousness was born in the conflict between the North West Company and the Hudson's Bay Company, see especially Arthur S. Morton, *A History of the Canadian West to 1870–71* (Toronto: 1939) and G.F.G. Stanley, *The Birth of Western Canada: A History of the Riel Rebellions* (London: 1936; reprint edition, Toronto: University of Toronto Press, 1960). See Irene Spry, this volume.

3 See Joe Sawchuk, *The Métis of Manitoba: Reformulation of an Ethnic Identity* (Toronto: Peter Martin Associates Limited, 1978) for an important analysis of contemporary métis identity as a political reformulation of an older cultural identity which was more narrowly bounded. The early-nineteenth-century concept of a métis nation functioned, I would argue, as the Manitoba Métis Federation and its other provincial counterparts do today as a reference point for the realignment and enlargement of an ethnic constituency. For a discussion about the nature of tribes and ethnic groups, how they are formed, and how their membership is defined and bounded, see: Morton H. Fried, *The Notion of Tribe* (Menlo Park, California: Cummings Publishing Company, 1975), especially pp. 101–05; Elizabeth Colson, "Contemporary Tribes and the Development of Nationalism," in June Helm, ed., *Essays on the Problem of Tribe: Proceedings of the 1967 Annual Spring Meeting of the American Ethnological Society* (Seattle and London: American Ethnological Society, University of Washington Press, 1963), 201–06; and Fredrik Barth, ed., *Ethnic Groups and Boundaries: The Social Organization of Cultural Difference* (Boston: Little, Brown and Company, 1969). See, most recently, the forceful suggestion that not all ethnic identities are similar and may be ambiguous, fuzzy, unarticulated, situational, and "tangled," in Karen I. Blu, *The Lumbee Problem: The Making of an American Indian People* (Cambridge, England: Cambridge University Press, 1980), 200–35.

4 I am grateful to Dr. Lionel Demontigny, assistant surgeon general of the United States Public Health Service and a participant and speaker at the 1981 Newberry Library Conference on the Métis in North America for the suggestion that Napoleon Bonaparte and his Continental System were important early-nineteenth-century influences upon métis self- and group definition.

5 For a description of the "foreign" aspects of métis ways, see, for example, William H. Keating, *Narrative of an Expedition to the Source of St. Peter's River, Lake Winnepeek, Lake of the Woods, etc. etc. Performed in the Year 1823, by order of the Hon. J.C. Calhoun, Secretary of War Under the Command of Stephen H. Long, Major U.S.T.E. Comp. from the Notes of Major Long, Messr*, 2 vols. (Philadelphia: H.C. Carey and I. Lea, 1824) 1:75–76. For changing attitudes about race, see: Jennifer S.H. Brown, "Linguistic Solitudes and Changing Social Categories," in Carol Judd and Arthur J. Ray, eds., *Old Trails and New Directions: Proceedings of the Third North American Fur Trade Conference* (Toronto: University of Toronto Press, 1980), 147–59; Robert E. Bieder, "Scientific Attitudes Toward Indian Mixed-Bloods in Early Nineteenth Century America," *Journal of Ethnic Studies* 8(1980)2:17–30. The term *halfbreed* was in use among English-speakers in Canada at least as early as 1773. References to métis and Métifs in the Illinois country date from the 1750s. See, for instance, Father Vivier's letter of June 8, 1750, in Reuben Gold Thwaites, ed., *The Jesuit Relations and Allied Documents: Travels and Explorations of the Jesuit Missionaries in New France, 1610–1791*, 73 vols. (Cleveland: The Burrows Brothers Company, 1896–1901; New York: Pageant Book Company, 1959), 69:145. Henry Rowe Schoolcraft referred to the Métif (his brother-in-law, William Johnston, used *half-breed)* in 1825. See his *Personal Memoirs of a Residence of Thirty Years with the Indian Tribes on the American Frontiers: With brief Notes of Passing Events, Facts, and Opinions, A.D. 1812 to A.D. 1842* (Philadelphia: Lippincott, Grambo, and Company, 1851; reprint edition, New York: AMS Press, 1978), 206. See also: Keating, *Narrative of an Expedition,* 1:106; Caleb Atwater, *The Indians of the Northwest, Their Manners, Customs etc. etc., or Remarks Made on a Tour to Prairie du Chien and Thence to Washington City in 1829* (Columbus, Ohio: 1831), 180.

6 George Croghan, quoted in Joseph Jablow, *Indians of Illinois and Indiana: Illinois, Kickapoo and Potawatomi Indians* (New York and London: Garland American Indian Ethnohistory Series, 1974), 248–49.

7 There is a sizeable secondary literature on the fur trade in Canada and, by extension, the Great Lakes region under French and British rule. For a review of the literature of the last fifteen years, see Jacqueline Peterson and John Anfinson, "The Indian and the Fur Trade," in W.R. Swagerty, ed., *Scholars and the Indian Experience: Critical Reviews of Recent Writing in the Social Sciences* (Bloomington: Indiana University Press, 1984), 223–57. A comprehensive history of the fur trade in the Great Lakes region has yet to be written. Several older works, although dated, still deserve consultation. They are: Harold A. Innis, *The Fur Trade in Canada,* rev. ed. (Toronto: University of Toronto Press, 1970); Louise Phelps Kellogg, *The French Régime in Wisconsin and the Northwest* (Madison, Wisconsin: State Historical Society of Wisconsin, 1925); Louise Phelps Kellogg, *The British Régime in Wisconsin and the Northwest* (Madison: State Historical Society of Wisconsin, 1935); Wayne E. Stevens, *The Northwest Fur Trade, 1763–1800* (Urbana: University of Illinois Press, 1928); Kenneth W. Porter, *John Jacob Astor, Business Man* (Cambridge, Massachusetts: Harvard University Press, 1931); and Ida A. Johnson, *The Michigan Fur Trade* (Lansing, Michigan: Michigan Historical Commission, 1919). Useful collections of documents and first-hand accounts include Charles M. Gates, *Five Fur Traders of the Northwest* (St. Paul, Minnesota: Minnesota Historical Society, 1965); L.R. Masson, *Les bourgeois de la Compagnie du Nord-Ouest: Recits de voyages, lettres et rapports inédits relatifs au Nord-Ouest canadien,* 2 vols. (New York: Antiquarian Press, 1960); E.B. O'Callaghan, ed., *Documents relative to the colonial history of the state of New-York, procured in Holland, England and France by John Romeyn Brodhead, Esq., agent under and by virtue of an act of the legislature,* 15 vols. (Albany, New York: 1856–57), particularly vol. 10 (hereinafter cited as *NYCD*); "The French Regime in Wisconsin" and "Fur-trade on the Upper Lakes, 1778–1815," in *Collections of the State Historical Society of Wisconsin,* 31 vols. (Madison, Wisconsin: 1854–1931), 16–18, 19 (hereinafter cited as *WHC*); W.S. Wallace, ed., *Documents Relating to the North West Company* (Toronto: The Champlain Society, 1934); William Johnston, "Letters on the Fur Trade," in *Michigan Pioneer and Historical Society Collections,* or *Michigan Historical Collections,* 40 vols. (East Lansing, Michigan, 1874/76–1929)37:132–207 (hereinafter cited as *MPHC*).

8 The most comprehensive work on the Canadian métis, their origins and emergence as a distinct ethnic group, is still Giraud, *Le Métis Canadien,* to be reissued in English translation by the University of Alberta Press.

9 Lyle M. Stone, *Fort Michilimackinac 1715–1781: An Archaeological Perspective on the Revolutionary Frontier,* Publications of the Museum (East Lansing, Michigan: Michigan State University, 1974), 355. For the contrasting view that French civilization in the Great Lakes region "was an adaptation of that of the St. Lawrence valley," see Kellogg, *The French Régime,* 402.

10 Stone, *Fort Michilimackinac,* 354–55.

11 Ibid, 356.

12 Etienne Carheil to de Callières, August 30, 1702, in Thwaites, ed., *Jesuit Relations,* 65:239; E.M. Sheldon, *The Early History of Michigan, From the First Settlement to 1815* (New York: A.S. Barnes and Co.; Detroit: Kerr, Morley and Co., 1856), 306.

13 Carheil to de Callières, August 30, 1702.

14 Jablow, *Indians of Illinois and Indiana,* 120, 123; Natalia Maree Belting, *Kaskaskia under the French Regime* (Urbana, Illinois: University of Illinois Press, 1948), 12–15.

15 E.M. Sheldon, *Early History of Michigan,* 91; "Memoir on Detroit," 1714, probably attributable to Captain de la Forest, *NYCD,* 10:866–67. La Forest said that Cadillac had been given 150 soldiers, rather than sixty, which he thought excessive. He said he needed only twenty plus a sergeant, but the post was essential for fending off the Iroquois and the British traders and for preventing the coureurs de bois from taking their peltry to the British.

16 Clarence M. Burton, *Cadillac's Village or Detroit under Cadillac* (Detroit: 1896), 15; Sheldon, *Early History of Michigan,* 93, 99, 103–04.

17 *WHC* 8:242–50, 291; Kellogg, *The French Régime,* 291; for a comment on the effect of intermarriage in the Illinois country by 1750, see Thwaites, ed., *Jesuit Relations,* 69:20.

18 Kellogg, *The French Régime,* 292–311; Ernest Voorhis, *Historic Forts and Trading Posts of the French Regime and of the English Fur Trading Companies* (Ottawa, Ontario: 1930); Richard Asa Yarnell, *Aboriginal Relationships between Culture and Plant Life in the Upper Great Lakes Region,* Museum of Anthropology Papers No. 23 (Ann Arbor: University of Michigan Press, 1964), 127.

19 Sieur d'Argremont, 1708, in Eugene T. Peterson, *France at Mackinac, 1715-1760* (Mackinac Island: Mackinac Island State Park Commission, n.d.), 3; for travellers' descriptions of Mackinac Island from 1669–1899, see "Mackinac Island Tourist Map," *Mackinaw History* (1964)3. Denis Raudot, in Vernon W. Kinietz, *The Indians of the Western Great Lakes, 1615-1760* (Ann Arbor: University of Michigan Press, 1940), 379, said that according to the Ottawa, Mackinac Island was the abode of "Michapoux, the place where he was born and taught his people to fish." See "Nanabozho (Michibou, Mieska, Wisakdjak)" in Frederick Webb Hodge, ed., *Handbook of American Indians,* Bureau of American Ethnology, Bulletin 30, Part 2 (Washington: 1910), 19–23. See also: Kellogg, *The French Régime,* 291; "The Mackinac Register," *WHC* 19:2; *NYCD* 10:889; "The Memoir of La Mothe Cadillac" in *The Western Country in the 17th Century,* ed. Milo M. Quaife (Chicago: The Lakeside Press, 1947), 68–69; Peter Scanlan, *Prairie du Chien: French, British, American* (Menasha, Wisconsin: George Banta, 1937), 23.

20 For an historical treatment of Michilimackinac, supplementary to Stone, see Eugene T. Peterson, *Michilimackinac: Its History and Restoration,* rev. ed. (Mackinac Island, Michigan: 1968).

21 Stone, *Fort Michilimackinac,* 7–8.

22 The term, *Panis* or *Panis-Maha,* referring to the Pawnee and Omaha tribes, was used interchangeably with *Indian slave,* since raids upon these tribes provided the majority of slaves in the Great Lakes region owned by Indians and Canadians. See Russell M. Magnagni, "Indian Slavery in the Great Lakes Region," paper read at the Great Lakes Regional History Conference, Grand Rapids, Michigan, April 30 to May 1, 1975.

23 "The Mackinac Register," *WHC* 18:469–513; *WHC* 19:1–161. The original transcription of the register is deposited in St. Anne's Catholic Church, Mackinac Island, Michigan.

24 "Relation trés abregé de Mon Voiage de michillimackinac," attributed to Michel Chartier de Lotbinière, 1749. Original manuscript is in the library of the New York Historical Society, negative photostat in Public Archives of Canada, MG 18, K3, vol. 3.

25 Ibid.

26 Ibid.

27 Lotbinière, "Relation trés abregé"; Stone, *Fort Michilimackinac,* 349–51.

28 "The Mackinac Register," *WHC* 18:469–513; *WHC* 19:1–161.

29 *WHC* 19:1–161.

30 *WHC* 19:1–161; Edwin Osgood Brown, *Two Missionary Priests at Mackinac* (Chicago: 1889), 39–40. Reference to L'Abbe Cyprien Tanguay, *Dictionnaire genéalogique des familles cana- diennes,* 7 vols. (Montreal: 1871–1890) was not especially useful in tracing the ethnic and regional origins of Michilimackinac's first generation of traders. Perhaps erroneously, I have treated all of these traders and voyageurs as Canadian rather than métis. Wives have likewise been treated as either Canadian or unknown, unless their Indian affiliation is specifically mentioned in the register or in travellers' accounts.

31 Peterson, *France at Mackinac,* 9; Stone, *Fort Michilimackinac,* 312–21, 350–51.

32 Edward V. Cicotte Ledger 1749–1752 Containing Accounts of French Settlers at Detroit, Burton Historical Collection, Detroit Public Library, Detroit, Michigan. Not until the Proclamation of 1749 were many non-trading families induced to migrate to Detroit, and even with subsidies of cattle, grain, seed, tools and land, the fur trade proved irresistible for most. See also *Registre de fort Pontchartrain de Detroit, 1703–1754,* Public Archives of Canada, FM 8, G 8, vol. 1 (microfilm), "Concessions 1734 à 1753." For Michilimackinac, see *WHC* 8:211, signed Lecuyer: "We concede with the good pleasure of the General to Mr. Bourassa, Sr., dwelling at this fort, a meadow or marsh, which lies on the road leading to Grand Lac, three-fourths of a league in depth at the distance of some arpents from the pinery where we cut the wood for his house in the eighth concession for him in property, or for his use as long as it pleases the General. Done at Michilimackinac, the first of June, 1754." See also Stone, *Fort Michilimackinac,* 354.

33 Peterson, *France at Mackinac;* George S. May, "The Mess at Mackinac," *Mackinac History* (1964) 1:5; Lotbinière, "Relation trés abregé."

34 May, "The Mess at Mackinac."

35 John Portheous Ms, August 16, 1767. Letter to John Portheous of voyage to Michilimack- inac dated there, Burton Historical Collection, Detroit Public Library, Detroit, Michigan. See also La Forest for an early comment on the unsuitability of Michilimackinac for colonization owing to the bad soil at the straits, *NYCD* 10:866–67.

36 Nearly every traveller visiting Mackinac in the eighteenth and early nineteenth centuries was struck by the summer lagniappe of peoples and wares. Among the best descriptions are those by Henry Rowe Schoolcraft, *Summary Narrative of an Exploratory Expedition to the Sources of the Mississippi River in 1820* (Philadelphia: Lippincott, Grambo and Company, 1855), 68–69 and by Gurdon S. Hubbard in 1818. See Gurdon S. Hubbard Collection, Recollec- tions, First Year, Chicago Historical Society, Chicago, Illinois, especially pp. 11–13. In 1818, according to Hubbard, "the permanent population on this picturesque island was about 500 – old voyagers, worn out with the hard service incident to their calling, lived there with their families of half breeds, subsisting mostly by fishing." During the summer the traders congregated at the island "so that when all were collected together they added 3,000 or more to the population." The Indians from the upper lakes, "who made this island a place of resort, numbered from 2,000 to 3,000 more – Their wigwams lined the entire beach 2 or 3 rows deep. . . ." See also: Elizabeth Therèse Baird, *WHC* 9:319; Caleb Swan in Kellogg, *The British Régime,* 236; Sheldon, *Early History of Michigan,* 337. English troops took possession of the island fort on July 15, 1780.

37 Portheous Ms; John Parker, ed., *The Journals of Jonathan Carver and Related Documents 1766–1770* (St. Paul, Minnesota: Minnesota Historical Society Press, 1976), 66.

38 Registre de fort Pontchartrain de Detroit, 1703–1754, "Concessions 1734 à 1753," vol. 1, illustrates that farms allotted at Detroit were two to four arpents wide. A French arpent equals 192.5 feet.

39 Portheous Ms.

40 *MPHC* 9:474, 469, 649. Detroit's population in 1773 was 1,400. By 1778, however, it had grown dramatically to 2,144, of which 564 were free male householders.

41 Russell F. Bidlack, "The Yankee Meets the Frenchman, River Raisin, 1817–1830," *Occasional Publications* 2 (Lansing, Michigan: Historical Society of Michigan, 1965), 4. By the turn of the eighteenth century, the old creole population of Detroit was also moving north toward Grosse Pointe, on the shore of Lake St. Clair. Thomas McKenney, touring the lakes in 1827, commented that the British side of the straits looked the same as it probably had a half century earlier, with no improvements in land or buildings. On the American side, however, "a new face is put on things . . . save where, here and there, an old French family lingers. And wherever that is, the picture of inactivity and barrenness is visible. . . ." The town was still laid out along the river, buildings scattered upon the bank for nearly a mile in length. Thomas L. McKenney, *Sketches of a Tour to the Lakes, of the Character and Customs of the Chippeway Indians, and of Incidents Connected with the Treaty of Fond du Lac* (Baltimore, Maryland: Fielding Lucas, Jr., 1827), 109.

42 Although Vincennes' creole inhabitants received their land patents earlier than did towns to the north and west, the original title, gained from the Piankeshaw and Miami in 1742, was never legally registered. Like other corporate trading towns, Vincennes was without a royal notary and register although the commandant, St. Ange, did issue patents for tenure and meritorious service after 1742. See: Joseph Henry Vanderburgh Somes, *Old Vincennes* (New York: Graphic Books, 1963), 34; and Leonard Lux, "The Vincennes Donation Lands," *Indiana Historical Society Publications* 15 (1949):431–32. Under the Quebec Act of 1774 the British attempted to extend legal jurisdiction over the trading population of the Great Lakes region, but these efforts were frustrated by the American Revolution. Not until the organization of Indiana Territory in 1803 did towns like Green Bay actually see an officially appointed justice of the peace. Usually, such early justices were traders with no legal training. For British policy in the West prior to the Revolution, see Marjorie G. Reid, "The Quebec Fur-traders and Western Policy, 1763–1774," *Canadian Historical Review* 6(1925):15–32, especially p. 30.

43 Scanlan, *Prairie du Chien,* 42; *WHC* 18:281–83, 263–67; *American State Papers, Documents of the Congress of the United States in Relation to the Public Lands, from the First Session of the Twentieth to the Second Session of the Twentieth Congress enclusive, commencing December 3, 1827, and ending March 3, 1829,* vol. 5 (Washington: Gale and Seaton, 1860), 56–328. See also vols. 1 and 2 for land patents at Prairie du Chien, Vincennes, Detroit, Sault Ste. Marie and Mackinac.

44 Bidlack, "Yankee Meets the Frenchman," 5–9.

45 Barnhart and Riker, 95–96, 156, 164, 170, 318n., 320–22. In 1746, Vincennes had forty male inhabitants and five blacks; in 1765, George Croghan estimated the population at eighty or ninety families. In 1769, Father Gibault claimed there were 700 to 800 persons there who desired a priest, and in 1787 Josiah Harmar found nine hundred Canadians and four hundred Americans there. For the communities on the St. Joseph's River in Michigan, see: Powell A. Moore, *The Calumet Region: Indiana's Last Frontier* (Indianapolis: Indiana Historical Bureau, 1959), 26; R. David Edmunds, "A History of the Potawatomi Indians 1615–1795" (Ph.D. dissertation, University of Oklahoma, 1972), 68; Rev. George Pare and M.M. Quaife, eds., "The St. Joseph Baptismal Register," *Mississippi Valley Historical Review* 13:201–39; Rollo B. Oglesbee and Albert Hale, *History of Michigan City, Indiana* (Edward J. Widdell: 1908), 29–30, 54–55.

46 Major Robert Rogers, "Rogers' Michilimackinac Journal," ed., William Clements, *Proceedings of the American Antiquarian Society,* n.s., 28:271; contract between Didace Mouet de

Moras and Courtemanche for trade at La Baye, dated June 9, 1732, Schmidt Collection, No. 252, Chicago Historical Society, Chicago, Illinois; "Augustin Grignon Recollections of Wisconsin," *WHC* 3:241–42; Durrie, 5; *WHC* 7:126–27.

47 Kellogg, *The British Régime*, 13, 95; Paul Trap, "Charles Langlade," *Dictionary of Canadian Biography*, ed. Francess G. Halpenny and Jean Hamelin, 11 vols. (Toronto: University of Toronto Press, 1979)4:563–64.

48 Kellogg, *The British Régime*, 22; *WHC* 12, 134–35.

49 Hon. James H. Lockwood, "Early Times and Events in Wisconsin," *WHC* 2:105; Thomas Forsyth counted "nearly forty French settlers" at Green Bay in about 1812, Thomas Forsyth Papers, Missouri Historical Society, St. Louis, Missouri, Forsyth to Ninian Edwards, n.d.

50 Scanlan, *Prairie du Chien*, 60, 67, 71–73; Joseph Tassé, *Les Canadiens de l'Ouest*, 2 vols. (Montreal: Cie. d'Imprimerie canadienne, 1882), 1:172–73.

51 Jonathan Carver in *WHC* 18:281–83; John Long in *WHC* 7:176.

52 A.R. Fulton, *The Red Men of Iowa, Being a History of the Various Aboriginal Tribes Whose Homes Were in Iowa* (Des Moines, Iowa: Mills and Company, 1882), 405–07; Reynolds, 121; Scanlan, *Prairie du Chien*, 71–72; "Personal Narrative of Col. John Shaw," *WHC* 2:226; for a post-War of 1812 estimate of twenty-five to thirty houses, see Lockwood, "Early Times," 124–25.

53 Stephen H. Long, *Voyage in a Six-Oared Skiff to the Falls of Saint Anthony in 1817* (Philadelphia: Henry B. Ashmead, printer, 1860), reprinted in *Collections of the Minnesota Historical Society*, 17 vols. (St. Paul, Minnesota: 1872–1920) 2:61–62 (hereinafter cited as *MHC*).

54 Long, *Voyage in a Six-Oared Skiff* 2:61–62. At Prairie du Chien, fields stretched nearly a mile behind the village; at Green Bay and elsewhere to the north, one-quarter of a mile was usual. For the Sauk farmers, see Ellen B. Whitney, ed., *The Black Hawk War, 1831–1832*, 3 vols. (Springfield, Illinois: Illinois Historical Society 1972–75).

55 Reid, "Quebec Fur Traders," 26; *Alexander Henry's Travels and Adventures in the Years 1760–1776*, Milo M. Quaife, ed. (Chicago: The Lakeside Press, 1921), 64.

56 Long, *Voyage in a Six-Oared Skiff* 2:57; Tassé, *Les Canadiens de l'Ouest*, 1:105–17; McKenney, *Sketches*, 191–92; personal conversation with F.K. Hatt, Department of Sociology/Anthropology, Carleton University, Ottawa, Ontario. The métis families of J.B. Nolin and J.B. Cadotte were among the most influential early Red River settlers.

57 Wayne E. Stevens, *The Northwest Fur Trade, 1763–1800* (Urbana, Illinois: University of Illinois Press, 1928), especially chap. 4, "Expansion and Monopoly, 1783–1800," 89–119; Jacqueline Peterson, "Prelude to Red River: A Social Portrait of the Great Lakes Métis," *Ethnohistory* 25 (Winter 1978):51.

58 For an exception, see the half brothers Thomas Forsyth and John Kinzie, Chicago traders, who both married white captives (Thomas Forsyth Papers, Genealogy Folder, Missouri Historical Society, St. Louis, Missouri). For John Kinzie, see A.T. Andreas, *History of Chicago from the Earliest Period to the Present* (A.T. Andreas, 1884), 101–02; John Kinzie Papers, Chicago Historical Society, Chicago, Illinois; Kinzie Family Papers, same source.

59 Antoine Ouilmette 1790 Reminiscence, Antoine Ouilmette to John H. Kinzie (written by James Moore), June, 1839, in Edward Everett Ayer Collection, The Newberry Library, Chicago, Illinois; Antoine LeClaire's statement, *WHC* 11:238–44; "Narrative of Peter J. Vieau," *WHC* 15:458–69.

60 Letter Book of William Burnett, New York Historical Society, New York, New York, printed as *Letter Book of William Burnett,* ed. William M. Cunningham (Fort Miami Heritage Society of Michigan, 1967); Journal of a Voyage Made by Hugh Heward to the Illinois Country, Hugh Heward Collection, Chicago Historical Society, Chicago; LeClaire, *WHC* 11:238–44; Peter J. Vieau, *WHC* 15:458–59; John H. Fonda, "Early Wisconsin," *WHC* 5:219; McKenney, *Sketches,* 261–64; Kellogg, *The British Régime,* 95; Charles Grignon Papers, Wisconsin Manuscripts, Wisconsin State Historical Society, Madison, Wisconsin; "Early Times at Fort Winnebago," *WHC* 8:316–20; "Narrative of Andrew J. Vieau," *WHC* 11:224; *History of Columbia County, Wisconsin* (Chicago: Western Historical Company, 1880), 347.

61 Andrew J. Vieau, *WHC* 11:224; Leclaire, 239–40; Peter J. Vieau, *WHC* 15:466; "The Beaubiens of Chicago," Frank Gordon Beaubien Papers, Chicago Historical Society, Chicago, Illinois; Jeanne Kay, "Wisconsin Indian Hunting Patterns, 1634–1836," *Annals of the Association of American Geographers* 69(1979):402–18.

62 Kay, "Wisconsin Indian Hunting Patterns," 402–18; Harold Hickerson, "The Genesis of a Trading Post Band: The Pembina Chippewa," *Ethnohistory* 3(1956):289–345.

63 Grace Lee Nute, *The Voyageur* (New York and London: D. Appleton Co., 1932), 7; Kellogg, *The British Régime,* 189; William Henry Puthoff to Lewis Cass, Mackinac, March 4, 1818, *WHC* 20:32 for "foreigners" in American territory: "The great mass of such as have descended from them mostly from a Connection with the aboriginal inhabitants. . . ."; Returns of Licenses Granted to Trade with the Indians at Michilimackinac, Detroit and the Northwest posts for 1780, photostat from the Public Archives of Canada deposited in the Missouri Historical Society, St. Louis, Missouri. While his estimates are based purely upon impressionistic evidence, Arthur Donald Gast claimed that "the records suggested that approximately one out of every two Euro-American traders acquired an Indian wife." See his "The Impact of the Fur Trade upon Chippewa-American Culture and Education" (Ph.D. dissertation, Indiana University, 1940), 208.

64 Lewis Cass to John Calhoun, May 27, 1819, Lewis Cass papers, Burton Historical Collection, Detroit Public Library; John Johnston to Col. Trimble, St. Mary's Falls, January 24, 1822, in Henry Rowe Schoolcraft, *Archives of Aboriginal Knowledge, Containing all the Original Papers Laid Before Congress Respecting the History, Antiquities, Languages, Ethnology, Pictography, Rites, Superstitions and Mythology of the Indian Tribes of the United States,* 6 vols. (Philadelphia: J.B. Lippincott and Co., 1868), 2:524; Gast, "Impact of the Fur Trade," 208–09; Anna Jameson, *Sketches in Canada, and Rambles Among the Red Men,* new ed. (London: Longman, Brown, Green and Longmans, 1852) for an interesting 1837 account of the métis residents of Lakes Huron and Superior. She noted: "In 1828, Major Anderson, our Indian agent, computed the number of Canadians and mixed breed married to Indian women, and residing on the north shore of Lake Huron, and in the neighbourhood of Michilimackinac, at nine hundred. This he called the *lowest* estimate." See p. 188n.

65 Kohl, *Wanderings Round Lake Superior,* 259. "Chicot" is a synonym for *bois brûlé* or métis. Its derivation is uncertain. Kohl was told that it meant "half burnt stump."

Some questions and perspectives on the problem of métis roots

John E. Foster

The emergence of the métis in the region of the Upper Great Lakes and on the Northern Great Plains in the latter half of the eighteenth century is directly related to the presence of the fur trade. As did other native peoples involved in the fur trade, the métis found that the consequences of that involvement could be disruptive as well as rewarding. The métis were unique among native peoples in the sense that as distinct entities they did not antedate the fur trade. They alone could look to the fur trade for their origins and not simply for significant formative influences.

Historically the term *métis* is applied to those individuals, frequently of mixed Indian, western European and other ancestry, who arose in the St. Lawrence-Great Lakes trading system, including its extensions to the Pacific and Arctic coasts, and chose to see themselves in various collectivities distinct from their Indian neighbours and, in some instances, distinct from members of the "white" community. The meaning of the term here is extended to include those of the Hudson Bay trading system who held similar views of their relations with Indians and others. The instances where the more limited and historical sense of the term *métis* is intended should be obvious from the context in which it is used.[1]

In spite of the enduring interest of scholars, the origins of the métis remain obscure. Recent works, however, particularly those of Jacqueline Peterson and Trudy Nicks, have made progress in clarifying this obscurity.[2] In addition to introducing new documents, Peterson and Nicks have applied new techniques of analysis. Their work and similar studies represent the first major development in a generation. They are reason enough to re-address the question of the extent to which the documents will support the study of métis roots.

While the papers of the métis prophet and leader Louis Riel constitute an invaluable source for métis studies, few other métis-authored materials have survived as part of the documentation on métis history and origins.[3] "Outsiders" have played a major role in determining what information would survive to this century. In most instances these outsiders have not chosen to record the mundane, the ordinary and the familiar; the exceptional, the noteworthy and the different have called forth their pens. Even when everyday subjects are of interest they frequently have been cast unfavourably in the light of the reader's own cultural antecedents. This problem is evident in the works of Alexander Ross, a leading recorder of the events that made up a significant part of the history of the Red River.[4]

While Ross's first-hand account of a métis buffalo hunt early in the 1840s and other aspects of métis life are invaluable to scholars today, it is as the first interpreter of the meaning of the métis experience that Ross has significance in western Canadian historiography. His use of the image of the alpine chamois hunter as a vehicle for conveying values and attitudes fundamental to their life is as effective as any interpretation offered on métis ways.[5] His juxtaposing of the poverty and hunger (which occurred frequently in the lives of the métis) with the buffalo hunters' council and the classical images to which the council could give rise, is equally effective.[6] Yet his "cost-analysis" of the buffalo hunt, while useful, reflects the perspective of an outsider unfamiliar with, and unsympathetic towards, significant aspects of métis life.[7] While Ross's interpretive comments are more sophisticated than those found in various other writings of the era, they tend to confirm the assessments of earlier observers and to prepare the way for both observers and scholars who would follow.[8] In sum, an assessment of the interpretive tradition beginning with Ross must conclude that it lacked success in delineating the origins of the Red River métis people in particular and the métis people in general.

Until recently, historians of the métis relied almost exclusively upon the analysis of documents that generated qualitative data. With the appearance of studies utilizing various techniques of quantification, documents which previously had been ignored became central to historical analysis. The "hard" evidence in parish records, census returns, land titles and "half-breed" scrip applications can be useful as a corrective to material found in impressionist records as well as a source of new information. These data both complement and encourage a critical re-evaluation of the meaning and the validity of usual source materials.[9] It is this area of scholarly inquiry in métis studies that offers the most promise at the moment.

Another complementary source of information is métis "folk" history. Almost exclusively an oral tradition, it has suffered the ravages of life-style changes associated with the post–World War II years in Western Canada. With the exception of the Riel Papers‾and a few other documentary collections, little material authored by members of métis communities has survived; however, recent efforts to record and to collect this material offer some promise.[10] It is from these various folk histories that a sense of the métis view of their historical experience emerges. As with all people's perceptions of their past, the material must be approached with caution, in terms of both factual record and interpretive comment; but, as a vehicle for sustaining values and attitudes that span generations, folk history accounts can be extremely useful. Taken together, folk accounts, data amenable to quantitative analysis, and familiar impressionist records suggest the possibility that a far more precise and exact understanding of the origins of the métis can be realized.

In historical analysis, the questions that historians formulate preparatory to addressing the contents of their sources are as important as the contents themselves. Such questions are a function of how particular scholars conceptualize their subject matter and how they perceive the purpose of their study. Marcel Giraud's monumental contribution, *Le Métis canadien*, published in 1945, is a prominent case in point.[11] It begins as a study in miscegenation; but, within the first few chapters the emphasis shifts towards a narration of historical and cultural evolution. Giraud's initial definition is biological: métis are the offspring and descendants of Euro-Canadian fathers and Indian mothers.[12] But, since the focus of his analysis centres on those of mixed ancestry who remained in the West and who lived in "métis" communities and not those who lived with Indian bands or who moved their residence to the Canadas or to Great Britain, the biological basis of his initial definition shifts to one of community and way of life. Yet, reflecting the scholarly climate of Giraud's day, the emphasis on the biological definition of métis persists.

For Giraud, métis' behaviour was a function of their biological-cum-cultural antecedents expressed in the context of fur-trade events and circumstances. The fur trade served as a vehicle which elicited cultural elements from both the Euro-Canadian and Indian heritages which were, to Giraud, surprisingly similar and compatible.[13] On the Northern Plains this cultural compatibility emerged as the way of life of the métis buffalo hunters from the Red River Settlement and from the Northwest as far as Fort Edmonton.[14] Giraud's history of these people remains fundamental to any scholarship on the subject. It is with other métis people, some of whom did not identify themselves as métis, that difficulties arise.

A legacy of Giraud's biological-cum-cultural explanation for the origins of the plains hunters is the impression that those métis who were not plains hunters were in essence merely variants of this main stock.[15] His definition of métis obscures the different processes through which métis people as diverse as the "Hudson Bay English" and the "Peace-Athabaska Iroquois" came into existence. This problem reflects, in part, the temporal and regional biases of a major part of his documentation, Hudson's Bay Company materials dating from the post-1820 period. But equally pertinent to the problem is the nature of Giraud's conceptualization of his subject matter and of the purpose of his study.

Giraud's pioneering study of the métis remains a beacon for scholars studying the métis nearly half a century after it was initiated. His method consisted of matching patterns of behaviour identified in the documents with what scholars then understood to be aspects of Euro-Canadian and Indian cultures and observing their expression and elaboration in the context of the events and circumstances that marked the history of the fur trade. Much of Giraud's work has stood the test of time and, no doubt, will continue to do so. But the thrust of his work emphasized the identification and description of "full-blown" métis communities with analysis geared to explaining their major behavioural traditions. The process or processes of origin were not central to his study.

In its emphasis on origins, more recent scholarly attention has shifted to individuals having similar cultural repertoires collectively recognizing the successes and failures of various adaptation experiences and acting on the basis of these experiences. The type and sequence of these adaptation experiences become central. Individual and small community life histories are most valuable. From such a perspective the associations and relationships among adult males, both formal and informal, may be seen to have been possibly responsible for much that became métis. The "company of men" becomes a focal entity in the study of métis origins.[16] Similarly the Indian women of the trading posts can be seen to have had their community which cannot be understood in terms of generalized comments about the behaviour of Indian males. And what of relations between women and men? Surely the familial context, no matter how fragile, was of greater interest than was the passing sexual encounter in terms of shared individual experiences. Giraud addressed these subjects, in some instances at length; but since his major concern was to understand more than a century of a particular people's history, the details of several different "origin experiences" were clearly beyond the scope of his study. His work remains, nevertheless, the invaluable point of departure for any quest for métis roots.

Recent works by Peterson and by Jennifer Brown draw attention to the writings of the anthropologist Fredrik Barth as being useful for our understanding of the métis. Two features of Barth's work seem particularly helpful. The first is his orientation toward ethnic rather than cultural groups or, for that matter, biological groups.[17] Barth notes that some cultural elements expressed by a people may appear or disappear with seemingly little consequence for a people's distinctiveness. At the same time some cultural practices will be mirrored in the lives of others who are viewed as separate entities. In other instances a people which occupies more than one ecological niche will manifest some distinctive cultural practices within its ethnic boundaries and yet remain, even for an extended time, a single entity in the eyes of the historical actors.[18] Thus a focus on cultural elements without reference to the *ethnos* tends to produce seemingly endless cultural inventories. In scholarly work to date, such inventories have not been very helpful. When the focus is put on the ethnic group rather than on a way of life, the analysis shifts to those cultural elements which serve to define a people's boundaries. As Barth notes, distance and antagonism are not necessary to maintain distinctions between peoples. Frequently relations may be close and friendly; cultural elements as well as individuals may pass relatively freely among communities.[19] Yet practices are maintained that perpetuate distinctions. Such practices are of particular interest in following the historical evolution of a particular people.

Barth emphasizes the importance of ascription in dealing with questions about who is and who is not a member of a particular people.[20] Answers to the questions are a function of the views of the historical actors, both "insiders" and "outsiders." Thus among the factors responsible for the origins of the métis are those associated with a time (and a place) when a particular population saw itself as métis and when outsiders shared this view.

In identifying particular populations that eventually came to see themselves as métis or some equivalent, it is useful to make a basic division between populations associated with the Hudson Bay trading system and those linked to the St. Lawrence-Great Lakes trading system. Although there was a blurring of distinctions between the two traditions after 1820 and although individuals occasionally passed between the two traditions, distinctions between the two populations survived well into the Confederation period after 1870.[21] At the same time, it is useful to subdivide each of the two basic populations, although any such subdivision must be considered tentative in view of the current state of research on the subject. In considering the St. Lawrence tradition it remains to be determined whether the distinctions between the métis of the Upper Great Lakes and the Northern Plains were such that the two should be considered separate social groups. Peterson has demonstrated how the tangled lineages which characterized the métis of the Upper Great Lakes after three or four generations caused "Métis identity . . . [to] become regionalized rather than place-specific."[22] Did the "region" extend to the plains? Some factors of circumstance and event suggest that it did not.

Prior to the conquest of New France in 1763 the Upper Great Lakes experienced more than a century of French presence and prominence; on the Northern Plains the duration of the French presence was limited to less than a generation. In the Upper Great Lakes region, fur-trade interests came to emphasize the importance of relations with Ojibwa peoples, while to the northwest the Cree and Assiniboine were the principal objects of fur trader interest. As well, the intimacy of association between the Great Lakes region and the Southwest trade, later evolving into the Missouri River trade, was not shared by the traders in the Northwest. These few examples of what could be an inventory of distinctions between the regions suggest the possibility of significant distinctions between the métis populations of each area. For instance, is it merely coincidental that Louis Riel, whose grandparents derived from the Northern Plains experience, should receive the enthusiastic support of the buffalo hunters and the tripmen in the Red River Settlement but less support from some métis families who appear to have had roots in the Great Lakes métis experience?[23] These same men were strong supporters of Riel's father during the free trade agitation that culminated in the Sayer trial in the Red River Settlement in 1849.[24] Is the "conservatism" of these men twenty years later to be explained, in part, by their added years? Or are some factors functions of community distinctions within the métis population that interacted in Red River?

Historians cannot ignore the possibility of further subdivisions within the métis populations. Some of these subdivisions would reflect the effect of events after métis populations were in existence as particular communities. What were the ramifications for the Great Lakes métis of the signing of Jay's Treaty in 1794? With this agreement the de facto British military and commercial presence in the American Old Northwest came to an end. Historians have seen the treaty as radically restructuring the Montreal fur trade, and particularly its hinterland.[25] Grand Portage and Sault Ste. Marie became part of a trading system that linked the Canadian Northwest with Montreal, and their traders supposedly lost interest in the region to the south. As a result, did their métis populations come to see themselves as separate from their kindred to the south?

Another area in which the mixed blood population may be subdivided is the Northern Plains. Evidence would suggest distinctions between the buffalo hunters of the prairie and parkland and the hunter-trappers of the boreal forest.[26] Within the latter group, a distinction between the "Peace-Athabaska Iroquois" and métis to the east seems warranted. And what of the métis of the Great Slave Lake-Upper Mackenzie River region – should they be distinguished from their kindred to the south?[27]

There is also a need to examine possible limits or boundaries of discrete populations among those mixed-bloods in the Hudson Bay tradition who eventually recognized their separateness from the Indian community. Were the mixed-blood populations in the vicinity of the Hudson's Bay Company's coastal factories a single entity or were they more than one social group? And what about the populations in the interior who were descended from these coastal groups – what boundaries set them apart from other mixed-blood populations?[28] Such questions emphasize the importance of identifying populations before attempting to discern the events and developments that brought the métis into existence. At this point, the question is of such complexity that just the existence of a "Euro-Canadian" father and an Indian mother no longer constitutes sufficient explanation for métis origins.

Having identified populations from which métis communities would arise, it becomes necessary to determine the factors responsible for their emergence at a particular place and time. What historical factors or mechanisms served to select the men and women who would in time become métis or an equivalent people? Louis Hartz has emphasized the fact that migrants are neither a social nor a cultural mirror of their parent community.[29] The circumstances of migration act as a highly selective device which causes the new community to diverge from its origins. The "Hartzian" effect is clearly evident in the fur trade, the needs of which were highly selective in terms of age, sex, occupation, social class and physical capability. The communities derived from the various migration processes reflected aspects of the parent cultures but were not a microcosm of them. Louise Dechêne has provided a graphic account of the types of individuals who filled the various roles in the fur trade in the St. Lawrence-Great Lakes tradition during the French period.[30] John Nicks has begun similar work on the Orcadians in the Hudson Bay tradition.[31] Sylvia Van Kirk offers a thorough examination of women in the fur trade in her book, *"Many Tender Ties"*; in it she affords several insightful comments on the changes in the behaviour of some Indian women who became wives to fur-trade officers and servants.[32] The question of how individuals were recruited for the populations that produced métis communities is of critical importance. It was these populations which experienced the adaptations and accommodations that gave rise to a new people.

Fundamental to Fredrik Barth's method of identifying social groups is the point of view of the participants.[33] In the cases of those populations who came to call themselves métis or an equivalent term, how did the historical actors determine who was a member and who was not a member? This question draws attention to mixed-blood populations who did not see themselves as distinct from the Indian. A number of Homeguard Cree and their descendants would certainly fit this description.[34] The corollary to the question of why these people did not see themselves as distinct from an Indian context is: when did those populations who in time saw themselves as métis first begin to do so? What constellations of events and circumstances led these people to alter their view of themselves in relation to other communities?

A comparison of Peterson's description of Upper Great Lakes métis communities with Dechêne's description of communities oriented towards a fur-trade interest in the environs of Montreal suggests interesting similarities.[35] A definitive statement must await further research but it would appear legitimate, at the moment, to describe the Upper Great Lakes communities as Canadien men living with native women and their children in a lifestyle that, in many respects, was imitative of the ways associated with some villages around Montreal. A sense of "eyes turned towards Montreal" emerges from Peterson's descriptions of life histories associated with several of the lineages she follows.[36] One has a sense of Canadien communities which happen to have mixed-blood components but do not see themselves as distinct from Canadien. For the métis to attain a self-consciousness in the population or populations of mixed-bloods who inhabited the Upper Great Lakes they would have to see themselves as distinct from the communities in and around Montreal. For historians, the event that would have engendered such a response would logically be the conquest of New France. The victory of the British on the Plains of Abraham outside Quebec in 1759 and its consequences for the subsequent generation have called forth much debate in French Canadian historiography, but the socio-cultural implications for the métis are more clear. In the generation following the Conquest the increasing dominance of the "anglais" not only as *bourgeois* (district heads) in the fur trade but as agents representing the London metropolis in Montreal was clearly evident. While Upper Great Lakes trading families could seek to protect their interests by extending their lineages to include anglais *commis* (clerks) and bourgeois,[37] it seems apparent that Montreal, in myth and in fact, could no longer occupy a central position in their sense of themselves. When they shifted the focus of their world from Montreal to the Upper Great Lakes did they, in effect, become métis?

On the Northern Plains a different situation existed. The Conquest proved disruptive; most Canadiens had abandoned the region by the end of the Seven Years War.[38] But since their presence had been established less than a generation earlier, their departures appear to have had minimal historical consequences. The critical factor when the St. Lawrence-Great Lakes fur trade re-established itself in the region was the predominance of the anglais in the bourgeois and, later, in the commis roles.[39] Young, ambitious Canadien tradesmen, who in the Great Lakes in previous years could envisage becoming commis and leading trading parties *en derouine* (circulating to Indian groups),[40] perhaps with sufficient success to become bourgeois, could no longer have such hopes within the fur-trade structure that was emerging. Yet the tradition of Canadien labour, which saw service merely as a temporary condition until one became a master, appears to have been as strong as ever.[41] In the context of the St. Lawrence–Great Lakes fur trade on the Northern Plains, the sole avenue of expression for this ethos was for these men to take the role of "freemen" purveying provisions and furs to the trading posts. By the closing decade of the eighteenth century it was clear to the Highland Scots bourgeois and commis that their former *engagés* (servants) who traded meat and furs with them were their most productive and dependable suppliers. *Les gens libres* (or as the Cree termed them, *O-tee-paym-soo-wuk,* "their own boss"),[42] were of pre-eminent interest to the fur trade. The traders recognized their pre-eminence by paying prices superior to those paid to Indians.[43] Clearly these freemen were distinct from the various Indian peoples around them, particularly with respect to the assiduity with which they hunted provisions and furs. Clearly they were distinct from the engagés, whose daily tasks were dictated by the commis and bourgeois. As yet, it is not possible to identify particular events as responsible for these populations holding such a view of themselves. It is certain, however, that this awareness predated by a number of years the Battle of Seven Oaks in Red River in 1816, the incident usually associated with the Red River métis' sense of themselves as the "New Nation."

In emphasizing the distinction between social groups and cultures, Fredrik Barth does not disdain cultural concerns. For him, behaviour that delineates boundaries between social groups is of critical importance. Thus he formulates a concept of cultural formation that seems admirably suited to the question of métis origins. Barth writes:

I find it reasonable to see social institutions and customs as the outcome of a complex aggregration of numerous micro-events of behaviour, based on individual decisions in each person's attempts to cope with life. . . . If a number of persons in communication share a similar opportunity situation, experience the same confrontations with reality, and have the same conceptualizations falsified, one would expect them to develop shared understandings and modify their collective culture and expectations in accordance with this.[44]

Although this statement "is not a complete theory of cultural change," it seems to serve the purposes of students who seek to understand the origins of the métis.[45] The shared experiences in a particular population create the social group; the shared understandings arising from these experiences are expressed as behaviour that distinguishes the métis from others.

The circumstances of mixed-blood populations in the fur trade suggest three distinct worlds of experience. The first and the most fully detailed in the literature is that of adult males. Although the record is far from complete, particularly outside the ranks of the officers, it is clear that a fundamental feature of this world was the manner in which it structured itself socially. In the St. Lawrence–Great Lakes trading system, the social structure reflected French and Canadien traditions. The process of acquiring furs through trade with the Indians did not dictate the social system but it did set limits that demanded accommodations and adaptations. The particular roles that marked the social hierarchy from bourgeois through commis to engagé, including tradesmen and unskilled labourers, reflected this circumstance. Mechanisms existed for individual males to alter their positions in the hierarchy through achievements appropriate not only to the trading of furs but to being a man of consequence among other males. Evidence to date suggests a similar social world in the Hudson's Bay Company's coastal factories.[46] Social differences between the two trading systems, reflecting differences in environment and hinterland-metropolis relations, are clear. But the existence of a hierarchical society, in which the interests of the participants as members of a collectivity of adult males contributed significantly to shared experiences, is clearly evident in both systems.

J.J. Gunn's brief but graphic biography of the legendary tripman, Paulet Paul, a folk history entitled "The Tripman of Assiniboia" in his book, *Echoes of the Red*,[47] demonstrates a dimension of the world of adult males in the fur trade that goes beyond the needs of the trade as a resource exploitation activity. Although Gunn's account reflects the post-1820 period when the voyaging tradition of the St. Lawrence-Great Lakes trading system had been blended into the tripping tradition of the Hudson Bay trading system and when métis communities were already in existence, he details a society whose traditions had roots in the previous century, in the fur trade. Gunn's Paul Bunyanesque account should not be allowed to obscure the fact that Paulet Paul occupied the position of brigade guide and as such was responsible for the crew's conduct on the trip and for handling all business pertinent to the brigade while it was tripping. Gunn writes:

[Paulet Paul] was a giant in stature and strength, beardless but shock-headed and black as erebus; with a voice like thunder and a manner as blustery as March, eyes like an eagle and a pair of fists as heavy, and once at least, as deadly as cannon balls. . . . Besides being guide of his brigade Poulet [sic] was its champion. . . . When the different brigades met at York Factory, and the question which could produce the best man, came to be mooted over a regal[e] of Hudson's Bay rum, he was ever the first to strip to the waist and stand forth to claim that honour for the Blaireau[x] ["Badgers," supposedly the principal food of the Saskatchewan brigade]. Michael [sic] Lambert who on such occasions would step forward in the interests of the Taureaux [Pemmican made from the meat of a Buffalo Bull, supposedly the food of the Red River brigade] [would] shake hands with Poulet [sic] and then for the next half hour or so, proceed to enhance his picturesqueness. . . . Such encounters . . . came to be a recognized institution of the trip. . . . Of course, there were other minor events at such points as Norway House or Portage La Loche with the Poisson-blanc [Whitefish, supposedly the food of the Athabaska or more properly, the Portage La Loche brigade]; but it was on that of York Factory when Paul and Lambert stood up for the honour of their respective districts, that interest chiefly centered – when the championship of all the west tossed back and forth with Poulet's [sic] ferocious pounding and the lightning-like science of Lambert.[48]

Yet in spite of his stature as brigade champion, Paul was subject to the discipline of the interests of his peers. When his brigade protested the actions of an officer against one of their fellows and dumped their cargo on shore, Paul was clearly expected to risk his occupational tenure in order to lend his stature, physical and occupational, to their cause. He did, and they were successful.[49] Gunn ends his account by noting that, while still a relatively young man, Paul was shot and killed near Fort Edmonton at the instigation of a rival who sought his position.[50]

A significant part of Paulet Paul's world was the company of adult males in the fur trade. Their behaviour was, in part, a function of the shared experiences of earlier generations that had become institutionalized as cultural elements and served to distinguish at least some of the métis of the Northern Plains from other social groups. The particular needs of the fur trade influenced but did not dictate the shared experiences of these men. Perhaps French and Canadien traditions, derived from the world of the military, influenced the institutionalization that was reflected in the behaviour in which Paul and Lambert participated.[51] But the ranks of an earlier generation of fur trade engagés did not consist solely of Canadiens.

Among them were Highland Scots, Irish, Iroquois, Ottawa and Ojibwa peoples.[52] These men of diverse origins appeared to be equally functional in an adult male world derived apparently from Canadien tradition. Lambert, Paul's perennial opponent, was Swiss-born.[53] Perhaps the significance of the Canadien tradition lies more in the terms used than it does in the institutions themselves. Perhaps a number of the institutions that arose in the fur trade post owed as much to the fact that the society consisted almost solely of adult males as it did to the needs of a commercial trade and Canadien tradition.

Among mixed-blood populations, the world of adult females was of some, if not equal or greater, importance in the sharing of experiences that became institutionalized as métis ways. Unfortunately the male bias of the documents renders it most difficult to garner an appreciation of these experiences. The relevant existing literature emphasizes the experiences of the officers' wives and daughters in the years after 1820.[54] Yet, in spite of these difficulties a few works, particularly Van Kirk's "*Many Tender Ties,*" provide insights into the world of women associated with the mixed-blood populations that emerged as métis.

The preponderance of Ojibwa-speaking women in the Upper Great Lakes and Cree-speaking women on the Northern Plains and the survival of both languages in the métis communities that emerged suggest the survival of many traditional ways in the shared experiences of these women.[55] Similarly, many women appear to have maintained close ties with their bands, possibly viewing such ties as of greater long-term importance than those they formed with personnel in the post.[56] Such behaviour again implies the survival of traditional ways. Other factors, however, such as the motives of individual women and the bias toward younger women imposed by fur trade circumstances, suggest the possibility of behaviour that may have emphasized shared experiences distinct from traditional ways.[57] It is most difficult to gain an appreciation of the shared experiences of the women when individual experience seemed to range from those who were items of barter among the men to those who managed their circumstances so as to establish positions of respect and influence.[58] Van Kirk urges caution in accepting the assumptions of European males that the trading post constituted a superior environment for Indian women.[59]

Further quantitative studies will no doubt confirm the startling apparent increase in fertility among native women living in the trading posts. Evidence suggests that women living in Indian hunting bands could expect four live births during their child-bearing years while those in the trading post frequently experienced live births double and triple that number.[60] The question that remains unanswered is the extent to which such behaviour was a function of "choice" and the extent to which it was a function of circumstance. Did increased fertility reflect improved circumstances for the women which enhanced reproductive success, or did it represent more difficult circumstances, perhaps a loss of knowledge of "women's medicine" or the constraints of a social system dominated by males unacquainted with and insensitive to Indian practices associated with sexual behavior, lactation, and child-rearing? Useful insights would be offered should comparative data for "homeguard" bands living in close proximity to the trading post become available.

The third area of shared experiences bearing upon the origins of the métis is that of family life, particularly the nature of the relationship between husband and wife. In both trading systems there were occasions when sexual licence was permitted; but, in most instances constraints of some type prevailed.[61] These constraints, together with the economic compatibility of traditional male and female roles in the circumstances of the fur trade, serve to explain the basis of family formation. The Anglican missionary, Reverend William Cockran, evokes a somewhat exaggerated image of these factors in a letter to the Church Missionary Society:

When a young voyageur comes to his winter quarters, he finds he wants many things to fit him for this new existence which he has entered upon. He wants his leather coat, trowsers [sic], mittens, duffle socks and shoes, all then must be made and kept in repair. He has no time to do this himself; he applies to an Indian who has got some daughters, or two or three wives; here he is quickly served, he makes a present to the head of the family, they set to work and make all ready for him, he comes at a certain time for his clothes, brings a little rum, and makes the principal persons of the family merry. He sleeps there. . . . He goes off in the summer, returns in the autumn, and perhaps finds the same young woman given to another. This does not distract his mind, he forms another connexion as speedily as possible; by this time he believes that he cannot get on without a woman.[62]

Cockran's statement is significant for several reasons. While it was written in 1833, the circumstances he described were fast altering as the Hudson's Bay Company's employment practices after 1830 limited the hiring of permanent servants to skilled tradesmen.[63] "Voyageurs," as Cockran termed them, were hired with increasing frequency on temporary contracts from among natives of the country. Cockran's description may better fit the world experienced by many of his Hudson Bay English parishioners prior to 1820.[64] In addition, Cockran's description reflects the "family life" of a male relatively low in the occupational hierarchy. At an earlier date in the Hudson Bay trading system a family life within the trading post had been reserved for the chief factor.[65] Other officers and senior skilled servants, such as Augustine Frost at Moose Factory in the 1730s and 40s, formed family relationships with women who continued to reside in the surrounding home-guard bands. These relationships appear to have been very similar to that described by Cockran.[66] After 1790, circumstances altered; officers and senior servants, with the chief factor's knowledge, established families within the post.[67] In the St. Lawrence tradition, family formation was apparently accomplished with greater ease; nevertheless, an engagé required the permission of his bourgeois.[68]

It would seem that the financial means and personal commitments of the male were instrumental in determining the extent to which the woman remained attached to her parental band. Brown's concept of patrifocality in *Strangers in Blood* reflects the capacity of officers, who were thus inclined, to place significant constraints on their wives' behaviour.[69] Males of lesser rank would lack such a capacity. With reference to the origins of the métis, a debatable point emerges. As Brown demonstrates, in most instances the families of old Hudson's Bay Company officers did not give rise to métis or, for that matter, Hudson Bay English.[70] Many children born of those family relationships described by Cockran grew to maturity as Indians. Questions remain as to the nature of the family relationships that enculturated children as métis.

Before leaving the question of the nature of shared familial experiences in the fur trade, it is useful to note instances where men and women functioned as economic units rather than merely as members of reciprocal economic relationships. From the earliest days of the fur trade, Indian women provided technical skills that had economic benefit. Such skills ranged from the preparation and care of pelts and hides to the processing of foods such as pemmican and to simple bullwork such as clearing a post of snow.[71] In some circumstances, a Euro-Canadian male and a native female presented themselves together as an economic unit in the fur trade. The most obvious example is that of the male buffalo hunter who, contrary to usual Indian practice, butchered the animal in preparation for the woman, who dried and further processed the meat into pemmican.[72] The resulting product was as much hers as his.

Another instance of the two operating as a single economic unit, this time as hired hands, may be evident in the trials and tribulations marking the Hudson's Bay Company's penetration of the interior. A particular problem faced by the company during the generation following the construction of Cumberland House in 1774 was the shortage of skilled labour to paddle the canoes into the interior.[73] Those servants skilled in this activity used the circumstances to demand increased wages.[74] The London directors apparently adamantly refused these demands for increased wages, yet the chief factors seemed willing to accommodate them.[75] Perhaps the willingness of the factors to accept some of these demands was a reflection of the fact that the company was, on occasion, hiring two pairs of hands rather than one.[76] In the Canadian Shield region, Cree women were skilled at steering small Indian canoes. As wives of servants, women offered skills in food preparation and in the care of furs and hides; but, in the critical area of transportation, as skilled canoeists, they would have been valued "unofficial" additions to the post complement, without drawing the attention of the governor and committee in London. Together, such husbands and wives would have been most welcome in the fur trade. In later times and in other places, such economic teams were most functional in the fur trade.[77] Their shared experiences are surely pertinent to the origins of the métis peoples.

In the face-to-face communities that became métis in the latter years of the eighteenth century, the worlds of adult males, of adult females, and of the family (when it existed) served to define the social circumstances of shared experiences. Among the men, attributes associated with occupation, experience, age and kin, or ethnic ties not only determined ascribed status but generated the existence of smaller social groupings within the population of a trading post. Similarly, among the women, small units of female association probably developed within the posts' populations. Yet, as the métis arose out of such populations, it would seem obvious that these social distinctions did not obscure the "post-wide" nature of many shared experiences nor for that matter the "trading system-wide" nature of some experiences. Thus, in conceptualizing the "proto-métis" populations as societies, an examination of the conjunction of these three worlds of shared experiences seems a most useful focus in the scholarly quest for métis origins.

NOTES

1 Much of the unprofitable debate on terminology could be eliminated with reference to the excellent discussion in Jennifer S.H. Brown, "Linguistic Solitudes and Changing Social Categories" in C.M. Judd and A.J. Ray, eds., *Old Trails and New Directions: Papers of the Third North American Fur Trade Conference* (Toronto: University of Toronto Press, 1980), 150–58.

2 See: Jacqueline Peterson, "Prelude to Red River: A Social Portrait of the Great Lakes Métis," *Ethnohistory* 25 (Winter 1978)1:41–67; Trudy Nicks, "The Iroquois and the Fur

Trade in Western Canada" in C.M. Judd and A.J. Ray, eds., *Old Trails*, 85–101; and Trudy Nicks, "Demographic Anthropology of Native Populations in Western Canada, 1800–1975" (Ph.D. dissertation, University of Alberta, 1980).

3 A team of scholars, headquartered at the University of Alberta under the general editorship of G.F.G. Stanley, is editing *Louis Riel, Collected Papers, Critical Edition/Louis Riel, Ecrits complets, édition critique*, in five volumes, for publication in 1985.

4 Alexander Ross, *The Red River Settlement* (Minneapolis: Ross and Haines Inc., 1957; first edition, London, 1856).

5 Ibid., 260.

6 Ibid, 251–53.

7 Ibid., 264.

8 For an example, see J.J. Hargrave, *Red River* (Montreal: 1871).

9 Douglas Sprague and Ronald Frye, "Manitoba's Red River Settlement: Manuscript Sources for Economics and Demographic History," *Archivaria* 9 (Winter 1979–80):179–93.

10 Several métis organizations, such as the Métis Association of Alberta and Federation of Métis Settlements, have undertaken oral history projects of varying sophistication and success in an attempt to record and to preserve this oral tradition. Recent offerings of Pemmican Publications in Winnipeg reflect a similar interest.

11 Marcel Giraud, *Le Métis canadien: son rôle dans l'histoire des provinces de l'Ouest* (Paris: l'Institut d'Ethnologie, 1945).

12 Ibid., v–vi.

13 Ibid., 331–64 and 867–80.

14 Ibid., 501–12.

15 Ibid., 429–75. Here, Giraud acknowledges métis origins in regions distinct from the Saskatchewan and the Red and Assiniboine River valleys; yet, his subsequent discussion concerns itself almost exclusively with the Plains buffalo hunters.

16 Ibid., 293–475. This section contains the essence of Giraud's discussion with reference to "origins."

17 Fredrik Barth, ed., *Ethnic Groups and Boundaries: The Social Organization of Cultural Difference* (Boston: Little, Brown and Co., 1969), 10.

18 Ibid.

19 Ibid., 9–10.

20 Ibid., 10. In this regard note as well O.P. Dickason, this volume.

21 Victoria Callihoo, "Early Life in Lac Ste Anne and St. Albert in the 1870s" *Alberta Historical Review* 1 (November 1953)3, reprinted in *The Pioneer West* (Calgary: Historical Society of Alberta, 1970), 10.

22 Peterson, "Prelude to Red River," 59.

23 This question, of course, remains to be studied in detail; but, the career of Pascal Breland, married to a sister of Cuthbert Grant, is a case in point. One of their daughters married Chief Trader Richard Grant, son of William Grant of Three Rivers. William Grant had married Margaret Laframboise and had engaged extensively in the Southwest trade prior to 1800. Breland, an active participant in the Red River events of the 1840s, was absent from the events of 1869–70 although he emerged later to sit on the council of the North West Territories after Confederation. See: A.G. Morice, *Dictionnaire historique des Canadiens et des Métis français de l'Ouest* (Quebec: J.P. Garneau, 1908), 48; W.S. Wallace, ed., *Documents Relating to the North West Company* (Toronto: Champlain Society, 1934), 451, 452; R.H. Fleming, ed., *Minutes of Council, Northern Department of Rupert's Land, 1821–31* (Toronto: Champlain Society, 1940), 452; and W.L. Morton, Introduction in E.E. Rich, ed., *Eden*

Colvile's Letters (London: Hudson's Bay Record Society, 1956), lxxxix, as quoted in Irene Spry, this volume.

24 An examination of the métis activists as distinct from the Hudson Bay English participants in the events of 1846 to 1849 and 1869–70 suggests, with the exception of the Riel and Goulet families, a lack of continuity between the activists of the free trade movement and those of the first Riel rising (Provincial Archives of Manitoba, Red River Settlement, Red River Correspondence, 1845–1847, James Sinclair et al. to Alex Christie, August 29, 1845 and PAM, RRS, "Peter Garrioch Journal," manuscript edited by H.G. Gunn, p. 261).

25 A.S. Morton, *A History of the Canadian West to 1870–75* (Toronto: University of Toronto Press, 1973; first edition, London, 1939), 489–90.

26 A particularly significant example of this distinction can be found near Lac La Biche, Alberta. There, "Mission Métis," originating in a migration from the Red River Settlement with Roman Catholic missionaries in the middle of the last century, were, until World War II, clearly distinguishable from the métis indigenous to the region. See Patrick C. Douaud, "Métis: A Case of Triadic Linguistic Economy," *Anthropological Linguistics* 22 (December 1980)9:392–414.

27 Richard Slobodin, *Métis of the Mackenzie District* (Ottawa: St. Paul University, 1966), is a basic source on this question.

28 At the point of writing, I have merely an impression of distinctions in the nature of labour-management relations as they existed at posts on the west coast of Hudson Bay and as they existed at the "bottom of the Bay." But from the circumstances associated with the arson at Moose Factory (staffed from Fort Albany) on Christmas Day, 1735, to the mutiny at Brandon House (staffed from Fort Albany) on February 24, 1811, I sense an aggressiveness in the assertion of servants' interests that is not reflected at posts on the west coast. The question remains as to the legacy of these traditions among various populations of Hudson Bay English. See: E.E. Rich, *The History of the Hudson's Bay Company, 1670–1870* (London: Hudson's Bay Record Society 1958), 547; and Hudson's Bay Company Archives, B.22/a/18a, Brandon House Journal, 1810–1811, February 24 entry.

29 Louis Hartz, ed., *The Founding of New Societies: Studies in the History of the United States, Latin America, South Africa, Canada and Australia* (Toronto: Longman's, 1964), 4.

30 Louise Dechêne, *Habitants et Marchands de Montreal au XVIIᵉ Siècle* (Montreal: Librairie Plon, 1974), 220–26. Also see Gratien Allaire, "Fur Trade *Engagés*, 1701–1745" in Thomas C. Buckley, ed., *Rendezvous: Selected Papers of the Fourth North American Fur Trade Conference, 1981* (St. Paul, Minn.: North American Fur Trade Conference, 1984), 15–26.

31 John Nicks, "Orkneymen in the HBC, 1780–1821" in Judd and Ray, eds., *Old Trails,* 102–26.

32 Sylvia Van Kirk, *"Many Tender Ties": Women in Fur Trade Society, 1670–1870* (Winnipeg: Watson and Dwyer Publishing Ltd., 1980).

33 Barth, ed., *Ethnic Groups and Boundaries,* 10.

34 J.E. Foster, "The Home Guard Cree and the Hudson's Bay Company: The First Hundred Years" in D.A. Muise, ed., *Approaches to Native History in Canada* (Ottawa: National Museums of Canada, 1977), 59–60.

35 Dechêne, *Habitants et Marchands,* 183–87, 220–26; Peterson, "Prelude to Red River," 50–53, notes "living arrangements . . . [which] set them apart from . . . European society to the east." For the "Canadien," the question arises as to the extent to which the "living arrangements" were distinct in "kind" and not "degree," particularly in terms of "stage of development." Note as well Jacqueline Peterson, this volume.

36 Peterson, "Prelude to Red River," 57.

37 Ibid., 43

38 Rich, *History of the Hudson's Bay Company*, I, 646.

39 E.E. Rich, *Montreal and the Fur Trade* (Montreal: McGill University Press, 1966,) 63.

40 Dechêne, *Habitants et Marchands*, 223.

41 Peter N. Moogk, "In the Darkness of a Basement: Craftmen's Associations in Early French Canada," *Canadian Historical Review* 57 (December 1976)4:419.

42 Trudy Nicks, "Demographic Anthropology of Native Populations," 61.

43 Ibid., 59.

44 Fredrik Barth, "Descent and Marriage Reconsidered" in Jack Goody, ed., *The Character of Kinship* (London: Cambridge University Press, 1973), 5.

45 Ibid.

46 J.E. Foster, "The Indian Trader in the Hudson Bay Fur Trade Tradition" in Jim Freedman and J.H. Barkow, eds., *Proceedings of the Second Congress, Canadian Ethnology Society* (Ottawa: National Museums of Canada, 1975).

47 J.J. Gunn, *Echoes of the Red* (Toronto: Macmillan Co., 1930), chap. 3.

48 Ibid., 54–56.

49 Ibid., 41–42.

50 Ibid., 57.

51 To this end see: Peter N. Moogk, "Rank in New France: Reconstructing a Society from Notarial Documents," *Social History* 8 (May 1975)15:34–53; and W.J. Eccles, "The Social, Economic, and Political Significance of the Military Establishment in New France, *Canadian Historical Review* 52 (March 1971)1:1–22.

52 Carol Judd, " 'Mixt Bands of Many Nations,' " in Judd and Ray, eds., *Old Trails*, p. 129, details the ethnic mix of labour in the Hudson's Bay Company prior to the end of competition. Some movement of labour between the two companies on the expiration of contracts ensured an ethnic mix although the Canadiens were overwhelmingly predominant in the North West Company.

53 Gunn, *Echoes of the Red*, 57.

54 Jennifer S.H. Brown, *Strangers in Blood: Fur Trade Company Families in Indian Country* (Vancouver: University of B.C. Press, 1980), is an excellent recent example.

55 On the use of languages see A.C. Garrioch, *The Correction Line* (Winnipeg: Stoval and Co., 1933), 199, 201, 208.

56 This seems to be a legitimate conclusion arising from the behaviour of the "Indian wife" as described in Public Archives of Canada, Church Missionary Society, Incoming Correspondence, Rev. William Cockran to the Secretaries, July 25, 1833, excerpts in L.G. Thomas, ed., *Prairie West to 1905* (Toronto: Oxford University Press, 1975), 35–36. Also see Jennifer S.H. Brown, this volume.

57 W.K. Lamb, ed., *Sixteen Years in The Indian Country: The Journal of Daniel William Harmon, 1800–1816* (Toronto: 1957), 98. Harmon's country wife, Lizette Duval, was about fourteen years of age.

58 Van Kirk, "*Many Tender Ties*," 47, 83–84.

59 Ibid., 7, 85–86.

60 Van Kirk, "*Many Tender Ties*," 86–87, and Jennifer S.H. Brown, "A Demographic Transition in the Fur Trade Country: Family Sizes and Fertility of Company Officers and Country Wives, ca. 1750-1850" in *Western Canadian Journal of Anthropology* 6 (1976)1:61–71.

61 Van Kirk, "*Many Tender Ties*," 47.

62 PAC, CMS, Cockran to the Secretaries, July 25, 1833.

63 Judd, " 'Mixt Bands of Many Nations,' " 138–41.

64 Only one third of the families in Cockran's parish at St. Andrew's, Red River Settlement, were headed by a European-born male. The bulk of the families originated before 1820.

65 Glyndwr Williams, ed., *Andrew Graham's Observations on Hudson's Bay, 1767–91* (London: Hudson's Bay Record Society, 1969), 145, 248.

66 Williams, *Andrew Graham's Observations,* and Van Kirk, "*Many Tender Ties,*" 43.

67 Alice Johnson, ed., *Saskatchewan Journals and Correspondence* (London: Hudson's Bay Record Society, 1967), xcix–xcx, 76n.

68 Moogk, "Rank in New France," 44.

69 Brown, *Strangers in Blood,* 218.

70 Ibid.

71 Van Kirk, "*Many Tender Ties,*" 53–74.

72 Herman Sprenger, "The Métis Nation: Buffalo Hunting vs. Agriculture in the Red River Settlement (circa 1810-1870)," *The Western Canadian Journal of Anthropology* 3 (1972)1:173.

73 Richard Glover, "The Difficulties of the Hudson's Bay Company's Penetration of the West," *Canadian Historical Review* 29 (September 1948)4:240–54.

74 A.M. Johnson, ed., *Saskatchewan Journals and Correspondence,* lxvii.

75 Ibid., xxviii.

76 HBCA, B.60/a/10, Fort Edmonton Journal, 1810–11, Wm. Auld to James Bird, September 28, 1811.

77 A noteworthy example is Paul Boucher dit Lamallice and his wife. See Van Kirk, "*Many Tender Ties,*" 84–85.

Communities in Diversity

II

The métis and mixed-bloods
of Rupert's Land before 1870

Irene M. Spry

Were the English-speaking mixed-bloods and French-speaking métis of what is now western Canada separate and mutually hostile groups? Or were they friendly and closely linked with each other? Frits Pannekoek contends that the *country-born* (as he terms the English-speaking mixed-bloods)[1] and the métis of Red River Settlement "were at odds years before the [Riel] resistance, and the origins of that hatred lay in the nature of Red River society." He concludes: "In fact, upon closer examination of the origins of Métis Country-born hatred, it becomes apparent that the first Riel resistance was in part caused and certainly exacerbated not by racial and religious antagonisms introduced by the Canadians, but rather by a sectarian and racial conflict with roots deep in Red River's past."[2]

This view of the divisions within Red River Settlement is directly contrary to what a métis, Louis Goulet, remembered. Writing of 1867, when his family returned to Red River from the far western plains, he recollected:

Something was missing in the Red River Colony: There wasn't the same feeling of unity and friendship that had always been felt among those people of different races and religions. And he [his father] wasn't the only one unhappy with the way things were going.

The old-timers seemed to feel a strange mood in the air. Newcomers, especially the ones from Ontario, were eagerly sowing racial and religious conflict, banding together to fan the flames of discord between different groups in the Red River Settlement. These émigrés from Ontario, all of them Orangemen, looked as if their one dream in life was to make war on the Hudson's Bay Company, the Catholic Church and anyone who spoke French. . . . The latest arrivals were looking to be masters of everything, everywhere.[3]

Continuing tradition among twentieth-century English-speaking descendants of the Selkirk settlers supports Louis Goulet. As Miss Janet Banner-

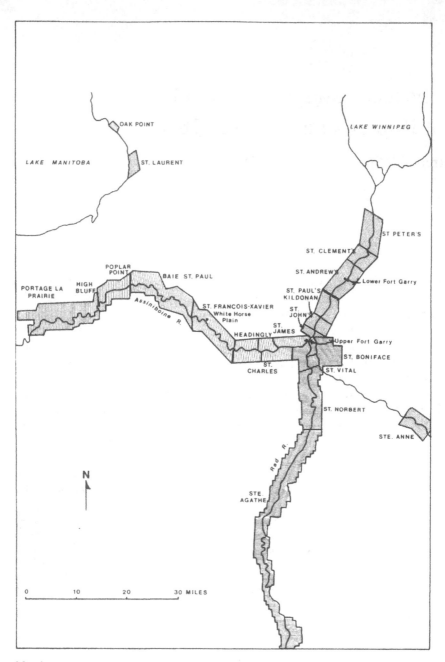

Map 1
The Red River Settlement, 1870. (Map by Victor Lytwyn.)

man of Old Kildonan recalled, "The relations between the French-speaking families and the rest of us in Red River were always of friendliness and goodwill. In the very earliest and hardest days of the settlement that friendship was established upon a lasting foundation by the French-Canadians and the métis who showed warmhearted kindness to the poor Scottish people when the lack of food at the Forks compelled them to go down to the buffalo hunters' headquarters at the mouth of the Pembina river in the winter time."[4] This, in turn, is consistent with Miss Anne Henderson's memories of walks, when she was a child early in this century, with her grandfather who introduced her to all the friends he met, many of whom were French-speaking.[5] Similarly, George Sanderson, Jr., writing of his boyhood in Portage la Prairie, mentioned among his chums the "Pochas" [Poitras] and "Demers" [Desmarais] boys.[6]

Very little evidence of conflict, let alone "hatred," has come to light except in the clerical sources on which Pannekoek's conclusion seems in large measure to be based. Such sources, it is submitted, must be used with great reserve. Independent evidence is needed to test the testimony of writers who were concerned to convert the adherents of rival dogmas and to protect their own flocks from counter-conversion. Hostility between Catholic and Protestant divines was a byword in Rupert's Land.[7] Such antagonism as there may have been between French- and English-speaking communities was, indeed, largely sectarian, but it does not seem to have been racial in origin.

A preliminary survey of such non-clerical evidence as is available concerning the nature of the relationships of the natives of the country of Indian and French and Indian and other white descent,[8] suggests that, far from being mutually hostile, métis and mixed-bloods were, as W.L. Morton put it, linked by "ties of blood and of long association on hunt and trip."[9]

Alexander Ross's celebrated statement may, perhaps, be taken with a pinch or two of salt, but it must at least be considered:

We have now seen all the different classes of which this infant colony was composed brought together. The better to advance each other's interest, as well as for mutual support, all sects and creeds associated together indiscriminately, and were united like members of the same family, in peace, charity, and good fellowship. This state of things lasted till the Churchmen began to feel uneasy, and the Catholics grew jealous; so that projects were set on foot to separate the tares from the wheat. . . .

Party spirit and political strife has been gaining ground ever since. The Canadians became jealous of the Scotch, the half-breeds of both; and their separate interests as agriculturalists, voyageurs, or hunters, had little tendency to unite them. At length, indeed, the Canadians and half-breeds came to a good understanding with each other; leaving then but two parties, the Scotch and the French. Between these, although there is, and always has been, a fair show of mutual good feeling, anything like cordiality in a common sentiment seemed impossible; and they remain, till this day, politically divided.[10]

Significantly, Ross said nothing about the mixed-bloods as a separate group, except as he described where each community lived; on the contrary, in his book, *The Red River Settlement,* he noted a number of apparent affinities among and cooperation between métis and mixed-bloods. Thus, in his account of talk among Rupert's Landers, Ross mentioned their "narrations." These were "made up of an almost unintelligible jargon of the English, French and Indian languages."[11] This suggests at least some mingling of the English- and French-speaking elements in the population of mixed descent, an impression borne out by a traveller's observation concerning a cart train south of Red River Settlement: "In the 'polyglot jabber' " of the métis drivers "he heard 'fine broad Scotch,' a scattering of Gaelic and Irish brogue, and a plentiful mixture of 'rapidly uttered French *patois.*' "[12] Another traveller in the Red River Valley in 1864 joined a cart train under the command of Antoine Gingras who "knew English" as well as French, though his drivers spoke only Indian and French.[13] J.G. Kohl in the 1850s recorded a bilingual statement by a métis: "Ou je reste? Je ne peux pas te le dire. Je suis Voyageur – je suis Chicot, monsieur. Je reste partout. Mon grand-père était Voyageur: il est mort en voyage. Mon père était Voyageur: il est mort en voyage. Je mourrai aussi en voyage, et un autre Chicot prendra ma place. Such is our course of life."[14]

Louis Goulet, in describing the Frog Lake massacre, mentioned that he and his friends, André Nault and Dolphis Nolin, conversed in English mixed with a little French when they were held by the Cree.[15] He noted, too, that a French-speaking métis of Scottish descent, Johnny Pritchard, was interpreter to Tom Quinn. Presumably this meant that he could speak English.[16] A granddaughter of Norbert Welsh (an Irish-French métis), in enumerating the languages that her grandfather had at his command, ended the list with "and, of course, English."[17]

Similarly, some mixed-bloods spoke French, people such as Charles Thomas who was in charge of the Hudson's Bay Company post at Reindeer Lake when Father Taché visited it in 1847.[18] "Big Jim" McKay, later to become the Honourable James McKay of Deer Lodge, whose father came from Sutherlandshire, spoke French,[19] as did members of another family of McKays, the "Little Bearskin" McKays, William McKay, his brother John ("Jerry") McNab Ballenden McKay, and his son

Thomas.[20] Joseph Finlayson, one of the Roderick Finlayson family, also wrote and spoke French fluently.[21] It would appear, therefore, that many métis and mixed-bloods, at least among the elite, spoke both French and English, as well as one or more of the Indian languages, in which tongues those who did not speak both French and English could and did communicate. The English-speaking pioneer settlers of Portage la Prairie, for instance, were fluent in Cree, which "enabled them to associate freely with the French Half-breeds" of White Horse Plain, among whom most of them could claim cousins.[22]

No doubt the métis and mixed-bloods of Rupert's Land spoke this diversity of languages at least in part because they were the descendants of a rich diversity of ancestors. Their maternal forebears included Cree, Ojibwa and Chipewyan, as well as French Canadians and Scots; while their paternal ancestry included not only French and English, but also Orcadian, Scots, Irish, Shetland and other European strains, notably the Danish ancestry of the numerous progeny of Peter Erasmus Sr.[23] Baptiste Bruce, for instance, the guide with Dr. John Rae's Arctic expedition of 1848–49, claimed Highland and French, as well as Indian descent.[24] Alick Fisher's mother was a métis.[25] Baptiste Robillard, a former guide with the Cumberland boat brigade, was accompanied out on the plains by a son-in-law, John Simpson, said to be the natural son of Thomas Simpson, the ill-fated Arctic explorer.[26] A long roster of names like Baptiste Kennedy attests the complex mixture of origins among the métis. Among the mixed-bloods, similarly, there were many with French ancestry. "Big Jim" McKay had French antecedents through his mother who was a Gladu(e).[27] Joe McKay, a "Little Bearskin," married one of the Poitras girls.[28] George Sanderson had two French grandmothers and a niece named Desmarais.[29]

It would be interesting to have a count of all mixed marriages, both *à la façon du pays* (according to the custom of the country) and those solemnized by the clergy. The fragmentary nature of the documentary record makes this impossible, but, even without such comprehensive information, it is evident that many marriages spanned the alleged gulf between the mixed-blood and métis groups. Among the marriages recorded in the Protestant parishes of Red River Settlement, a number involved couples with French and non-French names. It cannot, of course, be assumed that having a Scottish name meant that an individual was a mixed-blood, nor that all métis had French names. Some whose fathers came from Scotland or the Orkneys grew up speaking French and were assimilated to the culture of a French-speaking, Catholic métis mother, as in the case of the

Bruce and Dease families.[30] In other cases, seemingly non-French marriages had in them a strong French element, as in the case of James McKay's marriage to Margaret Rowand[31] and Jeanette [Janet] Tate's marriage to Alex Birston.[32] Moreover, dominance in a family of French, Catholic culture did not necessarily exclude non-French influences any more than a dominant non-French culture excluded French or Catholic influences.

A further complication in an attempt to analyze marriages listed in the parish registers is that not all the apparently French-non-French marriages were between métis and mixed-bloods of whatever descent. At least a dozen Swiss-Swiss and a half dozen French-French (or, more likely, Canadien-Canadienne) unions have been identified. Further, an apparently métis–mixed-blood marriage may turn out to be a Canadian-Scottish marriage. This adds uncertainty to the relevance of seeming cross-marriages to the question of métis–mixed-blood relationships. Norman Kittson, for example, who came from Quebec, married a daughter of Narcisse Marion, also from Quebec.[33]

Unfortunately, it has not been possible to analyze marriages in the Indian settlement, although some of the settlers there, such as Joseph Cook and his children,[34] were of mixed origin. Nor has it been possible to include data from the French-Catholic parishes. The fire that destroyed St. Boniface cathedral in 1860 destroyed most of the early formal records. There is, however, a list in the Provincial Archives of British Columbia of men married by the Catholic missionaries from the time of their arrival in 1818 to February 15, 1831.[35] Among the almost three hundred names listed, nearly twenty are non-French: mostly McDonnells, McLeods and the like. Undoubtedly, some of their descendants had been assimilated to the culture of métis mothers, though the wives' names are not given.

Other scattered records that survive show that non-French names were, in some instances, changed to a spelling better suited to French pronunciation than the original spelling was. For example, "Sayer" became "Serre"[36] and "McKay" became "Macaille."[37] Similarly, French spelling was sometimes anglicized. Thus, the descendants of Michel Reine (Rayne and other variants), from Strasbourg, became "Wren."[38]

Despite all these gaps and ambiguities, the records in the Hudson's Bay Company and church registers of what appear to be cross-marriages between métis and mixed-bloods in the Protestant parishes of Red River Settlement from 1820 to 1841[39] are of considerable interest (see table 1).

The spelling of names in these records varies from one to another and even from index to entry. It is, moreover, phonetic in character, and in

TABLE 1
Apparent marriages between métis and mixed bloods.

Entry number	Cross-marriage with date and reference number
13	Michael Lambere to Peggy (January 25, 1821 SJM 1820–1835)
18	George Saunderson to Lisset Lajimoniere (March 30, 1821 SJM 1820–1835)
23	William Dickson to Justine Pacquette (June 9, 1821 SJM 1820–1835)
36	John Warring to Lydia Fournier (November 11, 1821 SJM 1820–1835)
37	Martin Norte to Catherine Treathey (November 11, 1821 SJM 1820–1835)
58	Joshua Halcro to Francoise Laurain (November 18, 1823 SJM 1820–1835)
82	Henry Hallet, Jr., to Catherine Parenteau (October 18, 1824 SJM 1820–1835)
83	David Sandison to Louisa Giboche (October 19, 1824 SJM 1820–1835)
111	John Anderson to Mary (Murray?) [Desmarais] (January 31, 1826 SJM 1820–1835)
122	William Mackay to Julia Chalifoux (August 13, 1826 SJM 1820–1835)
124	James Swain to Margaret Racette (October 3, 1826 SJM 1820–1835)
125	William Birston to Hazelique Marchand (December 8, 1826 SJM 1820–1835)
129	William Bruce to Frances Andre (1827 SJM 1820–1835)
134	Andrew Spence to Susette L'Eunay (October 30, 1827 SJM 1820–1835)
167	George Kipling to Isabella Landrie (November 19, 1828 SJM 1820–1835)
176	Peter Pruden to Josette (Susette) Gothvier (May 7, 1829 SJM 1820–1835)
177	James Monkman to Nancy Shaboyee (May 12, 1829 SJM 1820–1835)
194	Pierre St. Pierre to Susannah Short (February 8, 1830 SJM 1820–1835)
202	Francis Desmarais to Harriet Spence (date and reference number missing)
212	John Batish Shurdan to Mary Lewis (January 6, 1831 SJM 1820–1835)
215	Aimable Hogue to Margarette Taylor (March 24, 1831 SJM 1820–1835)

TABLE 1   *continued*

Entry number	Cross-marriage with date and reference number
221	Hugh Cameron to Mary Jordan (October 26, 1831 SJM 1820–1835)
236	John Aimable McKay to Lizette La Vallee (March 12, 1832 SJM 1820–1835)
253	Charles Desmarais to Harriet Favel (February 7, 1833 SJM 1820–1835)
272	William Spence to Loraine Truche (March 6, 1834 SJM 1820–1835)
287	James Swain to Josette Couteau (January 7, 1835 SJM 1820–1835)
289	William Sutherland to Suzette Truche (December 26, 1834 SJM 1835–1854)
308	James McNab to Sarah Michael (January 21, 1836 SJM 1835–1854)
331	John Swain to Mary Alerie (January 18, 1837 SJM 1835–1854)
332	Baptiste De Champ to Margaret Johnston (January 19, 1837 SAM 1835–1860)
376	Baptist DeMarais to Sophia Erasmus (December 28, 1837 SJM 1835–1860)
390	Andrew Dennet to Mary Martinois (September 25, 1838 SAM 1835–1860)
434	Peter Warren Dease to Elizabeth Chouinard (August 3, 1840 SAM 1835–1860)

Sources: The index of the Provincial Archives of Manitoba; HBCA E.4/lb; parish registers of marriages.
SJM (St. John's Marriages)
SAM (St. Andrew's Marriages)

many cases difficult to make out. Some marriage entries in the parish registers differ from those in the company registers and some either do not appear in the latter or are illegible. The usage adopted by the Provincial Archives of Manitoba in its index has therefore been followed.

Some of the men whose names appear in this list may have come from Europe. Certainly men from the Orkneys, Scotland, England and elsewhere married women of mixed Indian-French ancestry, such as Hugh Gibson from the Orkneys who married Angélique Chalifoux; Francis Heron and Henry Hallet, Sr., from England, who married Isabella Chalifoux and Catherine Dansee respectively; while Louis Gagnon from France married Jane McKay. John Wasuloski, probably a de Meuron, married Justine Fournier. George Saunderson (Sr.), from Scotland, married Lisset Lagimonère (Lagimodière) both of whose parents came from Quebec. There are other uncertainties in the list, but, imperfect as it is, it suggests that some thirty marriages among a total of 450 were marriages of men and women with French names to men and women with non-French names, probably five percent or more. This surely indicates that the métis and mixed-blood communities cannot have been rigidly isolated from each other. Indeed, the Reverend William Cockran bears witness to a French element in the mixture of origins among his parishioners at St. Andrews: In ninety-two families there were thirty-nine European males and one female. The rest were "Orkney, English, Scotch, French, Welsh, Norwegian, Negro, and Jewish half-breeds."[40]

The Company's register of marriages for 1841 to 1851[41] shows proportionately fewer apparent cross-marriages, only some nine or ten out of a total of more than four hundred, but even this must have meant that there was a certain amount of going and coming between the métis and mixed-blood groups.

Further, marriages recorded in the parish registers were only those formally solemnized by the clergy. Unregistered marriages, *à la façon du pays,* may well have involved a greater proportion of cross-marriages since the clergy were not, in general, sympathetic to members of their own congregation marrying into a rival sect. Fragmentary evidence of marriages which do not appear to be listed in the official registers has come to light. A paper on James McKay mentions two such cross-marriages: John Rowand to Julie Demarais; Angus McKay to Virginia Boulette.[42] John Moar married Matilda Morrisseau at Lac Seul in 1859.[43] Angus Harper married Peggy La Pierre at Oxford House in 1830,[44] and Joseph Everette married Nancy McKay in 1846.[45] The financial records for Red River Settlement mention one Louise McLeod, widow of Baptiste Larocque.[46] Nancy McKenzie, the discarded country wife of Chief Factor J.G. McTavish, married Pierre Leblanc.[47] One of the Carrière sisters of St. Boniface married Roger Marion (son of Narcisse Marion), while the other became Mrs. Henry Donald Macdonald.[48]

That Protestant Anglophones and Catholic Francophones did, indeed, associate with each other is made still more clear by reminiscences recorded in W.J. Healy's *Women of Red River.* Father Louis-François Laflèche used to visit the Sinclair house to play the piano there and to exchange music with the Sinclair girls. Everybody in the Settlement seems to have gone to St. Boniface cathedral to hear Sister Lagrave play the organ built by Dr. Duncan, medical officer of the Sixth Regiment of Foot[49] and "Christmas midnight mass at St. Boniface cathedral was always attended by many parties from across the river."[50]

On the St. Boniface side of the river, the Narcisse Marion home was a centre of hospitality that included English-speaking Protestants. Mrs. Henry Donald Macdonald (née Angélique Carrière) related that it was a "great house for dances. . . . Many of the Kildonan people and the other people across the river used to come to our parties, and we went to theirs. We knew them all."[51] Indeed, it was Narcisse Marion who hospitably received the Reverend John Black, when he arrived to become the first Presbyterian minister in the Colony, and arranged for him to be taken across the river to the home of the leading Presbyterian, Sheriff Alexander Ross.[52]

Not only did colonists from the different parishes go to each others' parties, but also their children mixed with each other at school. Miss Janet Bannerman recalled that there were several children from well-to-do, French-speaking families at her first school, St. John's parochial school. Among them she remembered Joseph and Marguerite Leclair, Emile Bouvette, Ambroise Fisher, Henri Laronde and Baptiste Beauchemin.[53] By the same token, some Anglophone children went to school in St. Boniface, notably James McKay's three children.[54]

Mrs. W.R. Black, granddaughter of Kate and Alexander Sutherland of Kildonan, rounded off her recollections in this way: "I have said so much about the Riels and the Lagimodières because they and the other French-speaking families who were our neighbours are associated with my earliest memories almost as much as the English-speaking families of Red River." Her father, John Sutherland, built a new house across the river after the flood of 1852 swept away the original Sutherland house at Point Douglas. The whole family spoke French as well as English and John Sutherland became a confidant of his French-speaking neighbours and a link between them and the Kildonan settlers.[55]

Business transactions also linked the French- and English-speaking communities: grain from the Carrières' farm at St. Boniface was taken to Robert Tait's mill to be ground;[56] Moise Goulet, a noted plains trader, when illness forced him to retire, sold his whole outfit to A.G.B. Bannatyne;[57] Norbert Welsh, another prominent trader of Irish and Quebec descent, after a disillusioning transaction with "Bobbie" (Robert) Tait, took charge of Bannatyne's cart trains en route to St. Paul and, when he set up in business for himself, dealt with Bannatyne.[58] On January 1, 1846, Peter Garrioch went to see his friend Pascal Berlan[d], about getting some buffalo for him, in company with Peter Pruden and two others.[59]

Frederick Bird was apprenticed to a Catholic blacksmith named Bovette.[60]

Although the evidence is scanty, it would appear that métis and mixed-bloods joined together in the great Red River buffalo hunt. Alexander Ross records that in 1840 the captain of the hunt was one Jean-Baptiste Wilkie, "an English half-breed brought up among the French," while one of Wilkie's captains was a member of the Hallett family.[61] Ross himself travelled with the hunt that year; the late Miss Sybil Inkster once spoke to me of her relatives going to the buffalo hunt; and Henry Erasmus "accompanied the buffalo hunters on trips to the prairies after meat," of which he got a full share, even though he did not actually take part in the hunt itself.[62] The Reverend John Smithurst wrote in June 1840 that most of his parishioners (all Anglicans) had gone either on the buffalo hunt or with the boat brigades.[63] In June 1845, Peter Garrioch was with the buffalo hunt, which certainly numbered métis families among those in the one hundred tents. Of these, Garrioch mentioned Francis Lauze [Lauzon] and Morin.[64] George Sa[u]nderson, Jr., gives a lively description of the way in which Francophone boys were trained to hunt buffalo. He appears to have watched these proceedings. He states explicitly that the "Pochas" [Poitras] family were on one hunt in which his family took part.[65]

Besides the buffalo hunt, the major occupation of the mixed-bloods and métis was freighting, in boat brigades to York Factory and up the Saskatchewan; in the Red River cart trains to the south, to St. Peter's and St. Paul, and west by the Carlton Trail and other traditional overland routes; and in winter with dog trains carrying the winter packet or other urgent freight.

Scattered data about the personnel of boat brigades suggest a mixture of racial origins. In the Hudson's Bay Company's account books the names of some of the tripmen who received advances are listed, especially in the case of advances made at York Factory. The record of advances at York in the summers of 1826 and 1830, for example, gives a mingle-mangle of French and non-French names: In 1826, ten men with French names and four with non-French names received advances. Five others with French names and one uncertain did not have accounts.[66] In 1830, ten French names appear, with four names that originated in the United Kingdom, two mixed names (François Whitford and François Bruce), and one Indian name.[67] It is possible, though not documented, that the crew of each boat was separated on the basis of French or of non-French origin.

Information about the personnel of the cart brigades is also limited, but suggests a similar mixture. The *Daily Minnesotan* for July 22, 1854, stated that "Messrs. Kittson, Rolette, Caviller, Grant and others had arrived at Traverse des Sioux with nearly two hundred carts." The same journal published a letter on September 13, 1858, stating that the Sioux had killed two men on the plains, "Busquer" [Louis Bosquet], in charge of Henry Fisher's carts, and John Beads.[68] *The St. Paul Daily Pioneer* reported on July 12, 1870, that the *St. Cloud Times* had recorded seventy arrivals of Red River carts since July 9. They belonged to Gingras and Bannatyne.[69] The voyageurs' signatures to a Hudson's Bay Company contract to make the journey from Fort Garry to St. Peter's in 1850 included nine French names and seven Orcadian and other non-French names.[70]

Only one document has been found containing information about mixed personnel travelling in winter with dog trains. The party left from Ile-à-la-Crosse, not from Red River, but it may be significant: Samuel McKenzie, writing on January 15, 1867, noted that "Peter Linklater and Michel Bouvier go with the North Packet to Carlton accompanied by Baptiste Payette and James Wilson."[71] A party was sent from Red River Settlement in 1832 to bring back a herd of sheep from the United States. It too was mixed, having had in it, besides Scots, a French Canadian and an Irishman, two French half-breeds and two young English half-breeds.[72]

Some information is available about the voyageurs and hunters who accompanied the increasingly numerous expeditions engaged in exploration, surveying and other official missions in the nineteenth century, to say nothing of pleasure parties travelling on the western plains in "search of adventure and heavy game."[73] John Rae's Arctic searching expedition of 1848–49, for example, included, besides Canadians and Shetlanders, Baptiste Bruce, the guide already mentioned, Baptiste Emelin [Hamelin], Baptiste Fredrique, Xavier Laplante [Antoine Plante], William Sabiston and Edmund Stevenson, all natives of the country, and so, presumably, of mixed-blood or métis origin. The natives in his team in 1850–51 were John Fidler, John Hébert dit Fabien (not from Red River), Charles Kennedy, Alexandre Laliberté dit Lachouette, Peter Linklater, Baptiste Marcellais, Baptiste Peltier, and Samuel Sinclair, who was probably a native of the country. However, none of the Rupert's Landers with Rae's 1853–54 expedition had a French name. They were Jacob Beads, John Beads Jr., Henry Fidler and James Johnstone.[74]

Palliser's expedition set out from Red River in 1857 with the following men, besides James Beads, the expedition's servant: John Ferguson, first guide; Henry Hallet[t], second guide; Pierre Beauchamp; Samuel Ballenden[dine]; George Daniel; Baptiste Degrace; Perre Falcon; Amable Hogue; Donald Matheson; [Antoine] Morin, John Foulds; George Morrison; Charles Racette; John Ross; John Simpson; Thomas Sinclair; Robert Sutherland; George Taylor; Joseph Vermette; and Pascal.[75] At least some of Palliser's "Red River contingent" in 1858 were of French origin: among the Red River men who stayed with him at Fort Edmonton during the winter of 1858–59 were Pierre Beauchamp and Baptiste La Graisse, while Chief Factor W.J. Christie, who, on behalf of Palliser, paid off those who returned to Red River, called out "*assez*" to each man when he had taken all the trade goods to which his wage entitled him. Others, such as Todd and Ballenden, were of at least partly non-French origin.[76] In the fall of 1858, James Beads returned from Edmonton to Red River, on hearing that his brother had been killed by the Sioux. When Beads came back in the spring of 1859 he brought with him the redoubtable hunter Jean-Baptiste Vital[le].[77]

When Henry Youle Hind set off in 1858 for the western plains, his party included "six Cree half-breeds, a native of Red River of Scotch descent [John Ferguson?], one Blackfoot half-breed, one Ojibway half-breed, and one French Canadian." It is noticeable that, with one exception, he did not consider the European derivation of the "half-breeds" of sufficient importance to be mentioned.[78]

The Boundary Survey of 1872–76 recruited a troop of native scouts styled "the 49th Rangers," under the command of William Hallett. The deputy commander's name was McDonald, and the names of the three sub-leaders were Gosselin, Lafournais and Gaddy. The rank and file, too, included men of both French and Scottish or other descent.[79]

Records of sportsmen travelling in the West for pleasure do not always give the names of their voyageurs and hunters, but Hudson's Bay Company accounts show that the Comte de la Guiche had in his employment John Ferguson, Alexis Goulait, and Goulait's son,[80] in June 1851, when he left Red River on a trip to the Rocky Mountains. Lord Dunmore's party set out on August 22, 1862, with Jim McKay (spelled Mackay by Dunmore) as hunter-in-chief, Baptiste Valet as hunter, James Whitford, Pierre(?) and (?) De Charme as buffalo hunters and drivers, and Joe Macdonald as hunter, cook and driver.[81]

None of this suggests any sharp segregation between Red River mixed-bloods and métis. Indeed, Palliser, describing the expedition's great buffalo hunt in 1858 in the neighbourhood of modern Irricana, Alberta, commented: "The run was magnificent, and there was considerable emula-

tion between my Saskatchewan and my Red River men,"[82] a comment
that indicates some solidarity of the group from Red River, regardless of
descent, vis-à-vis the group from Lac Ste. Anne; elsewhere, however,
Palliser commented on what seemed to him a remarkable difference in energy and progressiveness between the Canadian and French and the
Scottish "half-breeds."[83]

Other mixed ventures include the party of emigrants from Red River to
the Columbia River which in 1841 made the extraordinary journey across
the plains and through the mountains under James Sinclair's leadership.
Its members numbered among them an almost equal balance of men with
names suggesting French and non-French origin, all of them speaking either French or English. Table 2 shows the list of men in the original
agreement between the emigrants and the Company. Cash advances were
made to all but three of these men (whose names are marked with an aster-
isk) and to two not listed in the agreement: David Flett and Pierre
Larocque Jr.[84] John Flett is not in either list, but other evidence makes
it clear that he was with the party.[85]

In contrast, none (or, at most, one)[86] of the second group of Red
River emigrants to the Columbia, who, again under James Sinclair's lead-
ership, went in 1854 to Walla Walla (Washington), seems to have had a
French name, at least according to the list given by John V. Campbell,
Sinclair's brother-in-law, who, as a lad, was a member of the party.[87]

Of greater importance than evidence of mixed parties freighting, travelling and emigrating from Red River Settlement is the story of the joint
mixed-blood–métis struggle against the claim of the Hudson's Bay
Company to the exclusive right to trade in furs in Rupert's Land and, until
the License to Trade lapsed in 1859, in the Indian territories beyond. W.L.
Morton tells this story admirably in his introduction to *Eden Colvile's
Letters, 1849–52.*[88] With a brief lull, while the Sixth Regiment of Foot
were stationed at Red River from 1846 to 1848, the mixed-blood–métis
population of Red River Settlement agitated throughout the 1840s for recognition of their "rights," as natives of the country, to take part in the fur
trade and for redress of other grievances. The Sayer trial in 1849 established that, in practice, the joyful shout of the métis, "Le commerce est
libre," was justified, but the natives of Rupert's Land still wanted a voice in
the government of the colony.

Evidence in Peter Garrioch's diary of métis–mixed-blood friendship
and fraternization has already been cited. Garrioch also makes it clear that
the men who banded together in 1845 to resist the imposition by the
Council of Assiniboia of an import duty on goods brought in from

TABLE 2
Emigrants from Red River Settlement to the Columbia River, in the James Sinclair Party, 1841.

François Jacques	James Birston
Julien Bernier	John Cunningham
Baptiste Oreille or Rhelle	Alexander Birston
Pierre Larocque	Archibald Spence
Louis Larocque	François Gagnon
Pierre St. Germain	Joseph Klyne
John Spence	James Flett
Henry Buxton	John Tate
Gonzaque Zastre	Horatio Nelson Calder
William Flett	Toussaint Joyal
Charles McKay	[David Flett]

Sources: HBCA B.235/d/82, p. 56; A.12/7, fo.392d (agreement between emigrants to the Columbia River and Hudson's Bay Company, dated 31 May 1841); William J. Betts, "From Red River to the Columbia," *The Beaver* (Spring 1971), 50–55.

American territory were of diverse origins: Canadian, Irish, métis and mixed-blood. Besides Peter Garrioch, they were Peter Hayden, Alexis Goulet, St. Germain (which Garrioch spelled Chagerma), Dominique Ducharme, Henry Cook and Charles Laroque.[89]

On August 29, 1845, a larger group of mixed-blood and métis traders submitted a list of questions to Governor and Chief Factor Alexander Christie concerning their rights (see table 3).[90] In another version of this list of signatures, given by Alexander Begg in his *History of the North-West,* four of these names are omitted: Pierre Laverdure, Edward Harmon [or Harman], James Monkman, and Edward Desjarlais Sr.[91] Two others were added: Adal Trottier and Charles Hole [possibly Houle]. Again, this is a not uneven mixture of métis and mixed-bloods.

In 1846, two parallel petitions, one in French and one in English, were drafted at a meeting held on February 26 in Andrew McDermot's house. The petitions contained demands for free trade and representative government. James Sinclair carried both of them to England where Alexander K. Isbister submitted them to the Imperial Government.[92] As W.L. Morton noted: "The settlement was an Anglo-French colony, a European-Indian community, and the métis, excluded from public office like the English half-breeds, were only demanding that the institutions of the Colony should reflect its ethnic composition. In so doing they spoke for the English half-breeds as well as for themselves, as they were to do again in 1869."[93] As well, "English half-breeds" such as James Sinclair

TABLE 3
Signatories to the letter to Governor C.F. Alexander Christie, dated 29 August 1845.

James Sinclair	Peter Garrioch
Baptiste Laroque	Jack Spence
Thomas Logan	Alexis Goulait [Goulet]
Pierre Laverdure	Antoine Morin
Joseph Monkman	William McMillan
Baptiste Wilkie	Louis Letendre [dit Batoche]
Baptiste Farman (Famian)	Robert Montour
Edward Harman	Jack Anderson
John Dease	James Monkman
Henry Cook	Antoine Desjarlais, Snr.
William Bird	Thomas McDermot
John Vincent	

Sources: HBCA D.5/15, fos.139a–139b; PAM MG2 135, "Red River Correspondence"; Alexander Begg, *History of the North-West*, 3 vols. (Toronto: Hunter, Rose and Co., 1894–95)1:261–62. Begg omits Montour but adds Adel Trottier and Charles Hole.

spoke for their métis associates as, for instance, in the Sayer trial at which Sinclair represented the four métis defendants and their armed colleagues who had surrounded the court house.[94]

The younger generation of mixed-bloods and métis was frustrated and restless. The demand for representation on the council and for a free trade in furs was a demand for an outlet for ambition, energy and enterprise.[95]

The métis organized a "council of the nation" and pressed upon Sir George Simpson still another petition when he arrived in the Settlement in June, 1849. Sent with a covering letter from Sinclair, dated June 14, 1849, this petition was signed by William McMalen [McMillan], Louis Rielle [Riel Sr.] Pascal Berland, Baptiste Fairjeu, Baptiste Laroque, Antoine Morein, Louis Letendre, Solomon Amelin and Urbain Delorme.[96] A letter presented to Simpson when he was again in Red River Settlement in the summer of 1850, was signed by William McMillan, Solomon Amelin, Louis Riel and eighteen others. They demanded that Recorder Thom should go and that they should have representation on the Council "chosen from our nation by ourselves."[97]

Yet another petition in 1851 reached the Company via the Aborigines' Protection Society and the Colonial Office asking "that Red River be granted British liberty, a Governor appointed by the Crown, a judge similarly appointed and able to speak English and French, power in the Governor to appoint Councillors in an emergency, the dismissal of

Councillors who had forfeited public confidence or been subservient to the Company, and the removal of Thom to some other British colony." The 540 signatures were attested by five leading métis.[98]

These data, fragmentary and incomplete as they are, cannot be conclusive, but, as far as they go, they do suggest an intermingling of mixed-bloods and métis, fellow feeling and cooperation between the two groups, not separation or hostility. This impression is strengthened by yet another petition sent in 1857 to the Legislature of Canada "from Donald McBeath and others[,] inhabitants and Natives of the Settlement situated on the Red River, in the Assiniboine Country, . . ."[99]

This petition was promulgated by a mixed-blood, "Captain" William Kennedy of Arctic fame, who visited Red River in 1857 as an emissary of Canadian commercial interests. It bore the signatures of 119 men with French names or known to be French-speaking, as well as fourteen more who may have been of French origin, and two with mixed names, out of a total of 511, including a number with Indian or probably Indian names. Though not all the apparently French signatures were those of métis, that of Narcisse Marion, for example, the Francophone roster is considerable. This is surprising since, according to Alvin C. Gluek Jr., the Catholic clergy had discouraged their parishioners from signing the petition.[100]

As late as 1869–70, a contemporary observer, Walter Traill, commented: "The natives [of Red River Settlement], both English and French, though not resenting the newcomers from the newly formed Dominion, wonder why it is that they . . . should be slighted by Canadians who are coming to rule them." And again: "If the Canadian Government . . . had recognized the natives, both English and French, both would have given their loyal support."[101]

"Hostility" reported by rival clerics, if it existed, may well have reflected deference to the missionaries' wishes and pressures. However, at least one missionary, that turbulent priest, Father G.-A. Belcourt, cooperated closely with Sinclair and Isbister. Besides Sinclair, Thomas McDermot, John Anderson and Peter Garrioch attended the meeting on February 26, 1846, at which Belcourt presided, speaking in French. It appears that they were the only English-speaking people at this meeting.[102]

An observation made by Eugene Bourgeau, botanical collector with the Palliser expedition, is further evidence of mutual métis–mixed-blood friendship. A compatriot, Ernest St. C. Cosson, the eminent French botanist, said of Bourgeau: "Par l'influence que lui donnait sa double qualité de Français et de catholique, il se concilia l'amitié de ces peuplades [the natives of the West], qui ont gardé le souvenir de notre domination, comprennent notre langue, et sont restées fidèles aux principaux dogmes de notre religion."[103] This was the man whose account of the Sunday services held by Palliser (a staunch Protestant) led Charles Gay to write in *Le Tour du Monde*: "Touchant accord que celui de ces croyances si diverses, ailleurs si fécondes en antagonismes et en rivalités, se confondant, au pied des montagnes rocheuses, dans une même bonne foi et dans une commune simplicité!"[104]

Palliser, too, noted this harmony. The métis Catholics from Lac Ste. Anne asked leave "to attend Divine worship," despite the fact that the prayers read for the Red River men, who "belonged to the Church of England," were from that Church's service. Palliser, therefore, through an interpreter, "conducted the lessons and half the prayers in Cree." He mentioned "this circumstance to show the respectful tendency and absence of bigotry of these men, in their appreciation of Divine service."[105]

If, then, even religious differences did not go very deep, were there important cleavages in Red River society? The answer must surely be yes. There were two fundamental divisions,[106] but these were not divisions between métis and mixed-blood.

The first was a division between the well educated and well-to-do gentry, the officers and retired officers of the Hudson's Bay Company and those of their progeny who had achieved respectability, the clergy, and the prosperous merchants, in contrast to the mass of unlettered, unpropertied natives of the country – the "engagés" of the Hudson's Bay Company and of the Nor'Westers before them and their descendants. James Sinclair, for example, was recognized as a "gentleman"; he was a close friend of his British-born son-in-law, Dr. William Cowan, an officer of the Hudson's Bay Company, as well as of his brother, Chief Factor William Sinclair II, and even of Sir George Simpson, despite his battles with the Company.[107] This set him apart from the ordinary tripmen, whom he employed on his freighting ventures. The gap was one occasioned by ambition, affluence, education and social status as against poverty and the inferior status of employees or, at best, of hunters, petty traders or small farmers.

The second was the division between the professional farmer and the hunter and plains trader, between the sedentary population and those to whom the freedom of a wandering life out on the plains was more important than economic security and material comfort. This was the irreconcilable cleavage, so convincingly analyzed in George F.G. Stanley's classic, *The Birth of Western Canada*,[108] and described in Goulet's, Welsh's and Sanderson's reminiscences.

As Jennifer Brown concludes in *Strangers in Blood,* the "half-breed" descendants of the men of both the North West and Hudson's Bay Companies "combined to define and defend common interests and finally to take military action in the Rebellions of 1869 and 1885."[109] Western Canada, as we know it today, was indeed born of conflict, conflict not between métis and mixed-blood, but between a wandering, free life and settlement; a conflict between agriculturalists, especially the flood of newcomers in search of landed property and wealth, and the old way of life that both métis and mixed-bloods had had in common with their Indian cousins, a way of life based on adjustment to the natural environment and the shared use of the free gifts of nature. That way of life was doomed with the coming of surveyors, fences, police, organized government, settlers and private rights of property in real estate and natural resources.[110] With it went the prosperity and independence of all but a small elite of métis and mixed-bloods alike.

NOTES

1 Here the term *mixed-blood* is used (in spite of its biological ineptitude) instead of Pannekoek's term *country-born* to denote Anglophone Rupert's Landers of hybrid Indian and white ancestry. After all, the children of Jean-Baptiste and Julie Lagimodière and those of Kate and Alexander Sutherland and other Selkirk settlers were country-born even though they had no Indian ancestry. A possible alternative might be to use *métis* with a qualifying adjective as Alexander Morris did: "The *Metis* who were present at the [North West] Angle [of the Lake of the Woods] and who, with one accord, whether of French or English origin, . . ." (*The Treaties of Canada with the Indians of Manitoba and the North-West Territories* [Toronto: Belfords, Clarke and Co., 1880], 51). Similarly, Isaac Cowie wrote of one man being an Irish and another a French Métis in his book, *The Company of Adventurers: A Narrative of Seven Years in the Service of the Hudson's Bay Company* (Toronto: William Briggs, 1913), p. 191, and George F.G. Stanley of "English Métis," in "Indian Raid at Lac la Biche," *Alberta History* 24 (Summer 1976)3:25. It seems simpler, however, to use *mixed-blood* for the Anglophones of mixed ancestry as a reasonably close equivalent of *métis* for the Francophones of mixed descent.
2 Frits Pannekoek, "The Rev. Griffiths Owen Corbett and the Red River Civil War of 1869–70," *Canadian Historical Review* 57 (June 1976)2:134.
3 Guillaume Charette, *Vanishing Spaces: Memoirs of Louis Goulet* (Winnipeg: Editions Bois-Brulés, 1980; translated by Ray Ellenwood, from the original French edition, *L'Espace de Louis Goulet,* 1976), 59.
4 W.J. Healy, *Women of Red River* (Winnipeg: Russell, Lang and Co. Ltd., 1923), 88.
5 Personal conversation, Winnipeg, May 22, 1973.
6 George William Sanderson, " 'Through Memories [sic] Windows' as Told to Mary Sophia Desmarais, by her Uncle, George William Sanderson (1846–1936)," 2, Provincial Archives of Manitoba (hereinafter cited as PAM) MGI/A107.

7 John Palliser wrote from Edmonton of "the black looks of the hostile divines, I understand that sometimes hostilities have proceeded further than mere looks. . . ." (HBCA, D.5/49, 1859 (2), fos. 245–46. I am grateful to the Hudson's Bay Company for kind permission to use material in its archives. The Rev. John Smithurst wrote in his journal: "We see the eagle of Rome watching to seize as its prey these precious souls. . . ." (PAC, MG19, E6, vol. 2, June 12, 1841). Father A.G. Morice, in his *Histoire de l'Eglise catholique dans l'Ouest canadien* (St. Boniface and Montreal: Granger Frères, 1915), vol. 1, p. 216, commented on the arrival of the Methodist missionaries that they "allaient se mesurer plutôt avec les enseignements de la Robe Noire et les pratiques religieuses que ses néophytes tenaient d'elles, qu'avec les ténebres épaisses et l'immoralité révoltante dans lesquelles croupissaient encore plusieurs des nations barbares du Canada central" (i.e., western Canada). There are many similar passages throughout the work.

8 Since the European origins of mixed-bloods included Highland and Lowland Scottish, Orcadian, Shetland, Swiss, Danish and other strains, as well as French, the commonly used description, *English,* scarcely seems appropriate.

9 W.L. Morton, ed., *Alexander Begg's Red River Journal and Other Papers Relative to the Red River Resistance of 1869-1870* (Toronto: Champlain Society, 1956), 12.

10 Alexander Ross, *The Red River Settlement* (London: Smith, Elder and Co., 1856; reprinted, Edmonton: Hurtig, 1972), 80–81. References are to the Hurtig reprint.

11 Ibid., 79.

12 Cited in Rhoda R. Gilman, Carolyn Gilman and Deborah M. Stultz, *The Red River Trails: Oxcart Routes Between St. Paul and the Selkirk Settlement, 1820-1870* (St. Paul: Minnesota Historical Society, 1979), 14. This "polyglot jabber" was, no doubt, Bungay, which the late Mrs. J.L. Doupe told me was widely used when she was a child in Winnipeg.

13 J.A. Gilfillan, "A Trip Through the Red River Valley in 1864," *North Dakota Historical Quarterly* 1 (October 1926 to July 1927)4:37–40.

14 J.G. Kohl, *Kitchi-Gami: Wanderings Round Lake Superior,* trans. Lascelles Wraxall (London: Chapman and Hall, 1860, reprinted, Minneapolis: Ross and Haines, 1956), 260. I am indebted to Jacqueline Peterson for this reference.

15 Charette, *Vanishing Spaces,* 119.

16 Ibid., 116.

17 Television broadcast, Ontario T.V., 1981, "The Last Buffalo Hunter," featuring Norbert Welsh.

18 Barbara Benoit, "The Mission at Ile-à-la-Crosse," *The Beaver* (Winter 1980):46.

19 Inkster papers, typescript account of the career of "The Honourable James McKay – Deer Lodge," 1.and 5, PAM. See also: Allan Turner, "James McKay," *Dictionary of Canadian Biography,* ed. Francess G. Halpenny and Jean Hamlin, 11 vols. (Toronto: University of Toronto Press, 1972)10:473–75; N. Jaye Goossen, "A Wearer of Moccasins: The Honourable James McKay of Deer Lodge," annotated typescript published in substance in *The Beaver* (Autumn 1978):44–53; and Mary McCarthy Ferguson, *The Honourable James McKay of Deer Lodge* (Winnipeg: published by the author, 1972).

20 Cowie, *Company of Adventurers,* 191–92.

21 Ibid., 192.

22 A.C. Garrioch, *The Correction Line* (Winnipeg: Stovel Co. Ltd., 1933), 200–01. I am indebted to Mr. Brian Gallagher for this reference.

23 Irene M. Spry, "A Note on Peter Erasmus's Family Background" and "Family Tree," in Peter Erasmus, *Buffalo Days and Nights* (Calgary: Glenbow-Alberta Institute, 1976), 303–05, 324–28 and end papers.

24 E.E. Rich, ed., *John Rae's Correspondence with the Hudson's Bay Company on Arctic Exploration, 1844–1855* (London: Hudson's Bay Record Society, 1953), 353–54.

25 Cowie, *Company of Adventurers*, 220.

26 Ibid., 348. It is possible that Cowie was mistaken; Sir George Simpson also had a son called John.

27 Inkster Papers, "James McKay," 1, PAM.

28 Mary Weekes, *The Last Buffalo Hunter, As Told by Norbert Welsh* (New York: Thomas Nelson and Sons, 1939; Toronto: Macmillan of Canada, 1945), 23.

29 Sanderson, "Memories," title and p. 8, and list of marriages, table 1, p. 101, PAM, MGI/A107.

30 Lionel Dorge, "The Métis and Canadian Councillors of Assiniboia," *The Beaver* (Summer, Autumn and Winter 1974), especially Part 3, 56–57. Douglas N. Sprague, in his research on Sir John A. Macdonald and the métis, has analyzed cross-marriages on the basis of the 1870 census, from which he has been able to trace all marriages back for three generations.

31 Goossen, "James McKay," 47.

32 Charles A. Throssell wrote the following note on January 20, 1966: "John Tate – Who's [sic] only daughter, Jeanette married Alex Burston about 1830. . . . They were both of French Canadian descent." This note was sent by Alex Burston's daughter, Mrs. Mary Burston Throssell, to Mr. William J. Betts of Bremerton, Washington. He very kindly sent me a copy on November 14, 1971. An entry in St. John's parish register states that Alex Burston [Birston] married Janet Tate on June 28, 1832, No. 237, St. John's Marriage Register, 1820–1835.

33 W.L. Morton, Introduction in E.E. Rich, ed., *London Correspondence Inward from Eden Colvile 1849–1852* (London: HBRS, 1956), xlv, lxxx, 246.

34 HBCA, E.4/1b, also recorded in PAM, Parish records. Some cross-marriages are recorded in the Indian church register of marriages, such as that of Sally Erasmus to Antoine Kennedy, December 23, 1847 (no. 57d), HBCA E.4/2.

35 Provincial Archives of British Columbia (hereinafter cited as PABC), Add Mss 345, File 135.

36 Les Archives de la Société historique de St. Boniface has the record of the marriage of "Guillaume Serre," alias William Sayer. I am indebted to Lionel Dorge for a copy of this record.

37 Dorge, "Métis and Canadian Councillors," Part 3, 57.

38 PABC, Wren Family papers; Spry, "Note on Family Background" in Erasmus, *Buffalo Days and Nights*.

39 HBCA, E.4/1b and 2 and PAM microfilm of parish registers. There are some discrepancies between these two sets of records. Marriages of Barbara Gibson and Isabella Spence to James Louis have been omitted because James Louis was the son of a mulatto from New England, not, as might be supposed, of French extraction. A record of the marriage of Margaret Louis [or Lewis] is omitted for the same reason, (HBCA E.4/1b, fo. 221, and A.38/8, fo. 36). I am indebted to the keeper of the Hudson's Bay Company Archives for this information. Nancy Budd's marriage to Michel Reine is also omitted because he was from Strasbourg.

40 John E. Foster, "Missionaries, Mixed-bloods and the Fur Trade: Four Letters of the Rev. William Cockran, Red River Settlement, 1830–1833," *Western Canadian Journal of Anthropology* 3 (1972)1:110 and 112.

41 HBCA, E.4/2.

42 Goossen, "James McKay," 48.

43 The marriage contract is reproduced in Sylvia Van Kirk, *"Many Tender Ties": Women in Fur-Trade Society, 1670–1870* (Winnipeg: Watson and Dwyer Publishing Ltd., 1980), 118.

44 Ibid., 117–19.
45 HBCA, B239/Z/39, fo. 22.
46 HBCA, B.235/c/1, fo. 248d.
47 Van Kirk, *"Many Tender Ties,"* 188.
48 Healy, *Women of Red River,* 119.
49 Ibid., 34–35.
50 Ibid., 208.
51 Ibid., 119.
52 Ibid., 68.
53 Ibid., 87.
54 Ferguson, *James McKay,* 60.
55 Healy, *Women of Red River,* 59 and 61.
56 Ibid., 119.
57 Charette, *Vanishing Spaces,* 70.
58 Weekes, *Last Buffalo Hunter,* 35–45, 57, 60–72, and 201–02.
59 Garrioch Journal, January 1, 1846, PAM.
60 Sanderson, "Memories," 12, PAM, MGI/A107.
61 Ross, *Red River Settlement,* 248 and 271.
62 Erasmus, *Buffalo Days and Nights,* 6.
63 PAC, MG19 E6, vol. II, journal entry for June 21, 1840.
64 Garrioch Journal, June 10 and 16, October 1 and 2, 1845, PAM.
65 Sanderson, "Memories," 3, PAM, MG9/A107.
66 HBCA, B.235/d/26, fo. 2d, 1826.

John Ashburn	Louis Lapierre dit Brilliant
J. Bts [sic] Boisvert (no account)	Francois Laframboise (no account)
Alexis Bonamis dit Lesperence	William Malcolm
Rennes Cardinal (no account)	Simon Martin (no account)
Antoine Deschamps (no account)	Pierre Papin
Antoine Dagenais	Medard Poitras
Leon Dupuis	David Scott
Toussaint Joyal	Jacques St. Denis
Louis La Rive	David Sandison
Jacques Le'Tang (no account)	Louis Thyfault [sic]

67 HBCA B.235/d/44, 1830.

Francois Savoyard	Henry House [Howse?]
Carriole Lagrasse	Joseph Savoyard
Pierre Savoyard	Richd Favel
James Birston	Bte Boyer
Antoine Lambert	George Kipling
Alex Carrier	Charles Larocque
Francois Whitford	Amable Lafort
Francois Bruce	Joseph Delorme
Matouche	

Cowie wrote that Baptiste Kennedy was a guide in a brigade with steersmen from Red River Settlement named Cameron, Spence, Cunningham and William Prince, an Indian (*Company of Adventurers,* 117).
68 Minnesota Historical Society, St. Paul.
69 St. Paul Public Library, Minnesota.
70 PABC, Add Mss 345, vol. 2, file 70.

71 HBCA, B.27/c/1, fo. 20.

72 Robert Campbell, "A Journey to Kentucky for Sheep: From the Journal of Robert Campbell, 1832–1833," *North Dakota Historical Quarterly* 1 (October 1926 to July 1927)1:36.

73 A phrase used by Palliser of the two friends who joined him on his expedition, Captain Arthur Brisco and William Roland Mitchell (Irene M. Spry, ed., *The Papers of the Palliser Expedition* [Toronto: Champlain Society, 1968], 338–39).

74 Rich, ed., *John Rae's Correspondence*, 350–78.

75 Spry, ed., *Palliser Papers*, 37, n. 1.

76 Ibid., 340–41.

77 Ibid., 403.

78 *North-West Territory. Report on the Assiniboine and Saskatchewan Exploring Expedition* (Toronto: John Lovell, 1859), 39.

79 John E. Parsons, *West on the 49th Parallel* (New York: William Morrow and Co., 1963), 53.

80 HBCA, B.235/a/15, Upper Fort Garry Journal, June 16, 1851.

81 "Log of The Wanderers on the Prairies in Search of Buffalo Bear Deer &c in 1862," ms. in the possession of Lord Dunmore.

82 Spry, ed., *Palliser Papers*, 258.

83 Ibid., 169.

84 HBCA A.12/7, fo. 392d, Agreement between emigrants to the Columbia River and Hudson's Bay Company, dated May 31, 1841, and HBCA B.235/d/82, fo. 30, 56, cash paid to emigrants. Whether there were two Pierre Larocques is not clear. The accounts list Pierre Larocque Jr., the agreement simply Pierre Larocque.

85 William J. Betts, "From Red River to the Columbia," *The Beaver* (Spring 1971):50–55, reproduces John Flett's own account of the journey.

86 Toussaint Joyal may have been with the second group of emigrants.

87 John V. Campbell, "The Sinclair Party – An Emigration Overland Along the Old Hudson's Bay Company Route from Manitoba to the Spokane Country in 1854," *Washington Historical Quarterly* 8 (July 1916):187–201.

88 See also Irene M. Spry, "Free Men and Free Trade," unpublished paper submitted to the Canadian Historical Association meeting held in Saskatoon in 1979, and "The 'Private Adventurers' of Rupert's Land," in John E. Foster, ed., *The Developing West: Essays on Canadian History in Honor of Lewis H. Thomas* (Edmonton: University of Alberta Press, 1983), 49–70.

89 Garrioch Journal, March 1 and 9, 1845, PAM. See also E.H. Oliver, *The Canadian North-West, Its Early Development and Legislative Records*, vol. 1 (Ottawa: Government Printing Bureau, 1914), 315, which lists Charles Laurance, Dominique Ducharme, Peter Garriock, Henry Cook, Peter Hayden and Alexis Goulait as petitioners to the Council. It does not include St. Germain.

90 Christie to Simpson, September 5, 1845, enclosing the letter from Sinclair et al, dated August 29, 1845, HBCA, D.5/15, fos. 139a 139b. Sinclair's letter is reproduced in Lewis G. Thomas, ed., *The Prairie West to 1905* (Toronto: University Oxford Press, 1975), 56–57, with Christie's reply, 58–59. No source is given and the spelling of some of the names is different from that in the copy enclosed by Christie. Another copy of the letter is in PAM, RRS/RRC, 1845–47.

91 Alexander Begg, *History of the North-West*, 3 vols. (Toronto: Hunter, Rose, 1894–95), 261–62.

92 Correspondence Relating to the Red River Settlement and The Hudson's Bay Company, *British Parliamentary Papers*, vol. 18, 1849, Colonies, Canada (Shannon: Irish Universities Press, 1969).

93 Morton, Introduction in Rich, ed., *Eden Colvile's Letters,* lxxxix.

94 A good account of the trial and of the role of Sinclair and Garrioch is given in Morton, Introduction in Rich, ed., *Eden Colvile's Letters,* lxxxii–lxxxvi, and another in Roy St. George Stubbs, *Four Recorders of Rupert's Land* (Winnipeg: Peguis Publishers, 1967), 26–29.

95 Morton, Introduction in Rich, ed., *Eden Colvile's Letters,* lxxxix.

96 Ibid., citing HBCA D.5/25, June 2, 1849, enclosed in Sinclair to Simpson, June 14, 1849.

97 Ibid., p.c, citing HBCA D.5/28, June 1, 1850; HBCA A.13/4, fos. 519–20; and A.12/5, Simpson, July 5, 1850.

98 Ibid., pp. cvii–cviii, citing HBCA A.13/5, enclosure in a letter from F. Peel, C.O., to Pelly, dated December 30, 1851. Attempts to find the signatures in HBCA, the Public Record Office, London, England, and the Archives of the Aborigines' Protection Society, Rhodes House, Oxford, England, have failed, so it has not been possible to discover the origins of the signatories.

99 The original petition with all the signatures is in PAC, RG 14-C-I, vol. 64, petition no. 1176, received and filed May 22, 1857. Oddly, the signature of Roderick Kennedy is not among the 511 signatures attached to the petition, though he presented it to the Legislature, and his name is the only one given in the Select Committee version. It was printed in *The Toronto Globe* for June 12, 1857, and as Appendix 15 of the *Report of the Select Committee of the House of Commons on the Hudson's Bay Company, 1857.*

100 Alvin C. Gluek, Jr., *Minnesota and the Manifest Destiny of The Canadian Northwest* (Toronto: University of Toronto Press, 1965) 123–25.

101 Mae Atwood, ed., *In Rupert's Land: Memoirs of Walter Traill* (Toronto: McClelland and Stewart, 1970), 204 and 208. Sanderson wrote of the Rising when he was captured by Riel's men, when he was with the Portage party: "I was not afraid of the French half-breeds . . . I knew Riel and many of his adherents, in fact I was related to some of his leaders" (PAM, MG9/A107, Part 2, 1).

102 Garrioch Journal, February 26, 1846, PAM.

103 *Bulletin de la Société botanique de France,* vol. 13, 1866, liv cited in Spry, ed., *Palliser Papers,* xxviii, n. 5. The number of the volume is given incorrectly in this citation.

104 "Le Capitaine Palliser et l'Exploration des Montagnes Rocheuses, 1857–1859," *Le Tour du Monde. Nouveau Journal des Voyages* (Paris: 1861), 287, cited in Spry, ed., *Palliser Papers,* xxviii.

105 Spry, ed., *Palliser Papers,* 238, n. 5.

106 A third cleavage might be identified, namely, the generation gap between the children and grandchildren of the well-established Principal Settlers of the colony and their aging precursors. See Morton, Introduction in Rich, ed., *Eden Colvile's Letters,* lxxxix.

107 This impression is derived from a wide range of material by and concerning both James Sinclair and William Sinclair II, including Journal of Dr. William Cowan, PAC, MG19 E8.

108 George F.G. Stanley, *The Birth of Western Canada* (Toronto: University of Toronto Press, 1960; 1963; reprinted from the original edition, Longmans, Green and Co. Ltd., 1936).

109 Jennifer S.H. Brown, *Strangers in Blood: Fur Trade Company Families in Indian Country* (Vancouver and London: University of British Columbia Press, 1980), 173.

110 Irene M. Spry, "The Tragedy of the Loss of the Commons in Western Canada" in *As Long as the Sun Shines and Water Flows: A Reader in Canadian Native Studies,* ed. Ian A.L. Getty and Antoine S. Lussier (Vancouver: University of British Columbia Press, 1983), 203–28.

Waiting for a day that never comes:
The dispossessed métis of Montana

Verne Dusenberry

Too bad the Indians are not the lineal and direct descendants of Methuselah and inherit his longevity, coupled with the patience of Job, that they might live to see some of the just obligations, established by precedent and treaty stipulation, fulfilled by the government. John W. Cramsie, U.S. Indian Agent for the Turtle Mountain Indians, in 1886.

In the tiny gold-mining town of Zortman, Montana, lives a quiet, scholarly, graying man. He is Joseph Dussome, president of the Landless Indians of Montana. For nearly half a century, he has been collecting data and assembling material pertinent to the bands of "wandering Cree and Chippewa" that have too often, during the past seventy years, plagued the conscience of Montanans and North Dakotans. Now, in his old age, Dussome sits in his small, neatly kept home and pores over his collection of evidence. He has documents, he has a vast file of letters, he has his memories. He knows better than any other person – for he is one of them – who these people are who now reside in the State of Montana and who number, conservatively, at least four thousand displaced, disenchanted individuals. While these people insist upon being called Chippewa, perhaps to escape the scorn with which reservation Indians refer to them as "Cree," or as "bon jours," or "bon hommes from Lake La Biche," Dussome can point out to an interested visitor that these people are part of the métis, descendants of the Red River Hunters who lived not only in Canada, but also across the border in what is now Michigan, Wisconsin, Minnesota, North Dakota, and Montana.

* * *

To understand the Indians in Montana who are unaffiliated with any established reservations, it is necessary to go back to the early French colonization of North America. For it is from these early explorers that one finds the progenitors of the Landless Indians. Even the surnames are the same, since the French encouraged their men to marry Indian women. These mixed-blood descendants, at first concentrated along the Great Lakes, scattered throughout the Northwestern states and Canada, but maintained their greatest numbers along the Red River of the North which has its source in North Dakota and Minnesota, forming the boundary between much of those states, but which flows north into Lake Winnipeg and ultimately into Hudson's Bay. And so it is that these people living in Montana today, whose ancestry was predominantly a non-native [non-Montana] tribe – Chippewa, trace their ancestry back to the Red River settlements, especially to those on the American side of the now established forty-ninth parallel that forms the international boundary between Canada and the United States.

These people, now known generally as "The Landless Indians," have had various names. . . . The frontier English and the Americans referred to them chiefly as "half-breeds," while the French occasionally designated them *"bois-brûlé"* (burnt wood) from the translation of the Chippewa appelation for them, *Wisahkotewan Niniwak,* meaning "men partly burned." This name had been given them by the Chippewa because of the color of their skin: dark, but not quite as dark as that of the pure Indian. More frequently, however, the early French referred to them as the métis, a French adjective meaning "cross-bred."

Perhaps the word *métis* is the best for them, for their degree of Indian blood was seldom fixed at exactly one-half. The child of an Indian mother and a French father would be a "half-blood," but when that offspring reached maturity, he might marry either a fullblood Indian or a fullblood Caucasian. Thus, as the years went by, and intermarrying continued, the individual could possibly become almost pure Indian or pure white. So, too, did the blood become mixed between Indians of various tribes. For while in Canada it was the Cree with whom the Frenchman usually married, in the United States it was the Chippewa. Thus there emerged, along the Red River particularly, a group of people who were neither Indian nor white; neither Chippewa nor Cree nor French, but a mixture of all three. They represented, as Joseph Kinsey Howard pointed out,[1] the emergence of a new race indigenous to this continent.

And in this emergence as a new people, they adapted various traits from their French fathers and their Indian mothers. For their livelihood they depended primarily upon the buffalo, as did their Indian forebears. But unlike their Indian grandparents, the hunt stemmed from the Red River settlements, where they returned each fall with pemmican (for which they became famous), to be sold or traded to the Hudson's Bay Company for other food items to be consumed during the winter months. Their transportation was not confined to the horse alone, as was the Indian's, for their distinguishing characteristic was the half-breed cart, a unique invention of their own, made entirely of wood. Its wheels, oftentimes six feet in diameter, had very broad tires, while a small body rested on the axle and shafts. Each cart, drawn by a single pony, could carry from six to eight hundred pounds. Since no grease was used on the axle, the noise made by these carts was almost insufferable. Almost every northern plains historical writer has attempted to describe the horrible screeching that a train of such carts made; but probably none has been presented more graphically than [Howard's description]: "It was as if a thousand finger nails were drawn across a thousand panes of glass." Later, when metal was used in their construction and the wheels could be greased, the métis generally called their vehicles Red River Carts. In either case, however, the cart served a dual purpose. In the long winters, a man would lift the body easily from the wheels, hitch a horse to it, and have a *carriole*, or sleigh.

The housing of the métis was copied directly from their fathers. In the settlements, they lived in one-story houses, often gaudily painted. While on the plains hunting, they used tents. Frequently, however, their hunts took them far to the west, particularly along the Milk River in Montana, and since the distance was too great for them to return to the Red River but occasionally, the métis built frontier cabins, generally of cottonwood, there. They plastered the interior with clay mixed with buffalo hair and, in one end of the building, they always built a fireplace, likewise cemented with clay. Scraped skins of buffalo calves, carefully worked until they were translucent, covered the windows. Floors were left bare. Just as their Indian [ancestors] placed their tipis in a circle, so did the métis build cabins, but in the center of the enclosure they built a large structure with puncheon floors.

These larger buildings were primarily used for dancing, since the métis had inherited the Indian's love of the dance. But, instead of using the dance as a medium of religious expression, the métis danced for sheer pleasure. Nor was the music that of the primitive drum; rather, it was [provided by] the fiddle, sometimes a genuine one but more frequently one made from a hollow piece of wood with cat-gut strings attached. The tunes were generally adaptations of old French folk songs while the dance itself was a lively number which in time became known as the Red River jig.[2]

The dress of the métis, too, was a blend of both Indian and French. The men usually wore an overcoat with a hood made from a blanket and adorned with brass buttons, scallops, fringes, and beads. Known as a *capote*, it combined the warmth of the heavy, all-wool blanket with the tailored quality of a coat. (Its present counterpart, but generally shorter in length, is the parka.) In warmer weather, the men wore fringed jackets made from buckskin but always they had leggings. These again were made from a blanket and were fringed with a seam of beadwork embroidered along the outside.[3] The women wore black dresses, simply made. During their girlhood they had gaily-colored shawls; in adult life the shawl was always black.

From the influence of their French fathers, the métis devoutly followed the teachings of the Roman Catholic Church. So devoted to their Church were they that as a matter of general practice they seldom embarked upon a hunt without having a priest accompany them. When they stayed away from the settlements over a long period of time, they observed Sunday with recitations of the rosary and with prayers. Wandering Jesuit and Oblate missionaries looked for them on the plains, and when finding them conducted open-air services, baptized infants, and blessed marriages. In fact, the Church adopted the policy of recognizing marriages as being legitimate when they were contracted away from the settlements, providing such marriages were later blessed by the priests. One of the best sources [of information] about the métis may be found in parish registers of the early missions in Montana, where, as early as the 1850s, Jesuit priests such as Fathers DeSmet, Croke, Imoda, and Hoecken recorded baptisms, marriages and deaths of the métis.[4]

The métis also developed a language of their own – a composite of Indian tongues, usually Cree and Chippewa, and French. Often a few English words were added. Yet, while most of them understood English, few of them ever used it. The French they spoke was an obsolete form drawn primarily from the patois of Normandy and Picardy.[5] A Frenchman usually could understand them; but the métis, in turn, had difficulty understanding correct French. So it was with Indian languages such as the Cree. Mrs. Dussome, for example, nurtured on the métis tongue, understands only isolated words of Cree as spoken on Rocky Boy's Reservation today.

Their political structure was a blend, again, of Indian and French. Strictly democratic, like the Indian, restraint seemed needed principally when the métis were on the hunt. Then, the entire group was under the control of the soldier society, known among themselves as *Les Soldats*, who executed the orders of the chief. Both the chief and the members of the soldier society were elected by the people themselves. Punishments, such as banishment from the hunt or the payment of fines, resulted if individuals refused to obey orders. Generally, the chief was known as *governor,* a title they borrowed from the French. Jean Baptiste Wilkie was an outstanding governor of the early-day métis.[6]

While the geographical heart of this new race seems to have been along the Red River near present-day Winnipeg, Canada, and Pembina, North Dakota, not all of them, by any manner of means, lived in Canada. True, the majority of the French-Cree descendants lived there. On the American side of the line a goodly number also lived – those who were related a little closer to the Chippewa. Their center was Pembina, established as a trading center in 1780, a factor which gives it the distinction of being the oldest settlement in the Northwest. Pembina exists now, a drab, tiny village at that spot on the map where North Dakota and Minnesota come together at the Canadian border. With Pembina as their headquarters, the southern métis enjoyed, particularly, the hunting resources of the Turtle Mountains, some one hundred miles to the west, in mid-North Dakota, just south of the Canadian line. For their long-range hunting activities, however, they moved constantly westward in their pursuit of the buffalo – along the Missouri River and its tributaries, particularly to the Milk [River], but often west and south again to the valleys of the Teton, the Dearborn, the Sun, and the Marias Rivers. In 1842, Alexander Ross, when he accompanied the hunters, tells of being at the mouth of the Yellowstone. In his record, Ross mentions the names of several métis who were on the party – Wilkie, Valle, Courchene, and Parisien – all names familiar among these people in Montana today.[7]

Individual members penetrated the now-Montana region, too, often serving as guides for the fur traders. One of them, Jacob Berger (often spelled Bergier or Bercier and always pronounced so by the métis today) was in the employ of the American Fur Company in 1830. It was he whom Kenneth McKenzie, then in charge of Fort Union, sent into the Blackfeet country to induce the hostile tribe to trade with the American Fur Company. So successful was Berger (for he induced a number of the Blackfeet to accompany him to Fort Union) that the following year, McKenzie sent one of his most trustworthy men, James Kipp, to the Blackfeet country. Kipp established Fort Piegan at the mouth of the Marias River, near present-day Loma, Montana, to tap the rich resources of the Blackfeet trade. The largest and most influential fort operated on the Upper Missouri by the American Fur Company, Fort Union, was constructed by métis laborers.[8] Louis Revis, sometimes spelled Revais or Rivets, Augustin "Frenchy" Hamell, and Pierre Cadotte are other métis names significant in the opening of the fur trade in what is now Montana.

But it was not only with the fur trade that the métis came into Montana. As the years passed, more and more carts filled with Red River hunters came into the territory and settled in the regions where buffalo were always plentiful. In making this move, the métis followed somewhat the pattern of their Indian heritage, a nomadic tendency to follow the source of their food. Unlike the Indian, they built cabins and stayed, sometimes for several years. Then, group by group, they returned to relatives and friends in the Pembina region, where after a succession of years of residence, they moved again to Montana. Thus it was that during the decades of the 1850s, 1860s and 1870s the creaking carts groaned their way back and forth between the little settlement of Pembina and the unspoiled valleys of Montana.

From old parish registers one learns the names of some métis who were in Montana during this early period. Many of them remained along the Milk River; others went farther west. Along the tributaries of the Marias River, especially near Dupuyer Creek, the records reveal the names Guardipee, Morrin, Lespera, Larion, and Trembles. Somewhat southward, near present Choteau, the Champaignes, Vivies, Ducharmes, Cardinals, and Moriceaus camped, while in the Sullivan Valley near St. Peter's Mission and not far from the Dearborn River, Gabriel Azure, Modeste Gladeau, and members of the LaSerte and Cadotte families lived. When one of Montana's earliest cattlemen, R.S. Ford, established his holdings in 1872 on the upper reaches of the Sun River, near present Augusta, he employed métis families that included such names as Sangrey, Jarvais, Landre, LaRance, Swan, Nomee, and Paul.[9]

Perhaps one of the best known settlements (for it became more permanent than did the others who so frequently left their cabins and returned to the Red River) is the one at present Lewistown in central Montana. A group of métis left the Pembina district in 1870 and headed westward with no particular destination in mind save that of trailing the buffalo. One of the members of the group described facets of that expedition well when she wrote, shortly before her death in Lewistown in 1943, the following account:

While we roamed the prairies of western Minnesota and the Dakotas, we were always in the same company of people of part Indian blood, and travelled in many groups. We left Walhalla, North Dakota, in 1870 shortly after we were married, and set out travelling all over the Dakotas, just camping here and there without thought of settling permanently at any place, just following the buffalo trails. You might think we lived the life of the real Indians, but one thing we had always with us which they did not – religion. Every night we had prayer meeting and just before a buffalo hunt we would see our men on bended knee in prayer. Our men did all the hunting, and we women did all the tanning of the buffalo hides, jerky meat making, pemmican and moccasins. For other supplies, we generally had some trader with us like Francis Janeaux who always had a supply of tea, sugar, tobacco and so on.[10]

Leisurely, the party made its way across North Dakota and followed the Milk River westward into Montana. For nearly seven years the group camped at the big bend of the Milk River, northeast of present Malta. In 1877, they were living at Chinook when [Chief] Joseph surrendered his army at the Bear Paw battlefield south of that city. They assisted some Nez Perce stragglers who had eluded capture and were making their way to Canada. Along the Milk River the men hunted, but game became increasingly scarce until suddenly, in the spring of 1879, it seemed to have disappeared completely. Pierre Berger, leader of the group, called the members around him to discuss the situation. He recalled that previously a Cree Indian had told him of a spot across the Missouri River where small game and wild birds were abundant and where the grass grew high. The land sounded promising, so in May, 1879, twenty-five families left the familiar Milk River area in their squeaking carts and started for this new region. As it was necessary for them to go by way of Fort Benton and then eastward until they came to the Judith Mountains, it took most of the summer for the group to make the journey.

Here at their destination, the Judith Basin looked fertile and inviting. Berger decided that this area would provide an excellent home site. The twenty-five families built cabins and hurriedly made preparations for the approaching winter. True to the description given by the Cree, game was plentiful. So, during the decade of the 1880s (and at a time when the métis who remained behind in their accustomed haunts around the Turtle Mountains were starving) the Spring Creek colony flourished. Soon Janeaux established a trading post for them; in time other establishments sprang up, and a colorful Montana frontier village, destined later to become Lewistown, was born.[11] Early métis occupancy is reflected in the names of two Lewistown streets, Morasse and Oullette Avenues, while Janeaux Street bears the name of their trader.

In 1869, while Montana Territory was being colonized by Red River hunters – at least on a temporary basis – an . . . incident occurred that left its mark upon the Landless Indians of Montana. It has been a prime cause of confusion about them ever since. When the Hudson's Bay Company relinquished its charter to Rupert's Land (which comprised all of the prairie provinces of Canada as well as the North West Territories) and the Dominion of Canada was formed, the métis in the Red River settlements became dissatisfied. Finally, in 1869, they established a provisional government, a land they called Assiniboia – now Manitoba. Louis Riel, that remarkable métis, was their leader. When the British successfully overcame the métis government, Riel and many of his mixed-blood followers went to the United States. Riel himself eventually came to Montana Territory becoming a naturalized citizen of the United States, at Helena, in 1883.[12] A few years later, the métis who in the meantime had moved into Saskatchewan, became dissatisfied with the land policy of the newly formed province and again revolted against the Canadian government. Louis Riel was called upon to return to Canada and lead them. Their military leader, Gabriel Dumont, came from Saskatchewan to St. Peter's Mission, near Cascade, Montana, to convince Riel that he should leave his teaching at the mission and return to Canada to head the revolt. The year was 1885. When the British army crushed this second rebellion, more métis than ever came to the United States, particularly to Montana Territory. Riel, however, was captured by the British, tried for treason, and subsequently hanged in Regina. Gabriel Dumont lived for many years in the Lewistown area, particularly near Grass Range where he brought several boys orphaned by the Rebellion to his childless home, but later he returned to Canada, where he died.

No one knows the exact number of the Canadian métis who came to the United States following the two uprisings. They were of Cree extraction but reared in a cultural pattern much like the Chippewa métis who had lived south of the [Canadian-American] border for centuries. Their loyalties were with the Cree who had joined them in the 1885 rebellion. (Some of these Cree came to Montana, were granted political amnesty, and ultimately were placed on Rocky Boy's Reservation.)[13] These Canadian métis, however, have been the cloud that has obscured the American métis ever since, for it has been easy to dismiss any mixed-blood Indian, especially one with a French name, as being Canadian. Thus the fiction grew, until all métis were lumped together as Canadian Cree. True, the groups have intermarried, but available evidence indicates that the majority of the Landless Indians of Montana today are from the Pembina region – an area which has belonged to the United States since 1818. Hence it is that one must go to Pembina to establish the actual citizenship of the American métis.

The United States Census of 1850 for the Pembina District, Minnesota Territory, gives the names, ages, sexes, occupations, and birthplaces of the 1,116 residents of the area.[14] Reading the list today one recognizes the names of Montana citizenry. Only a random sampling of names indicates their familiarity – Azure, Batock, Beautinau, Belgarde, Bellgard, Berger,

Bushman, Cadotte, Caplette, Cardinal, Collins, Delorme, Demon, Falcon, Filcon, Fion, Gardipin, Gingrais, Gladau, Grandbois, Houl, Jerome, LaPierre, Laframbois, Landrie, Landy, LaRock, LaRocque, Laurente, Laverdue, Lonais, Monisette, Montoir, Montreau, Morin, Morrin, Nedeau, Papin, Pappin, Paranteau, Parente, Parisen, Peltier, Plouffe, St. Pierre, Trotter, Trottier, Valier, Valle, Vandall, Vivian, Wells, Wilkie.

Along with the métis in the Pembina area, there lived a small group of Chippewa – probably the [westernmost] Chippewa group. Many of them had probably intermarried with the Cree; some of them had French grandparents in their ancestry, while most of them had definite relatives among the American métis. Like all the other Chippewa, they had at some time or other occupied regions on both sides of the [Canadian-American] boundary. This small band, however, claimed for their area the land lying north of Devil's Lake in North Dakota, a region that included the Turtle Mountains. Their recognized chief and spokesman had been named Little Shell for three generations: grandfather, father and son. When the time came for the American métis to face the reality that they were Indians, because of the growing demands of the white settlers, it was Little Shell's band to whom they went. By proximity and by marriage they were closely related. Furthermore, since the United States Government consistently recognized the Chippewa as an American tribe and effected treaties with them, the métis felt that since they, too, were now considered Indians, their rights were as significant as were those of their maternal ancestors.

The United States Government designated this small Chippewa group in North Dakota as the Pembina Band. The first treaty with them [was signed] in 1863 when Alexander Ramsey went to Red Lake, in northern Minnesota, to meet a large delegation in that area. Representatives from the Pembina Band and métis were present, also, and while a right of way was ceded through their territory, Ramsey wrote that "the Pembina Band, who subsist by buffalo hunting, also retain for themselves a tract of country claimed by them, embracing some of the favorite pastures of that animal north and northwest of Devil's Lake."[15] They were, moreover, to receive an annuity of $20,000 per annum for twenty years, with one-fourth of it to be applied to agricultural and other beneficial purposes.

During the next twenty years, irritations mounted. The Pembina Band of Chippewa seemed too far away to receive much supervision from the U.S. Indian agents. The métis straggled away into Montana, again, to follow the buffalo or to find other subsistence as best they could. When, in the early 1880s, the buffalo disappeared, the Pembina Band of Chippewa and their mixed-blood relatives began to press strongly their claims upon

Washington. Despite the warning of the then Commissioner of Indian Affairs, H. Price, who maintained that the group had as good a title to their land as had any Indians in North America, the government, on October 4, 1882, officially opened nine million acres – the land claimed by the Pembina Band – to white settlement. At the same time, two townships, in the southeastern part of the Turtle Mountains, were retained and by an executive order became a permanent reservation. Two years later, John W. Cramsie, Indian agent at Devil's Lake Agency, wrote the commissioner and told him that thirty-one Chippewa and twelve hundred mixed bloods were living on the newly-created reservation. Prophetically, he added:

> If poverty and ignorance in abject form is to be found in this world, I know of no better place to seek it than among the half breeds of the Turtle Mountains. With but few exceptions, the half breeds have lived on the buffalo all their lives, and now that their means of subsistence have all disappeared, I cannot tell how they are to make a living without assistance. Fifty thousand dollars worth of stock and farming implements would hardly supply their wants, and without it they will starve or be compelled to steal. Unless generous aid and instruction are furnished these people, the near future will see our jails and penitentiaries filled to overflowing with their prolific rising generation.[16]

Despite their increasingly destitute condition, the Chippewa and the métis remained relatively quiet during these years. A sub-agent, E.W. Brenner, reported in 1883 that they did not wish to do anything to endanger their friendship with the government while their affairs were pending. "A great danger," he wrote, "is from the mixed bloods living away from the reservation. Many are entitled by blood to the same treatment as those residing here, and in many cases have even better claims than many of the residents."[17] The question, however, of who was an Indian, especially a Turtle Mountain Indian – as the group was beginning to be known – was becoming more acute. It's the same question that has plagued the métis continually, and unfortunately still does.

Finally, on August 19, 1890, Congress authorized the president [Benjamin Harrison] to appoint a commission of three persons to negotiate with these Indians for cessation and relinquishment of whatever right or interest they might have to their claim, and for their removal to a settlement upon lands to be selected subject to the approval of Congress. The commission was charged also to determine the number of Chippewa and the number of mixed bloods that were entitled to the consideration of the government.

But the commission did not come to the Turtle Mountains at once. The then current chief, Little Shell, like his half-breed relatives, had been forced to wander westward in order to find subsistence. From Wolf Point, Montana, on August 28, 1891, Little Shell wrote to the Commissioner of Indian Affairs and proposed an agreement whereby he would vacate the Turtle Mountain area in exchange for a reservation on the north side of the Missouri River above the mouth of the Milk [River]. Since the Turtle Mountain lands seemed much more valuable to the white men, Little Shell believed that a cash settlement should be made to his people in addition to their securing a strip of land lying adjacent to the Fort Peck Reservation. Commissioner Morgan disposed of the request with the statement that the land desired was part of the public domain and thus could not be given to Little Shell. Morgan did believe, however, that there was sufficient land on the Fort Peck reservation for the Little Shell group to live if they so desired.[18]

Perhaps in anticipation of the day that the commission would arrive, United States Indian Agent John Waugh appointed a committee of thirty-two men made up of sixteen full-blood Chippewa and sixteen métis to represent the interest of their people in any transaction with the government in the adjustment of their claims. This committee was appointed in August, 1891, over a year and a half after the establishment of the commission by Congress. Coincidentally, Waugh picked the committee during the same month that Little Shell and his party were on the Fort Peck Reservation. To many of the Chippewa group, as well as to a goodly number of the métis, the selection of a committee at this particular time indicated that Agent Waugh wanted a hand-picked group with whom he could work without interference. Furthermore, Waugh selected five members from his committee of thirty-two to go over the list of eligible names, both Chippewa and métis, and to delete those families or individuals who were not entitled to participate. As a result, 112 families, comprising 525 individuals were immediately [struck] from the rolls.[19]

Finally, in September, 1892, the commission arrived. It was composed of three members, headed by P.J. McCumber. The Commission met in session at the Turtle Mountain Indian Agency beginning September 21 and called for the standing committee's report. (This would be the report of the thirty-two men selected the year previously.) Since this report concerned itself primarily with eligible persons, Chief Little Shell and his assistant, Red Thunder, protested forcefully against the dropping of the names of many individuals. Little Shell first spoke to the commission and pled for the consideration of people who had moved away, particularly for those who had gone to Montana because of dire need for food. Red Thunder succinctly summed up the situation by saying: "When you (the white man) first put your foot upon this land of ours you found no one but the red man and the

Indian woman, by whom you have begotten a large family." Pointing to the métis present, he added, "These are the children and descendants of that woman; they must be recognized as members of this tribe."[20] Firmly, the commission chairman told Little Shell that only the committee appointed by Agent Waugh would be heard, but that once the rolls were established, Little Shell might receive a copy of it. In disgust, Little Shell replied that his group would leave and that he would place his authority in the hands of his attorney, John Bottineau, a member of the tribe and a métis.

On September 24, the commission finished hearing the report of the committee and then published the roll of eligible members. Instead of giving a copy to Bottineau, the roll was posted on the doors of the church. When Bottineau saw it, he was astounded at the number of people who had been dropped from the accepted group, and more flabbergasted, yet, when he received the following letter:[21]

U.S. Indian Service
Turtle Mountain Agency
October 15, 1892
John B. Bottineau, Esq.
Belcourt, North Dakota

Sir:

As per the enclosed you will observe that all persons except those mentioned in said notice are directed to withdraw from the limits of the reservation. I am instructed by the commission that in the matter of treaty for which a meeting has been called that they are instructed to deal directly with the people and will not recognize an attorney. Trusting that you will govern yourself in accordance with the directions of said notice, I remain,

Yours truly,

John Waugh, U.S. Indian Agent,
Per E.W. Brenner, Farmer in Charge.

The enclosure received by Bottineau was the same one that went to all métis whose names were not on the rolls:

To Whom It May Concern:

Notice is hereby given to all parties who are not residents of the Turtle Mountain Reservation, or enrolled as members of the Turtle Mountain Band and accepted by the Commission now present as entitled to participate in any proceedings with the said Commissioners having in view the making of arrangements for a treaty, are hereby directed to withdraw from within the limits of the Turtle Mountain Reservation at once or be arrested.

John Waugh, U.S. Indian Agent,
Per E.W. Brenner, Farmer in Charge.

The commission continued its deliberation with the committee and on October 22 announced its agreement. The Turtle Mountain Band of Chippewa, including the métis who were considered eligible members, agreed to withdraw all claim to the 9,500,000-acre tract of land in the region, except the two townships previously established as a reservation in 1882. For their withdrawal, the government promised to pay the tribe $1,000,000. (Here is the basis for the description of the treaty that is so often given by the métis of Montana when they mention the incident. The term, *ten-cent treaty,* refers to the government's action in taking 9,500,000 acres of land for the sum of $1 million.)

Little Shell was aghast. By this willful action his people's sole remaining resource was given away for a paltry sum. Moreover, he saw no logic, equity or reason in the arbitrary determination of persons "chosen" as constituted members of the Turtle Mountain Band, for eligible members often had full brothers or sisters denied membership. Furthermore, he was incensed with what he thought to be the general high-handed tactics of the commission. Immediately he announced repudiation of the treaty and called his council, *La Loge de Soldat,* together. On October 24, Chief Little Shell mailed a protest to Washington listing grievances. He reviewed carefully the regular method by which the Chippewa reached an agreement through its council, to which neither the appointment nor the action of this committee conformed. He protested against the manner in which his attorney had been ordered off the reservation. And finally, he made specific charges against the commission, the committee of thirty-two and the Indian agent, accusing all of coercion.[22]

There is no evidence to indicate that Little Shell's protest was ever considered. A few weeks later, [on] December 3, 1892, the secretary of the interior transmitted the agreement, as concluded by the commission, to President Harrison, who in turn sent it to Congress for ratification.

Then came long years of waiting. Congress failed to ratify the treaty. The years that followed were marked by unrest and acrimony, both by Indians and whites. At least one committee of white citizenry appealed to Congress to settle the issue. More Indians had to move westward to try to find a livelihood in a land that was fast becoming settled; and even the government Indian agents were discouraged, frustrated and outraged by the long delay. Finally, on January 26, 1898, Chief Little Shell wrote to his attorney, John Bottineau, who was then in Washington trying to secure some kind of settlement, an impassioned letter:

Belcourt, N.D.
January 26, 1898

The chief, Little Shell, here speaks: We are tired, fatigue since so long waiting for the settlement of our claims. Even though we are fatigue, we keep strong – firm – to stay by you and your efforts in our cause . . . In regard to the affairs and doings of the three commissioners – the ten-cent treaty commissioners – we are very much troubled in here about it; but I repeat to you here again . . . that I would never sign their affairs, the ten-cent treaty; I am all the same yet and now. My greatest fatigue is to see my people so poor and going hungry.

Little Shell, Chief
(his x mark)

Sasswein, Henri Poitrat
(his x mark)

Gaurin, Baptiste Champagne
(his x mark)

Bay-riss, Cuthbert Grant
(his x mark)

Written by John B. Reno, Secretary of the Council.[23]

The years passed. More métis moved west. Others came back to the Turtle Mountains to see what had happened during their absence. Despairingly, a sympathetic agent, F.O. Getchell, wrote to the commissioner of Indian affairs describing the reservation and its people:

Such is the place and such are nearly 2,000 of the people who are beseiged in their mountain fastnesses by the peaceful army of the plow that has settled their erstwhile hunting grounds. Here they are held in worse than bondage while they are waiting, waiting, waiting for a settlement with the Government for the lands so settled by the plowman, *waiting for a day that never comes*, while their chances in the land that was their own is fading, fading away from them. God pity their patient waiting and appoint that it may not have been in vain.[24]

At long last, on April 21, 1904, nearly twelve years after the McCumber Commission presented its report, Congress ratified the so-called treaty. In the final ratification, provision was made that all members of the Turtle Mountain Band who were unable to secure land upon the reservation could take homesteads upon any vacant land in the public domain without charge and would and should still retain their rights to tribal funds, annuities, or other property held by the Turtle Mountain group, provided that such right of alternate selection of homesteads should not be alienated.[25]

But this ratification did not even end the litigation, for on January 19, 1905, the assistant U.S. attorney general held that the document signed by the Indians did not give a general release of their claim to the lands in North Dakota, and that ratification could not be complete until such release was obtained. Word was sent to the agreeable Indians, who called a meeting on February 15, 1905, and executed the necessary release. Little Shell and his followers refused to sign.

Now that the final legal entanglements seemed cleared, it appeared that some kind of settlement could be effected. But again, such was not the case. Once more the spectre of the rolls confronted the Indian agents. One agent, Charles L. Davis, writing his report to the U.S. Indian commissioner for the year 1906, mentioned the trouble by saying that he was attempting to follow the report of the 1892 commission and that he was adding only [the names of people] who had been born to families listed on the original report. He also mentioned that he tried to eliminate such members who "seemed to have discontinued or forfeited their tribal rights by long abandonment."[26] Francis E. Leupp, commissioner of Indian affairs, listed the criteria in his report for 1906 by which Indians should be judged, and singled out, as well, those to whom no grants could be given. Those individuals, then, who should be excluded – aside from death – were to include:

1. Applicants coming from Canada after the date of the McCumber treaty.
2. Persons receiving land scrip or other benefits as Canadian Indians.
3. Applicants not living on the nine-million acre tract at the time of the McCumber treaty unless they can show they were born and raised there and were absent temporarily.
4. Those who may have been living on that tract at the time of the McCumber treaty and who have since permanently removed therefrom are debarred.[27]

How, the métis wondered, as they heard of the last provision, could they have existed during those fourteen years that had elapsed between the time of the McCumber Treaty and its final execution?

One of the provisions of the treaty was that Indians unable to secure land on the reservation could file for homesteads on the public domain. During . . . 1906, a total of 549 members of the Turtle Mountain Band filed on public land. The land office at Devil's Lake, North Dakota, recorded 10 such filings; the one at Minot, 390; the one at Great Falls, 142, and the one at Lewistown, 7. But, in his report for . . . 1907, Commissioner Leupp stated that there were at least 1,370 Indians for whom no provision had been made and that these included principally the wives and children of the reservation allottees. "If these Indians are to secure lands it must be from the public domain in North Dakota and Montana," he wrote. "But protests have been made against their taking so much of the public domain in these states, because the lands will remain untaxable as long as they are held in trust by the government."[28]

So the government concluded its responsibilities toward the Pembina band of Chippewa – full bloods and métis. What happened, then, to the métis who straggled back to Montana?

The wild game was largely gone, their cabins burned, barbed wire greeted them at every turn, for their timing coincided with the homestead boom that had struck the high plains that once had been their home. A few, like Joseph Dussome, tried to homestead but encountered difficulties – were they or were they not Turtle Mountain Indians and hence qualified to take land on the public domain without payment of fees? Some of them intermarried with enrolled Indians on established reservations where their children at least would have the benefits accorded to them by the government. But most of them were forced to sink deeper and deeper on the social scale. Always confronted by the stigma of being Canadian Cree, these early pioneers of Montana – these Azures, LaPierres, Collins, LaFrambois, Poitras, and all the rest – sought work where they could find it. Many of them congregated on a hill near the fast-growing city of Great Falls (later to be called Hill 57) while others went to the areas they knew and loved the best: Choteau, Augusta, Dupuyer, and the Milk River towns of Havre, Chinook, Malta, and Glasgow.

And here their descendants live today, scorned by both the white and the enrolled-Indian populations. All the assistance their forebears gave to the fur traders and to the early stockmen is forgotten. All of their struggle to receive recognition as American citizens after their exclusion from the rolls at the time of the McCumber Treaty is unknown. All that is remembered is the erroneous impression that they are Canadian Cree and therefore displaced persons, landless and unwanted.

*   *   *

Joseph Dussome still sits in his cabin with his good wife and goes over his papers. He remembers the things that have happened to him – the false hope that has so often been engendered. He remembers the first organization that he effected, "The Abandoned Band of Chippewa Indians," in 1927, which seven years later he had incorporated under the name of "The

Landless Indians of Montana." Without rancor, he recalls seeing a group of younger and more aggressive men split from his organization to incorporate one of their own, "The Montana Landless Indians."

He particularly remembers the hope of the 1930 Depression years, for then the government promised to buy 37,000 acres of land lying near Box Elder for the Landless Indians of Montana. The government fulfilled its contract, but the jurisdiction of the land was placed under Rocky Boy's agency, with the Cree inhabitants of that reservation making the decision as to who should be adopted. As he views the adoption, the Canadian Cree – those who came to Montana after the Riel Rebellion – were the adoptees, so another dream vanished. The American métis still wandered.

Dussome recalls, too, the purchase by the government of a forty-acre tract of land near Great Falls in the 1930s. Here was to be a chance for the Indians of Hill 57, the landless ones from the Turtle Mountains, to live in less squalid conditions and to have subsistence garden plots. Too vivid in Dussome's memory is the opposition from Great Falls' residents to the occupancy of the site by the Indians, so the opportunity passed.

And then there was the government Resettlement Plan that was almost accomplished, early in the 1940s. In Phillips County, where the Farm Security Adminstration did remarkable things for white farmers, the plan developed whereby all of the Ben Phillips' pioneer land holdings were to be purchased by the government for the Landless Indians. On this land, experienced Indian farmers would have separate units; inexperienced ones would work cooperatively. But the war came, and the idea became a forgotten one.

But hope, even now, is not entirely dead. Joe Dussome still believes that the federal government will eventually provide a rehabilitation program for his people; that the Indian claim to the hunting rights of the Turtle Mountain area will some day be recognized as being as significant as those cultivated rights of the white man; that eventually right will triumph and some of the inequities of the past will be rectified.

The trucks from the mines roar by his cabin by day. At night wind blows down from the little canyon past his door. Joseph Dussome sits in his cabin at Zortman and waits, perhaps for a day that never comes.

NOTES

This article was originally published in *Montana: The Magazine of Western History* 6 (1958). Reprinted with permission.

1 Joseph Kinsey Howard's remarkable book, *Strange Empire* (New York: William Morrow and Co., 1952).

2 For much of this information, I am indebted to Mrs. Joseph Dussome, Zortman, Montana, for personal interviews.

3 For an excellent early description of the métis see "The French Half Breeds of the Northwest" by V. Harvard, M.D. *Annual Report of the Smithsonian Institution for the Year 1879* (Washington: Government Printing Office, 1880), 309–27.

4 For this information I gratefully acknowledge the assistance given me by one of my students, Joseph D. Marion, Jr., whose acquaintance with the métis and their problems is unequalled by any other person in Montana.

5 Harvard, *Annual Report of the Smithsonian Institution,* 325.

6 Personal Interview, John Barrows, Zortman, Montana, September 14, 1957.

7 Alexander Ross, *The Red River Settlement: Its Rise, Progress, and Present State* (London: Smith, Edler and Co., 1856. Reprinted Minneapolis: Ross and Haines, Inc., 1957.)

8 J.M. Hamilton, *From Wilderness to Statehood* (Portland: Binfords and Mort, 1957) 83.

9 Joseph Marion gave me these family names from his notes concerning the movements of the early-day métis.

10 Obituary of Clemence Gourneau Berger, Lewistown *Democrat-News,* December 31, 1943.

11 Personal Interview, Mrs. Elizabeth Swan, a granddaughter of Pierre Berger and a resident of Lewistown, September 18, 1956.

12 For the complete and beautifully written story of the métis in Canada and of the Riel uprisings, see Howard, *Strange Empire.*

13 An account of the trouble the Cree had in securing Rocky Boy's Reservation appears in Verne Dusenberry, "The Rocky Boy Indians," *Montana Magazine of History* (Winter 1954).

14 *Collections of the State Historical Society of North Dakota* (Bismarck: Tribune State Printers and Binders, 1906) 1:384–405.

15 *Senate Documents* 154, 55th Congress, 2nd Session, 11.

16 *Report of the Commissioner of Indian Affairs for 1884,* 34–35.

17 *Report of the Commissioner of Indian Affairs for 1888,* 41.

18 *Senate Document* 154, 55th Congress, 2nd Session, 20.

19 *Report of the Commissioner of Indian Affairs for 1892,* 353.

20 *Senate Document* 444, 56th Congress, 1st Session, 33–36.

21 Ibid., 41.

22 Ibid., 31–36.

23 *Senate Document* 154, 56th Congress, 1st Session, 26.

24 *Report of the Commissioner of Indian Affairs for 1903,* 228–29.

25 *33 Stat. L.,* 58th Congress, 2nd Session, Chapter 1402, 1904, 194.

26 *Report of the Commissioner of Indian Affairs for 1906,* 281.

27 Ibid., 154–55.

28 *Report of the Commissioner of Indian Affairs for 1907,* 60–63.

Treaty No. 9 and fur trade company families: Northeastern Ontario's halfbreeds, Indians, petitioners and métis

John S. Long

We hear about the white man's fame
And of the Indian's need,
But seldom do we hear about
The little known halfbreed.

. . . .

Who helped the Whites and Crees to trade
And learn each other's ways?
The man of course who spoke their tongue
And shared the ventures of those days.
Gordon Moore[1]

The roles of native[2] people in the history of the James Bay region have finally received their due attention. Daniel Francis and Toby Morantz have discussed native peoples and the fur trade on the eastern side of James Bay, while Charles A. Bishop and Arthur J. Ray have focused more on the western margin and its hinterland. The familial situations of certain descendants of native women and European men around James Bay (and elsewhere) have been ably described through the scholarship of Jennifer Brown and Sylvia Van Kirk. These developments are so new that an otherwise excellent text entitled *Ontario Since 1867*, published as recently as 1978, contains two references to the western métis, but no mention of their Ontario counterparts. A history book distributed to all Ontario school children to mark Ontario's bicentennial in 1984 makes the same omission.[3] Yet in northeastern Ontario, within the James Bay hinterland, there exists a well documented "halfbreed" or métis identity. The legal basis for this unique situation is the signing of Treaty No. 9 in 1905, although its human dimension can be traced back more than two centuries earlier.

In 1668 a trading post was established at Fort Charles, later called Rupert House, at the mouth of the Rupert River. Two years later the Hudson's Bay Company (HBC or Company) received a British charter granting it the exclusive right, in the custom of the day, to exploit the James and Hudson Bay watersheds. In 1671, reaching westward, the renowned Pierre Esprit Radisson traded for the Company in the estuary of the Moose River, where a second trading post was established two years later. In 1674 further explorations proceeded along the coast towards the Albany River, where Fort Albany was later situated.[4]

The Cree were nomadic hunters and gatherers. The land would not support large concentrations of people except for brief periods. Beyond this, the seasonal movements of the Cree prior to the establishment of trading posts along the Bay are not known with any certainty, due to a dearth of archeological research. Bishop speculates that the Cree wintered inland near the Canadian Shield where big game was plentiful. It is equally possible that small numbers of Cree wintered near the coast. Some Cree, designated *Home Guard* by the traders, were induced to protect and provision the coastal posts during the winter. Depending on one's view of prehistory, these Home Guard Cree were inlanders enticed to the coast and/or an expansion of the previously small coast-oriented group. Bishop suggests that these Home Guard Cree quickly became dependent on the post in times of famine. In the spring of 1784, for example, there were eighty Cree being fed rations at Moose Fort and another one hundred at Fort Albany. Morantz has shown, however, that this was a temporary situation; the fur traders were the dependent ones over the years, at least on the eastern coast of James Bay.[5]

The Europeans did try to impose a formal system of ranking on the traditionally egalitarian Cree, hoping to induce esteemed hunters to exert their influence over their compatriots. Explorer Samuel Hearne considered the influence of these leading men to be "trifling," yet HBC post journals indicate that traders considered the burials of Cree trading captains, lieutenants and kings to be solemn events. These journals, carefully kept records of only the "most remarkable Transactions and Occurrences," chronicle the names of captains *Pusso, Uttum* and others at Moose Fort in the 1780s.[6]

Understandably, many natives were not considered economically significant as individuals. The 1815–16 District Report written at Moose Fort listed individually the names of three dozen male native hunters together with their respective contributions in "made beaver," which was the fur-trade standard. Their female counterparts, who processed furs, netted snowshoes and thus made an equally important contribution to the trade, were confined to obscurity by a brief reference to "the Women."[7]

In other cases the identities of native women were more consciously omitted, as in an account of the capture of Moose Fort in 1686. The Chevalier de Troyes led a band of one hundred Frenchmen to capture this post, Fort Charles and Fort Albany; the fur traders of New France had keenly felt the adverse effects of an English presence on James Bay. Governor Henry Sergeant, in charge of the HBC's establishments, neglected to identify a pair of natives involved accidentally in the takeover. In a deposition used to refute charges that he inadequately protected the forts, Sergeant alleged that at Moose Fort the French "found . . . Two Indian Women" in the men's rooms.[8]

Relationships between Company employees and native women were expressly forbidden by the HBC's London directors, yet non-native women were barred from Rupert's Land following the French seizure of the James Bay posts. Hence a policy which Jennifer Brown calls "military monasticism" could not be enforced. Most of these early, clandestine unions were not recorded among the remarkable events in post journals destined to be read in England. But by 1800 the fact of a new hybrid population living at these posts could no longer be ignored. Educational and employment policies were formulated in recognition of this situation. As a concomitant to the Company's school plans, systematic birth records began to be kept at some major posts – though only for employees, thus excluding the roving hunters.[9]

Early in the nineteenth century, prior to the 1821 union of the HBC and its arch rival, the North West Company, employment opportunities were expanding for youths of mixed ancestry such as Joseph Turner (or Turnor) Sr. and Thomas Richards Jr. in James Bay's relatively self-sufficient trading post communities. The officer in charge at Moose Factory, as the establishment was more frequently known after a district reorganization in 1810, reported favourably on the lads. Turner was a "very good cooper carpenter sailor & boat steerer" while young Richards was "very expert in the Canoes." Turner may have been a son of the Company's first full-time surveyor, the Englishman Philip Turnor, who probably took a native woman as his partner; less probably, he may simply have been named in honour of the Englishman.[10]

As missions became established after 1840, another vocational niche was created for James Bay's population of mixed ancestry. Bilingual catechists and clergy were needed to assist their European supervisors, supplementing the number of spiritual labourers and providing fluent translators. These native associates were supposed to be the leaven for a Christian native church, locally supported.[11] Clergy of mixed ancestry like Thomas Vincent and Richard Faries were unable, however, to rise above the rank of archdeacon. Sometimes described as "raised in the country," an allusion to their mixed origin, such clergy faced racial discrimination.

Bishop John Horden of Moose Factory considered Vincent "a first class native," and he objected to the term *country born* being used to describe such clergymen – "tending as it does to create a caste feeling." Though Horden himself used the expression *half caste* in his private correspondence, he felt the Church Missionary Society's almanac should not emphasize racial distinctions among indigenous clergy, all of whom ought to be considered "native."[12]

If a half caste mated with a European, the resulting offspring, according to Horden's racial views, would display intellectual hybrid vigour. Yet Horden warned of the prospect of hybrid *rigor mortis* unless the native strain was continually thinned. The children of Archdeacon John McKay, another James Bay half caste, the Bishop expected to be "of fair intellect as his wife is an European," whereas Vincent's sons were "all stupid." This perceived "declension of the European intellect in the second or third generation," drowned in nativeness, presented a challenge to the creation of a native church. Men like Vincent and McKay were "rare [birds] indeed," lamented Horden. The James Bay hinterland was "not the country for high intellectual power." The talent that did emerge was monopolized by the HBC: "At fifteen all boys, sons of HBC's servants are taken into the service of the HBC either as apprentices to some trade, or as laborers."[13]

Some offspring of mixed ancestry may have inherited a degree of disease immunity from their European forebears and may not have succumbed as readily as other natives to tuberculosis ("the fearful disease of consumption"). Horden observed: "Here is certainly seen the great difference between the constitutions of the natives and the Europeans. The latter enjoy exceedingly good health here, but the former soon after they engage in the company's service begin to fail. The former appear able to endure the sudden transitions from hot to cold and from cold to hot, while the latter is thereby subject to most severe and trying colds which frequently terminate fatally. But this effect is not so frequently produced as long as the native remains in his tent, but soon after his admittance into the house with European servants."[14]

HBC employees of mixed ancestry were prone to charges of unsteadiness or drunkenness. John Thomas Jr., one of the first young halfbreeds employed at Moose Factory, was inactive, lazy and "given to liquor" – but so was a European servant of the same age and occupation. For the conscientious halfbreed – obedient, respectful, sober, honest, active men like George Moore Sr. and Joseph Turner Sr. – a career was possible. If their children consistently emulated these virtues, over the generations a tradition of Company service developed for the boys, and the girls became eligible wives for European or halfbreed employees. By the mid-1840s, two-thirds of the servants and one-third of the officers in the service of the HBC in the James Bay region were men of mixed ancestry. A limit was set, however, by discriminatory personnel policies – as evidenced by the dead-end position of postmaster to which halfbreeds were sometimes consigned to discourage any expectation of their promotion.[15]

The ethnic composition of Moose Factory changed following union with Canada in 1870. Two years later Horden wrote, "There was formerly no Society here; now we have some European or Canadian ladies." Yet numbers of native women continued to marry Company employees: "Many, when they have made any advance whatsoever in civilization, will become amalgamated with the whites. A good deal of that has already taken place in this quarter, the European servants of the HBC marrying Indian women who are quite their equals in intelligence; and eventually on retiring from the service, taking them with them to various parts of Canada." In 1886, for example, Horden performed fourteen marriages at Moose Factory. Five of the grooms were European employees of the HBC – George Carey (English), Henry Bradburn (English), John Macaulay (Orkneyman), Augustus Beck (American) and William Shaw (Scot) – and all married native women.[16]

By the 1890s an important HBC post like Moose Factory, headquarters for the James Bay region, required thirty-six employees besides the officer in charge: a postmaster, a surgeon, three clerks, twelve mariners, five boat builders, three labourers, two carpenters, two coopers, two blacksmiths, two stewards, a storesman, a cattlekeeper and a sawyer. Seventy-two percent of the one hundred employees in the district had Hudson Bay listed as their parish of origin, an indication of mixed ancestry.[17]

Toward the end of the nineteenth century, further limits to the upward mobility of halfbreeds were imposed when economizing and modernizing measures led to staff reductions by the HBC in the James Bay region. The 1890s were difficult years for the Company. Commissioner Clarence C. Chipman reported that the Company's James Bay District needed "considerable reorganization and good management before its real value to the Company will be apparent." The poor financial situation was attributed simply to "diminishing Returns . . . with increasing Expenses." With the completion of the transcontinental railroad in 1885, inland posts could be more economically supplied by rail, yet a large trans-shipment centre was still maintained at Moose Factory.[18]

A Company report on sea transport in James Bay revealed the high cost of an inefficient system of trans-shipping and landing goods at Moose Factory. Silting of the Moose River hindered the movement of schooners. A large staff of Company servants was maintained – some eighty men, two scows and a steam tug were required to unload six hundred tons of supplies from the annual supply vessel from Montreal, and then to reload the barque with furs and ballast within three weeks. In addition to this crew, schooners were employed to deliver goods to dependent coastal communities such as Fort Albany, Rupert House and Fort George. Company employees and their families comprised nearly one-third of the entire population associated with Moose Factory. According to rational economic analysis, this "ship-time gang" constituted "a permanent staff twice as large as could be justified at any other Season of the year."[19]

To remedy the situation, a pier and warehouse were built at Charlton Island, about seventy-five miles northeast of Moose Factory. A steamer, the *Inenew*, was purchased to replace the schooners. The steamer required fewer skilled men, whereas two crews of accomplished sailors were needed for the *Mink* and *Marten*. With a new depot and the steamer, it was predicted that some $25,000 annually could be saved. Should opposing fur traders challenge the Company's virtual monopoly in James Bay, this would allow the HBC to double its fur prices. A small winter trading post had already been established at Long Portage House (also called New Post) some eighty miles inland from Moose Factory, to meet the further threat of rival traders to the south.[20]

Revillon Frères Trading Company Limited began to penetrate the James Bay region soon after 1900. Initially established at Ara Island, where the Moose and Abitibi Rivers meet, Revillon was relocated near the present town of Moosonee on the mainland north of Moose Factory by the spring of 1903. The opposition company hired the *Eldorado* to transport 1,450 tons of cargo to James Bay that summer, but the vessel ran aground and was wrecked near Fort George. Undeterred, Revillon established a depot at Strutton Island (near Charlton). Within a few years, this newer company had established posts at several locations on the James Bay coast. The arrival of this opposition dramatically altered the circumstances of many James Bay halfbreeds.[21]

Herbert F. McLeod, a retired HBC servant, stated during a conversation in the late 1970s that a number of Company employees had been dismissed at Moose Factory as economizing measures were instituted shortly after

1900. His recollections were confirmed by a missionary's account written in June, 1902, of having met, upriver from Moose Factory, "43 men, women and children of HBC's servants, who had been given a passage to the [railway] line. They will find many hardships before they settle. Moose Fort is half emptied of the Company's servants, some few Indians have left, and a few more are going." The Line, as the transcontinental railway was referred to, proved an attraction to a number of native hunters, some of whom were admitted into Treaty No. 9 at Chapleau and Missanabie. Most of the halfbreed servants had left James Bay involuntarily. When Revillon Frères appeared on the scene, the tide of immigrants reversed somewhat. In July, 1902, missionary observers met "a large party of new traders, French Roman Catholics . . . going to settle near Moose, and taking with them Indians and servants, nearly 40 canoes in all." Evidently some of the HBC employees who had been discharged at Moose Factory were rehired, either by the HBC or by Revillon Frères.[22]

Another retired Company servant, William R. Faries, stated that a similar exodus had occurred at Fort Albany. This too was confirmed by an HBC employee's account written from Fort Montizambert on the Canadian Pacific Railway (CPR) line, midway between Sault Ste. Marie and Port Arthur (Thunder Bay). The writer sympathized with the plight of the Fort Albany expatriates in July, 1902: "Wm. Etherington, Wm. Louttit, Wm. Corston, & James Louttit son of James Louttit B, arrived from Albany this afternoon . . . poor devils they were servants at Albany, but have got the quiet hint to move. They may get work along the Line & they may not." The Albany men found temporary work at odd jobs around Fort Montizambert post, cutting firewood or fixing the hen house.[23]

The same year another HBC servant from Fort Albany, Peter Louttit, began erecting a dwelling at Fort Montizambert in anticipation of relocating there. Two years later, one year before treaty time, a James Bay man named Corston arrived with his family from Moose Factory. Disabled, Corston faced an uncertain future. His sympathetic colleague wrote, "The poor devil will starve here for sure, I don't know what the poor man can do with a lame leg."[24]

Halfbreeds Peter Louttit, William Louttit and William Etherington returned to Fort Albany by treaty time, thanks to the arrival of Revillon Frères. From Pagwa, on the Canadian National Railway (CNR) line, to Fort Albany at its mouth, the Albany River provided an excellent transportation system at high water in the spring. Revillon Frères loaded its scows at Pagwa and towed them downriver to James Bay, where they were dismantled for lumber.

The halfbreed James Louttit, a one-armed man, moved from Fort Montizambert to the Dryden area. Many other halfbreeds moved to other settlements in Ontario or Manitoba, including Port Arthur (Thunder Bay), North Temiskaming, Sault Ste. Marie, Temagami and Winnipeg.

Given the clandestine or slightly documented origins of many early halfbreeds, the precise extent of James Bay's racially-mixed population at the turn of the twentieth century cannot easily be determined. E.B. Borron, Ontario's Stipendiary Magistrate, noted in his report for 1879–1880: "a large proportion of the natives appeared to have more or less European blood in their veins." In a later report, he added, "The European element is almost entirely Scotch, English and Scandinavian. There are very few French métis." A useful demographic baseline can be derived from the 1881 census for Eastern Rupert's Land which lists place of birth, probable racial origin and occupation for each individual at Moose Factory, Fort Albany and certain satellite posts in Ontario. When combined with parish registers and a sampling of HBC employee records, a preliminary census of fur trade Company families at treaty time can be reconstructed.[25]

The treaty signed in northern Ontario in 1905–06 was only partially prompted by the plight of native hunters, some of whom had experienced severe hardship in the 1890s. A few of these hunters (for example, Charles Cheechoo, a cook) had become full-time HBC servants. Some, like Andrew Butterfly, had temporarily moved to the Chapleau area. Many others were employed by the Company in the summer at odd jobs – cleaning the boats, digging gardens, mending fences, sweeping the yard or working on the hay boats. Native hunters like Simon Smallboy and John Cachegee were valued canoe makers. Still, their primary occupation was hunting. The federal government had been prompted to provide them with relief even before treaty obligations existed, when starving hunters were reported eating their furs in desperation. The fur trade had been declining for decades in the James Bay region.[26]

The immediate purpose of the treaty was to obtain a surrender of the territory north of the height-of-land, due to "the projected passage of the new transcontinental railway through their territory, and the increasing influx of prospectors." A number of natives living near the CPR had begun petitioning government agents for a treaty in the mid-1880s. In 1901 the Laurier government announced its intention to build a second transcontinental line through northern Ontario. One proposal, the Trans-Canada Railway, was contemplated running from Roberval, Quebec, through Moose Factory to Fort Simpson, British Columbia. Ontario's Premier George Ross determined, in the same year, to build a settlement railway from North Bay to

Temiskaming in order to service the newly discovered Great Clay Belt. Ontario's Crown Lands Department envisaged a population of one million people in the latter region, with its "healthful and invigorating" climate, and predicted that within three years "through trains will be carrying fish from Moose Factory . . . to Chicago."[27]

Three treaty commissioners were involved in the signing process, Duncan Campbell Scott and Samuel Stewart representing the federal government. The best known of these was Scott, of literary fame, who had joined the Indian Affairs Department in 1878. By 1905 Scott was in his early forties, halfway through what was to be a fifty-two year career in government service. Of Scott one biographer has written, "The poet in him and the civil servant agreed in believing that the future of the Indians . . . depended on their being brought more and more nearly to the status of the white population."[28]

Such a view meshed perfectly with the assimilationist assumptions of federal Indian legislation. The *Indian Act, 1880,* for example, specifically excluded halfbreeds from its provisions and from treaties except in "very special circumstances, to be determined by the Superintendent-General [of Indian Affairs] or his agent." In practice, the western métis had been given a choice between treaty and scrip. The object of the Indian legislation was to promote "enfranchisement," whereby individual Indians or entire bands relinquished Indian status and ceased to be wards of the government.[29]

The third commissioner was Daniel George MacMartin, a lawyer from Perth, who represented the Province of Ontario; Treaty No. 9 was the first post-Confederation treaty to have provincial representation. An 1894 agreement between the Ontario and federal governments had provided "that any future treaties with the Indians in respect of territory in Ontario . . . shall be deemed to require the concurrence of the Government of Ontario." Treaty No. 3, in northwestern Ontario and adjacent Manitoba, had given rise to several federal-provincial disagreements – St. Catherines Milling vs. The Queen (1888), Attorney General for Canada vs. Attorney General for Ontario (1896), Ontario Mining Company vs. Seybold (1903), Dominion of Canada vs. Province of Ontario (1910) – one of which was not resolved at the time of the Treaty No. 9 signing in 1905. These jurisdictional complications resulted in a delay in reaching an intergovernmental agreement on Treaty No. 9 arrangements.[30]

In 1903, when Treaty No. 9 was still in the planning stages, the Honourable Clifford Sifton (federal superintendent-general of Indian Affairs) received a report recommending that "if any claims be made by halfbreeds as distinguished from Indians, the Province to grant 160 acres *to each of such persons* in fee simple under conditions that will admit of land being located in advance of survey and being taken possession of at once, as without such conditions, owing to the remoteness of these persons from surveyed lands, the grant would be of little use to them [emphasis added]."

When the Province of Ontario was notified in confidence of the proposed treaty in 1904, however, no reference was made to the treatment of halfbreeds. Joint orders-in-council and an intergovernmental memorandum of agreement, drafted in June, 1905, similarly failed to mention halfbreed interests.[31] Thus the treaty commissioners were apparently dispatched without any instructions for handling halfbreed claims.

When the Treaty No. 9 commissioners visited Fort Albany on August 3, 1905, they admitted 375 native people into the treaty. Among these were over thirty halfbreeds, who thereby obtained Indian status. We may refer to them as Indian halfbreeds – halfbreeds by origin, Indians by decree of the commissioners. William R. (Willie) Faries, ten years old in 1905, stated in 1978 that four distinct Company families were admitted to treaty at Fort Albany – the Louttits, Faries, Hunters and Linklaters. They shared close ties of kinship.

Peter Louttit, Willie's stepfather, was a forty-five-year-old widower with five children. Peter was a former blacksmith and cattlekeeper for the HBC, and was of Scottish-Cree ancestry through his father and French-Cree through his mother. He had just married Mary (Wesley), widow of George Faries, and before Revillon Frères' arrival had anticipated a move to Fort Montizambert on the CPR.

Sixty-nine-year-old labourer Patrick Faries, descended from a North West Company trader, and reported by the 1881 census to be of Cree-Irish origin, was admitted to the treaty along with his wife Jane (Mark), their daughters, and four grandchildren (Willie, his brothers James and George, and his sister Jane).

John Hunter, a thirty-eight-year-old carpenter and son of an Orkneyman, was admitted with his wife Sarah (Linklater) and their eight children.

George Linklater, forty-one years old, post master at Attawapiskat and described as of Scottish-Cree origin, was admitted with his second wife Margaret (Faries) and two children. His brother James, age twenty-nine, steward at Fort Albany, was likewise admitted with his wife Charlotte (Linklater) and two children.

These Indian halfbreeds of Fort Albany and Attawapiskat shared four characteristics: mixed racial origins, a family tradition of employment with the HBC, membership in the English-speaking congregation of the Anglican Church and domicile. All resided north of the the Albany River, outside the province of Ontario. Many other halfbreeds, like petitioner James Louttit, had permanently left the region before 1905. Others were evidently admitted to the treaty at other posts on the Upper Albany River.

A different fate awaited the Moose Factory halfbreeds. The Reverend T. Bird Holland wrote in the parish records that "Treaty money . . . was paid on Thursday the 10th [of August, 1905] to or for 340 persons, halfbreeds not included." They could not have been excluded simply by virtue of their mixed racial origins, since the federal treaty agents acknowledged that halfbreeds were admitted at Fort Albany. It would have been illogical to exclude them on the basis of their employment with the HBC, since this was not a criterion at Fort Albany.[32]

A descendant of the Indian halfbreed Peter Louttit suggested that his father was admitted to treaty at Fort Albany at the request of the other Indians to whom he was related. It is true that some of the Indian halfbreeds were closely related to the Wesleys and Marks, two leading Indian families – but so were some of the Moose Factory halfbreeds. Fred Mark, selected as chief by the Moose Factory Indians, was married to a halfbreed, and his sister was married to a halfbreed petitioner. A descendant of the Indian halfbreed George Linklater speculated that his Moose Factory counterparts "didn't want in" to the treaty.[33]

After leaving Moose Factory, the treaty commissioners visited Abitibi where Duncan Scott photographed the halfbreed Louis MacDougall, admitting him to treaty while remarking on the man's Scottish ancestry in the photograph's caption. Though a halfbreed, MacDougall was evidently not as well educated or skilled in Company trades. John Horden had observed such a coastal/inland distinction years earlier at Timiskaming: "And what a difference between the half breed population of this quarter & that of the Moose District . . . here, not one, except such as have obtained their learning either directly or indirectly from Moose, can read English, while in the whole Moose district, with many of the posts hundreds of miles from the central mission, I do not think five half breeds can be found, excepting the old people who cannot speak, read & write in that tongue."[34]

The territory to which the treaty purported to obtain a surrender overlapped the northern border of the province. Indians living north of the Albany River, residents of the District of Keewatin, became a financial liability of the federal government and were designated on the paylists as Dominion Indians until 1912 when the province's northern boundary was extended. Those residing in Ontario, termed Ontario Indians, also received their treaty annuities from the federal paymaster on his annual visit – but the Ontario government bore the cost. In correspondence prior to the treaty signing, Hudson's Bay Company authority C.C. Chipman had recommended inclusion of these northern Indians, arguing that to include only the Ontario Indians would seem arbitrary to the Keewatin people since there was no real difference between the two groups.[35]

Faced with the commissioners' rejection, five Moose Factory halfbreeds petitioned the Government of Ontario for compensation. Their letter states:

We the undersigned, half breeds of Moose Factory, beg to petition the Government of Ont. for some consideration as we are told by His Majesty's Treaty Commissioners that no provision is at present made for us. We understand that script [sic] has been granted to the half breeds of the North West Territory.

We have been born & brought up in the country, and are thus by our birth and training unfit to obtain a livelihood in the civilized world. Should the fur traders at any time not require our services we should be obliged to support ourselves by hunting.

We therefore humbly pray that you will reconsider your present arrangements and afford us some help.

Andrew Morrison
George McLeod
William McLeod
William Moore
William Archabald

A postscript added by halfbreed John G. Mowat, HBC officer in charge at Moose Factory, stated that the petitioners also represented others who were absent at Charlton Island depot or aboard Company vessels.[36]

This petition, written at the time of the commissioners' visit in 1905, was forwarded by the Indian Affairs Department to the new provincial government in Toronto. George Ross's Liberals had just been soundly defeated, to be replaced by the Conservative government of James Whitney. A few dozen James Bay halfbreeds could not have ranked highly among the new government's priorities. Acting on the advice of its Attorney General, the province sent the petition back to Ottawa, stating, "the petitioners probably mean the Government of the Dominion." It was returned to the Ontario government with an explanation that "the Halfbreed title is of the same nature as the Indian title. . . . *They were refused treaty by the Commissioners* on the grounds that they were not living the Indian mode of life [emphasis added]. The only thing that might be done for these people is to admit them into the Indian treaty if you thought advisable to do so; but as they are residents of the Province and would come under the same category as the rest of your Indian adherents of Treaty No. 9 and would be paid by your

Government, it is a matter which you will have to decide." In April, 1906, Provincial Treasurer Matheson wrote that his government had decided "to allow these half-breeds . . . 160 acres of land reserving minerals" with two stipulations. The land had to be selected "in the District in which they at present reside" and the plots could not in any way "interfere with Hudson's Bay posts or Indian Reserves, or land to be required for railway purposes or for town sites."[37]

From other records it would appear that no sites were to be allotted until the region was properly surveyed. A survey of the Moose Factory Indian Reserve did not take place until 1912[38] when, concurrently, Ontario's boundary was moved north to its present location – thereby transforming the Dominion Indians of Keewatin into Ontario Indians whose annuities (under terms of the pre-treaty intergovernmental agreement) were now the responsibility of the province, and making the commissioners' exclusion of the Moose Factory halfbreeds even more arbitrary.

Matheson's letter unequivocally demonstrates that the Government of Ontario recognized a claim by the halfbreed petitioners of James Bay. His reply was *not* sent to the petitioners, however, but to the Indian Affairs Department in Ottawa. The department's Inspector J.G. Ramsden was twice instructed to inform the halfbreed petitioners of Matheson's offer. By 1909 Ramsden was informing the department that the proffered plots would be "of little use" to the one-armed James Louttit, a sixth petitioner then living near Dryden. Louttit knew of Matheson's offer and had written to the Indian agent at Kenora: "I would like to know if we are going to get enay thing four fore our land as they git Treatty now . . . I would like to git a little hilp. . . . I only have wune arm and I find it hard to make a living as I got a large family to seport so I hope you will looke into this thing four us[.] Ive asked befor and we ware Tolds that we would git Land scrp that is half [breed] [s]crip." Yet in Moose Factory there is no oral tradition of a petition nor of Matheson's offer. From all evidence Ramsden was a man of integrity. As late as 1909, Ramsden wrote the Indian Affairs Department, "The half-breed question at Moose will have to be dealt with. I would like some instructions with reference to this question." Again he was advised of Matheson's offer, but we have no proof that he communicated the province's offer to the Moose Factory petitioners.[39]

And what if he had? With the exception of a few isolated pockets of suitable soil situated near the river deltas, or well drained land along major river banks, Ontario's James Bay coast and hinterland are far from a homesteader's dream. Naturalist Fred Bodsworth described the territory as a "drowned and sodden land . . . a great shallow stagnant sea." Even surveyor

James Dobie, mapping the Fort Albany Indian Reserve in 1912, complained of its wetness. When traversing the Moose Factory Indian Reserve he grumbled at it being so bathed in water that it was "impossible to work in it." Dobie's reports make no reference to an enquiry from halfbreed residents anxious to have their land grant(s) surveyed.[40]

The petitioners, with the exception of James Louttit, lived in the island community of Moose Factory. At the time of the treaty, the HBC was utilizing about seventy acres of land and the Anglican mission another ten. Matheson does not seem to have specified 160 acres for each family, although this is a reasonable inference from the métis experience in western Canada and from a pre-treaty recommendation in the report to Sifton. Roughly a thousand acres might have remained on the island, enough for half a dozen halfbreed land grants, but this land was adjacent to a Company post and thus unavailable. The Company had acquired title to the entire island in 1886, though their original claim according to the 1869 Deed of Surrender was only one hundred acres; all of this was unsurrendered territory prior to 1905.[41]

The mainland to the north, near present-day Moosonee, was occupied by Revillon Frères and its employees, some of whom were halfbreeds. It was also a potential railway site. Much of the surrounding land is subject to spring flooding and erosion during break-up of the river ice. At best it is poorly drained. The school principal at Moose Factory, writing in 1914, considered nearby Haysey Island the only area close enough to the island for farm instruction.[42] It was likely the only land near enough for the halfbreeds to exploit as well, though it would accommodate only two 160-acre plots. Moreover, Haysey Island was used at treaty time as a summer pasture for livestock owned by the HBC.

Even if larger tracts had been available, no HBC servant (nor Revillon man for that matter) could seriously consider clearing the land and occupying it. A servant's contract required that he "perform all such work and services, by day and by night, for the Company, as he shall be required and directed to perform by the officers thereof." Indenture further stipulated that each employee would "diligently and faithfully devote his whole time and attention to their work and service; that he will not absent himself from the said service; nor engage nor be concerned in any trade or employment whatsoever except for the benefit of the said Company."[43]

The Anglican Bishop of Moosonee was aware that these halfbreeds deserved compensation, for his previous mission was in Athabasca's Treaty No. 8 region where there had been separate Indian and halfbreed treaty commissions. In 1907 Bishop George Holmes urged that the children of halfbreeds be allowed to enter Moose Factory's Indian residential school as grant-earning boarders. Although his primary concern was self-serving – filling the school with its quota of boarders, thereby subsidizing the mission – this suggestion shows that an alternative to a land settlement was proposed.[44]

Matheson's offer of 160 acres of land was a useless one, as Ramsden and Holmes indicated. It demonstrated the Ontario government's long-standing preoccupation with promoting settlement in its northland, and thus its preference for agricultural solutions. Free land grants were offered to Boer War returnees and World War I veterans. Similarly, farming the north was seen as a partial solution to the 1930s' depression. The dollar value of Matheson's proposal was approximately $80 at 1905 rates of 50 cents per acre. By coincidence, this was the exact sum which an Indian received upon relinquishing his or her status through enfranchisement. The offer was not overly generous, but it compared reasonably well with provincial precedents and with grants of 160 acres made to the western métis.[45]

What was the response of the Moose Factory petitioners? William Archibald and his family pressed for Indian status. Their persistence was rewarded and they were admitted to the New Post Indian Band. William's half brother, David Wynne, had already been admitted to this band. Another half brother, Tom Taylor, second engineer on the HBC steamer *Inenew*, was excluded.[46] William became the Anglican mission's catechist and servant. He did not have the limited security of a Company contract nor did he have a specialized trade.

The financial benefits of Indian status at the time, $4 per capita annually, though limited, must have been an attraction. Yet surely identity played an important role as well. The first treaty chief at Moose Factory was Fred Mark, a school teacher, catechist and later an ordained clergyman. He signed the treaty at Moose Factory, along with nine other headmen, in Cree syllabics. His beautiful flowing penmanship in the mission marriage register years before stands in sharp contradiction to the image conveyed by the treaty document of an Indian unfamiliar with written English. Most of those who signed in Cree syllabics could sign only that way. Mark *could* write in English, but chose not to. Perhaps he felt compelled to demonstrate his separateness, his Indianness, at treaty time by signing this way, given the exclusion of his halfbreed kinsmen who were not leading the "Indian mode of life." Treaty No. 9 was a tremendously important symbol of nativeness and exclusivity, separating Indians from petitioners, confirming or denying identity by government decree.[47]

What of the McLeods, Morrison and Moore? Denied Indian status, they (together with Archibald) had asked for "some help," perhaps in the form of scrip, a negotiable land or money certificate. Like the vast majority of western métis, offered a choice between land scrip and money scrip, they might have chosen cash. Farmland was a useless commodity given the local terrain and their Company lifestyle. Traplines and fishing grounds were valuable, and each servant or his wife exploited an area assigned by the Company. Though the men were refused Indian status, William McLeod's wife – a sister of Chief Fred Mark – was admitted to the treaty. They had been "refused treaty by the Commissioners." Denied Indian status, it is possible they might have rejected it anyway, because of the stigma of dependency or inferiority it may have implied at that time. The sixth petitioner, one-armed James Louttit of Dinorwic, stated categorically, "I prefer scrip to Treaty," though his wife Jane (Linklater) was later added to the Fort Albany paylist as a Dominion Indian.[48] Unlike Louttit and hundreds like him who had emigrated to Red River or elsewhere, the four petitioners felt "unfit to obtain a livelihood in the civilized world."

The halfbreed Andrew Morrison seems to have played a pivotal role in channelling the demands of the petitioners. He wrote the petition. When he died in March 1906 from a "prolonged & painful illness," the Moose Factory halfbreeds may have lost their most effective and literate spokesman.[49] Still, "demands" seems too strong a word. Obedience and respectfulness were character traits which Company families had inculcated for generations. The petitioners may simply have made a polite inquiry, unaware of the strength of their claim. These halfbreeds had no advocate such as Louis Riel, university educated and trained in law. Until 1980 when a legal clinic opened in Moosonee, the James Bay Indians and halfbreeds had little access to legal advice. Nor did they have an effective and persistent clergyman as advocate. When no answer to their petition was forthcoming, its authors may have shrugged briefly and forgotten the issue.

A newspaper article written in the 1930s when the number of fur-bearing animals had seriously declined in the region, due in part to an influx of non-native trappers and the use of poison bait, quoted petitioner William (Long Willie) McLeod. He favoured having "the old Indian treaty revised and the land returned to the Indians that the fur-bearing animals may multiply and increase once more. He wants to see the Indians trapping and trading as he has seen them 50 years and more ago." Though he "condemned the treaty whole-heartedly" in this respect, McLeod made no mention to the reporter of any halfbreed claim.[50]

The petitioners were relatively prosperous men. By 1909, William McLeod was earning a wage of $235 per year, plus lodging and rations. He and Andrew Morrison were carpenters. William Moore was an accomplished blacksmith and bear trapper. George McLeod was a shipwright.

These four had been among the few retained by the HBC after its economizing drive in 1902.[51] While stating the truth in asserting "we should be obliged to support ourselves by hunting" if no longer needed by the trading companies, they were unlikely candidates for dismissal and perhaps had little need for the financial benefits of Indian status.

They shared close ties of kinship as well. The two McLeods were brothers, descendants of a Scot and his halfbreed wife Jane (Turner). Blacksmith Moore was married to their sister. When William McLeod's wife Ellen (Mark) died, he married Andrew Morrison's daughter Frances.

Mowat's postscript to the petition stated that the signers represented "various absentees at Charlton & on HBC vessels." In addition to the previously mentioned Tom Taylor, a number of these absentees can be identified. They included slooper George Moore aboard the steamer *Inenew*, and his wife Emma (Morrison). Two of their sons married into the McLeod and Archibald families, while another married a daughter of Chief Fred Mark; the poet Gordon Moore was their grandson. Another prosperous halfbreed, George Moore, had a credit balance of £353 in 1905.[52]

The seeming prosperity of these halfbreeds contrasts with the bleak picture of poverty painted by Edward Barnes Borron two decades earlier:

As long as they remain unmarried they can live, and even save money. Few, however, do this; the far greater number marry Indian or half-breed women. The single ration, together with what the wife may be able to add by fishing and hunting, suffices the young couple for a while. But as child after child is born, the annual pittance of wages is drawn upon not only for clothing but for food. At the prices charged . . . in this territory, the man's wages will not go very far. The quantity of game and fish at or near the trading posts is neither great nor at all times to be procured. And when the families are large and chiefly girls, they are, I fear, sorely pinched to live. If the father dies, their condition is still more pitiable. . . . It is a mystery to me how many of them do live.[53]

Another seaman was Augustine (Gus) Untergarden, or Udgarden (now Gunner), son of a Norwegian and his halfbreed wife Harriet (Turner). Gus's brother Harold had moved to Great Whale River, on eastern Hudson Bay, and married an Inuit woman. Seven other Udgarden siblings evidently left the region for points to the south.

Other halfbreeds had moved to HBC posts in nearby Quebec. James Morrison Jr. had died in 1901, leaving his wife Mary (Turner) and five children who moved to Rupert House. Widower Robert Turner, boatbuilder at Moose Factory, married Annie McLeod and moved to Eastmain. Their son Robert Jr. settled at Rupert House.

Commissioner Duncan Campbell Scott estimated the number of halfbreeds at Moose Factory to be twenty-five to thirty. Reconstructed genealogies, however, suggest that their numbers are in the hundreds. They are scattered across the country. The frequency with which the surname Turner recurs indicates that virtually all were related by birth or marriage to patriarch Joseph Turner Sr. When Bishop David Anderson took Joseph Alexander Turner from Moose Factory to Red River for instruction in 1855, he noted that Turner's uncle was employed by the church as catechist to native missionary Henry Budd at Nepowin on the Saskatchewan River. "Thus," wrote the Bishop, "is the whole country bound together by close links, which are always reappearing here and there."[54]

Many descendants of these halfbreeds still live in the James Bay region. During the early 1970s, local affiliates of the Ontario Métis and Non-Status Indian Association (OMNSIA) were formed in Moosonee and Moose Factory. Voluntary members of these local associations include two categories of people. First are the "métis," descendants of the petitioners and other halfbreeds living in Ontario or Quebec when Treaty No. 9 was signed. (Many of the older generation are still uncomfortable about being called métis, a recent introduction.) The second category consists of non-status or enfranchised Indians and Indian women who have lost their status through marriage to non-Indians.

Advised of their claim since 1973,[55] descendants of Ontario's James Bay halfbreeds have been cautious in pressing for compensation. The offer from Matheson of 160 acres of land might be seen as an opening offer in their negotiations. More than three-quarters of a century after the signing of Treaty No. 9, the idea of a change in their status is a very difficult and complex issue for the petitioners' heirs to contemplate. If they press for special compensation as halfbreeds or métis, what form should their settlement take, for example, hunting rights, educational benefits or rights, a cash settlement, a land base, guarantees of political representation?

Pat Chilton (a descendant of Robert Chilton I, who served the HBC from 1793 to 1812), who has been actively involved in the Moose Factory and provincial OMNSIA organizations, referred the claim to OMNSIA's provincial office. OMNSIA president Duke Redbird subsequently requested that métis and non-status Indian rights be included in the 1982 Canadian constitution. Canada's then justice minister, Jean Chrêtien, rejected the request. Chrêtien argued that "the claims of métis were general and largely undocumented." OMNSIA was unwilling to press the claim, fearing that extinguishing the well-documented Moose Factory situation might jeopardize consitutional negotiations on aboriginal rights of native people not recognized under the *Indian Act*. In the end, Canada's Charter of Rights and Freedoms entrenched aboriginal, treaty and other rights, but failed to define them to the satisfaction of the métis.[56]

An argument might also be made that the Moose Factory and Revillon Frères halfbreeds were discriminated against, and should have been given Indian status as were their Albany River counterparts. There is a weakness in this argument, however. They *were* denied Indian status initially, but it might be argued that the other petitioners did not want to be included; if they had, they would have protested like William Archabald and might also have been successful. The chiefs of the Indian bands in the Treaty No. 9 region, the governing body of Grand Council Treaty No. 9 (formed in 1972 but restructured as the Nishnabe-Aski Nation in 1984), agreed to support the halfbreeds' claim in 1982. The whole question of Indian status is now undergoing a change as a result of the sexual equality provisions of the Canadian Charter of Rights and Freedoms. Numerous non-status Indians now living in Moosonee and Moose Factory could be repatriated to their former bands.[57] Alternatively, though it is a very remote possibility, the Moose Band could absorb these people, together with the halfbreeds, if it were to receive additional land and resources.

At the local level, in Moose Factory and Moosonee, there is a lively interest in the resolution of this legacy from 1905. The Moosonee OMNSIA local has become more formally organized, with an office in the town Friendship Centre. In the spring of 1981, it hosted a northeastern Ontario OMNSIA zone seminar in Moosonee. In 1983, the northeastern zone became incorporated as the Aboriginal People's Alliance of Northern Ontario. (The acronym APANO means "let's sit down" in Cree.) The Moosonee OMNSIA local presented a brief to the Special Committee on Indian Self-Government at hearings in Moose Factory in July, 1983, mentioning the halfbreed claim.

On the evening of February 16, 1984, APANO, in cooperation with the provincial office of OMNSIA and its national counterpart, the Native Council of Canada, hosted a public meeting on aboriginal rights and the constitutional process in the Anglican parish hall at Moose Factory. A newspaper advertisement explained that the purpose of the workshop was to inform "the Half-Breed Indian people of the region, recently known as Métis" and the non-status Indians of recent developments in constitutional talks.[58]

About two dozen individuals attended the February, 1984, meeting chaired by Earl Danyluk of Moosonee (a descendant of John L. Iserhoff, North West Company servant at Waswanipi in 1819–1820),[59] who has been active in leadership roles in the Moosonee OMNSIA local and in APANO. APANO treasurer Bert Morrison Jr. of Timmins (a grandson of Philip Morrison) and Shin Imai, APANO legal counsel, explained APANO's structure. Speeches were given by provincial and national native political leaders. Most of the meeting was videotaped, another indication of the organization and sophistication of the Moosonee OMNSIA local.

A slide presentation outlined the treaty-signing process and the exclusion of certain halfbreeds, their petition and government response, and their potential claim to Indian status or special compensation as halfbreeds. Legal counsel Shin Imai indicated that his preliminary research confirmed a solid basis for such a claim by descendants.[60] The meeting lasted from 7:30 until 11:30 p.m. It culminated in a motion, carried unanimously, to proceed with follow-up action on the petitions of George and William McLeod, Andrew Morrison, William Moore and those they represented in 1905. Following the meeting, fourteen people came forward to sign their names to a "new petition" – a descendants' and potential beneficiaries' list.

Some descendants have married Indians and are now members of the Moose Band. Others have married non-status Indians, who may seek repatriation of their Indian status. Others can trace their roots to northern Quebec, and are possible beneficiaries of the James Bay and Northern Quebec Agreement of 1975.[61] The latter have formed an organization known as MoCreeBec, which is investigating, among other questions, the establishment of a beneficiaries' land base in Moosonee or Moose Factory.

In addition to the complex personal issues at stake, future inter- and intra-community political relationships will be redefined if the claim is resolved. What would be the relationship between the Moose Band and a potential halfbreed or métis entity? What advantages and disadvantages would there be to the band in supporting the descendants' claim to Indian status? If the descendants sought a separate land base or reserve, would it be in Moosonee or in Moose Factory?

Declared a people apart by government rejection in 1905, these people have maintained a unique sense of identity over the years. Treaty commissioners denied them "Indian" status. The Cree refer to them as *wemistikosheekan* 'not really a Whiteman'[62] or as *apet'ililew* 'half Indian'. They refer to themselves by a variety of terms including *halfbreed, métis* and Earl Danyluk's *Indian halfbreeds*.[63] Hospitals in Moosonee and Moose Factory in the 1980s label them, and all other non-Indians, as "white status." What they will become is uncertain; they are now on the threshold of negotiating a new identity through a comprehensive land claim.

NOTES

Costs of attending the Newberry Library (Chicago) Conference on the Métis in North America, where an earlier version of this paper was presented, were offset by the generosity of the Social Sciences and Humanities Research Council of Canada, whose assistance is gratefully acknowledged.

I would like to thank a number of individuals and organizations for their help at various stages of my research. First and foremost, I am grateful to numerous friends and neighbours who are descended from the "halfbreeds" mentioned, and who have provided information. Herbert McLeod and Willie Faries (both now deceased), Willie Moore, Bert Morrison Sr., Harry Moore Jr. and Fred Moore were especially knowledgeable and hospitable. Pat Chilton and Earl Danyluk gave the final draft a critical reading. Just after this article was submitted for publication, David McNab offered numerous helpful comments and criticisms, most of which were incorporated into a revision; he also alerted me to the existence of additional Ontario government records, including the original petition. I am grateful for his assistance.

I am also indebted to Jennifer Brown and Sylvia Van Kirk, whose writings have contributed greatly to my understanding of James Bay social history. Thanks also to the Ontario Public School Teachers' Federation, the Moose Factory Island Public School Board, Munroe Linklater (former Chief of the Moose Band), the Ontario Métis and Non-Status Indian Association, Shirlee A. Smith (Hudson's Bay Company Archives), David Hume (Public Archives of Canada), John Leslie and Dennis F.K. Madill (Treaties and Historical Research Centre, Department of Indian and Northern Affairs), Teresa Thompson and Dorothy Kealey (General Synod Archives, Anglican Church of Canada), the Archives of Ontario, Bishop Caleb J. Lawrence (Anglican Diocese of Moosonee) and Canon Redfern E. Louttit, D.D. (St. Thomas Anglican Church).

1 Gordon Moore, *Poems of James Bay* (Cobalt: Highway Book Shop, 1977), 6.

2 The word *métis* could have been used as a convenient but arbitrary and historically inaccurate alternative for designating certain descendants of fur trade company families usually referred to as "halfbreeds" by contemporaries and by themselves. Another expression from folk biology, *mixed bloods,* has been avoided for two reasons. The first is that genes, not blood, mix when people from two racial groups produce children. Second, use of the term *mixed blood* implies that there are *full bloods,* and it would likely be impossible to identify a racially pure group. The word *halfbreed* was resorted to with some reluctance, due to its racial implications and possible derogatory connotations.

It could be argued that everyone has mixed ancestry, supplied by a mother and a father. The expression *people of mixed ancestry* is used in this discussion in reference to the descendants of what Jennifer Brown calls fur trade company families, and in particular to Hudson's Bay Company families. Emphasis is on their mixed or bicultural backgrounds, *not* their biracial characteristics. For convenience, the contemporary term *halfbreed* is used as a synonym. See: Jennifer S.H. Brown, *Strangers in Blood: Fur Trade Company Families in Indian Country* (Vancouver: University of British Columbia Press, 1980); "Linguistic Solitudes and Changing Social Categories" in *Old Trails and New Directions: Papers of the Third North American Fur Trade Conference,* ed. Carol Judd and Arthur J. Ray (Toronto: University of Toronto Press, 1980), 147–59.

The word *Indian* is used here only in its specialized legal sense, as defined in the *Indian Act.* Some James Bay Indians have a family tradition of bush-oriented hunting and gathering, while others have a post-oriented fur trade company family tradition. The former are here referred to as native or Cree hunters, the latter as Indian halfbreeds. In practice, the division is not this neat. Hunters can combine their hunting with seasonal employment or abandon the bush life. Alternatively, some descendants of (Hudson's Bay) Company families opted for the bush life. The *Indian Act* R.S., c. 149, s. 1, defines an Indian as "a person who pursuant to this Act is registered as an Indian or is entitled to be registered as an Indian."

All the above categories are included under the umbrella term, *native people*. Europeans or Euro-Canadians are referred to as non-natives.

The group name *Cree* is thought to be derived from the French pronunciation of *Kristinaux*, variously spelled. Jesuit missionaries learned of the Cree as early as 1640. At that time the Cree did not participate directly in the fur trade with Europeans, who were centred along the St. Lawrence River. Instead, they obtained trade goods through the Nipissings and other native middlemen. See: F.W. Hodge, *Handbook of Indians of Canada* (Ottawa: King's Printer for Geographic Board of Canada, 1912; reprinted by Coles Publishing Co., Toronto, 1971), 117-21; Bruce Trigger, *The Children of Aataentsic: A History of the Huron People to 1660*, 2 vols. (Montreal: McGill-Queen's University Press, 1976), 1:352.

3 Daniel Francis and Toby Morantz, *Partners in Furs: A History of the Fur Trade in Eastern James Bay 1600-1870* (Kingston: McGill-Queen's University Press, 1983); Charles A. Bishop, "Demography, Ecology and Trade Among the Northeastern Ojibwa and Swampy Cree," *Western Canadian Journal of Anthropology* 3 (1972):58-71; Arthur J. Ray, "Fur Trade History as an Aspect of Native History" in *One Century Later: Western Canadian Reserve Indians Since Treaty 7*, ed. Ian A.L. Getty and Donald B. Smith (Vancouver: University of British Columbia Press, 1978); Brown, *Strangers in Blood;* Sylvia Van Kirk, *"Many Tender Ties": Women in Fur-Trade Society 1670-1870* (Winnipeg: Watson and Dwyer, 1980); Joseph Schull, *Ontario Since 1867* (Toronto: McClelland and Stewart, 1978); Robert Choquette, *Ontario: An Informal History of the Land and Its People* (Toronto: Ministry of Education and Ministry of Colleges and Universities, 1984).

4 E.E. Rich, *Hudson's Bay Company 1670-1870,* 2 vols. (Toronto: McClelland and Stewart, 1960)1:36-81. Though known to the Company for years as Rupert House, the post is now officially designated Fort Rupert by the Government of Quebec. It is referred to as Rupert's House or Waskaganish (Small House) by most James Bay residents.

5 Bishop, "Demography, Ecology and Trade"; E.E. Rich, ed., *Moose Fort Journals 1783-85* (London: Hudson's Bay Record Society, 1954), xxix; Toby Morantz, "The Fur Trade and the Cree of James Bay" in *Old Trails and New Directions: Papers of the Third North American Fur Trade Conference,* ed. Carol Judd and Arthur J. Ray (Toronto: University of Toronto Press, 1980), 39-58. See also Charles A. Bishop, "The First Century: Adaptive Changes Among the Western James Bay Cree Between the Early Seventeenth and Early Eighteenth Centuries" in *The Subarctic Fur Trade: Native Social and Economic Adaptations,* ed. Shepard Krech III (Vancouver: University of British Columbia Press, 1984), 21-53; Francis and Morantz, *Partners in Furs.*

6 Morantz, "Fur Trade and the Cree"; Van Kirk, *"Many Tender Ties,"* 15-16; Rich, *Moose Fort Journals,* 208; Hearne quoted in June Helm and Eleanor Burke Leacock, "The Hunting Tribes of Subarctic Canada" in *North American Indians in Historical Perspective,* ed. Leacock and Nancy Oestreich Lurie (New York: Random House, 1971), 343-74.

7 Hudson's Bay Company Archives (hereinafter cited as HBCA), Moose District Report 1815-16, B.135/e/3. See also Van Kirk, *"Many Tender Ties,"* 72.

8 "Henry Sergeant's Deposition" dated November 4, 1687, is reprinted in W.A. Kenyon and J.R. Turnbull, *The Battle for James Bay 1686* (Toronto: Macmillan, 1971), 106.

9 Brown, *Strangers in Blood,* 159ff.; Van Kirk, *"Many Tender Ties,"* 173.

10 HBCA, Moose River Servants Requests and Resolves 1803, B.135/f/1; E.E. Rich, "Philip Turnor," *Dictionary of Canadian Biography* 4 (1979):740-42; Brown, *Strangers in Blood,* 62.

11 Jean Usher, "Apostles and Aborigines: The Social Theory of the Church Missionary Society," *Social History* 7 (April 1971):28–52.
12 General Synod Archives (hereinafter cited as GSA), Church Missionary Society (hereinafter cited as CMS), Horden to Fenn, February 20, 1889, St. John's Vicarage, Folkestone, microfilm reel (mr) A–115; Horden to Fenn, September 16, 1885, Moose Factory, mr A–113. See also my "Archdeacon Thomas Vincent of Moosonee and the Handicap of 'Métis' Racial Status," *The Canadian Journal of Native Studies* 3 (1983)1:95–116.
13 GSA, CMS, Horden's "Statement Respecting Moosonee" n.d. (1882), mr A–104; Horden to Fenn, February 19, 1884, Moose Factory, mr A–112; Horden to Wright, July 22, 1878, Moose Factory, mr A–103; Horden to Wright, September 9, 1875, Moose Factory, mr A–81.
14 GSA, CMS, Horden journal entry October 28, 1854, mr A–88.
15 HBCA, Moose List of Servants 1814–15, B.135/f/9; B.135/g/27; Brown, *Strangers in Blood,* 206.
16 GSA, CMS, Horden to Lay Secretary, September 11, 1872, Moose Factory, mr A–80; Horden to Fenn, August 22, 1883, Moose Factory, mr A–111; Horden to My dear friend, January 19, 1887, mr A–114.
17 HBCA, B.135/g/74.
18 HBCA, Chipman to Armit, January 14, 1892, B.135/e/31, fos. 2–3.
19 HBCA, B.135/e/33, fos. 7–8.
20 Ibid., fos. 11–12.
21 HBCA, Chipman to Ware, July 3, 1903, A.12/FT 217/2, fo. 19; L.F.S. Upton, "The Wreck of the Eldorado," *The Beaver* 299 (Autumn 1968):27–31; Alan Cooke and Clive Holland, *The Exploration of Northern Canada, 500 to 1920: A Chronology* (Toronto: Arctic History Press, 1978), 294, 297; Ontario Ministry of Natural Resources, "Revillon Frères Trading Company Limited," 17 pp., brochure.
22 Conversations with Herbert F. McLeod, Moose Factory, 1977–79; *Moosonee Mailbag* 2 (October 1902)9:142–43.
23 Conversations with William R. Faries, Moose Factory, 1977–78; Archives of Ontario, "Fur Trade Papers Fort Montizambert" (Ms. 415), July 18, 1902.
24 Archives of Ontario, "Fur Trade Papers Fort Montizambert" (Ms. 415), September 12, 1902, September 9, 1904 and October 25, 1904.
25 See Borron's "Report on the Basin of the Moose River" in Ontario *Sessional Papers* 87 (1890):82. This report, a partial reprint of his 1884 report, actually reads "French, Métis or Half-breeds." On Borron, see Morris Zaslow, "Edward Barnes Borron, 1820–1915: Northern Pioneer and Public Servant Extraordinary," in F.H. Armstrong et al., eds., *Aspects of Nineteenth Century Ontario* (Toronto: University of Toronto Press, 1974), 297–311.
      Parish registers of Anglican marriages, baptisms and burials for the communities of Fort Albany, Moose Factory, Rupert House, Fort George, Mistassini and other James Bay communites have recently been microfilmed by the General Synod Archives of the Anglican Church of Canada. I am grateful to Archivist Teresa Thompson and to Bishop Caleb J. Lawrence for taking this action. Anglican parish records already in possession of the Ontario Archives include Ms 161, Ms 192, Ms 311, and Gs 862287.
      The 1881 Census of Canada is available on microfilm from the Public Archives of Canada. Reel C–13286 includes Eastern Rupert's Land. HBC precursors of church records include the Eastmain records, B.59/z/1 and the Faries-Corston marriage contract, B.186/z/1, in addition to the Moose Factory register in Ontario Archives Ms 161. My sample of HBC servants' records included: Albany 1803 (B.3/f/1), Moose 1803 (B.135/f/1),

Eastmain 1810 (B.59/f/7), Albany 1810 (B.3/f/7), Churchill 1810 (B.42/f/5), Moose 1810 (B.135/f/8), Churchill 1811 (B.42/f/6), Eastmain 1811 (B.59/f/8), Churchill 1812 (B.42/f/7), Albany 1814–15 (B.3/f/8), Great Whale River 1814–15 (B.372/f/1/), Kenogamissi 1814–15 (B.99/f/1), Moose 1814–15 (B.135/f/9), Southern Department 1823–24 (B.135/g/4), Southern Department 1843–44 (B.135/g/27), Southern Department 1853–54 (B.135/g/37), Southern Department 1863–64 (B.135/g/46), English River 1866 (B.89/f/1), Southern Department Abstract of Accounts 1891–92 (B.135/g/74); the school records found in K.G. Davies, ed., *Northern Quebec and Labrador Journals and Correspondence 1819–35* (London: Hudson's Bay Record Society, 1963), 342; and Jennifer Brown, "A Colony of Very Useful Hands," *The Beaver* 307 (Spring 1977):44. It is apparent from the HBC records that there were successive and concurrent waves of male sojourners from certain families from Scotland and the Northern Isles to James Bay, e.g., the many Linklaters, Mowats and Louttits.

26 HBCA, B.135/a/189, f. 65d–74, 92d–95; Fortesque [sic] to Chipman, September 15, 1891, B.135/e/31, fo. 4; Chipman to Reed, December 18, 1894, A.12/FT 243/1, fo. 5; Reed to Chipman, December 26, 1894, and Chipman to Ware, December 29, 1897, A.12/FT 243/1, fos. 6, 20. Pre-treaty school grants were also extended: see John S. Long, "Education in the James Bay Region During the Horden Years," *Ontario History* 70(June 1978)2:75–89.

27 Canada, Sessional Papers, *Annual Report of the Department of Indian Affairs, 1904–1905* (Ottawa: King's Printer, 1906), xviii; John S. Long, *Treaty No. 9: The Indian Petitions 1889–1927* (Cobalt: Highway Book Shop, 1978); G.R. Stevens, *Canadian National Railways*, vol. 2 (Toronto: Clarke Irwin, 1962), 137; Ontario Crown Lands Department, *A Statement Concerning the Extent, Resources, Climate and Industrial Development of the Province of Ontario, Canada* (Toronto: King's Printer, 1901 and 1903); Donald Pugh, "Ontario's Great Clay Belt Hoax," *Canadian Geographic Journal* 90(1975):19–24.

28 E.K. Brown, quoted in E. Palmer Patterson, "The Poet and the Indian: Indian Themes in the Poetry of Duncan Campbell Scott and John Collier" *Ontario History* 59 (1967):69–78; quotation is from p. 73. See also Gerald Lynch, "An Endless Flow: D.C. Scott's Indian Poems," *Studies in Canadian Literature* 7 (1982)1:27–54.

29 Derek Smith, ed., *Canadian Indians and the Law: Selected Documents 1663–1972* (Toronto: McClelland and Stewart, 1975), 121, 145–148. See also *The Historical Development of the Indian Act* (Ottawa: Treaties and Historical Research Centre, Indian and Northern Affairs, 1978).

30 John S. Long, *Treaty No. 9: The Half-Breed Question, 1902–1910* (Cobalt: Highway Book Shop, 1978), 3–6. The legal disputes are abstracted and fully cited in Thomas S. Abler et al., *A Canadian Indian Bibliography 1960–1970* (Toronto: University of Toronto Press, 1974), 323–24.

31 Long, *Treaty No. 9: The Half-Breed Question,* 1–6.

32 Holland's comments are in the Moose Factory Preacher's Book 1904–1917 deposited at the Diocesan office, Schumacher, Ontario; Public Archives of Canada (hereinafter cited as PAC), Pedley to Matheson, November 21, 1905; and D.C. Scott and Samuel Stewart "Education, Treaty 9," RG 10, vol. 3093, file 289, 300.

33 Conversations with Canon R.E. Louttit, D.D. and Munroe Linklater, 1981.

34 The photographs are in the Ontario Archives (Acc. 2475, S7677 and S7678). Quotation is from GSA, CMS, Horden to Fenn, September 9, 1872, Moose Factory, mr A–80.

35 PAC, Treaty 9 Annuities Paylists 1905–09, RG 10, vol. 9550; Chipman to Pedley, May 11, 1904, RG 10, vol. 3033, file 235, 225–1. On the finances of annuity payments see PAC RG 10, vol. 3034, file 235, 225–24.

36 Copy of petition with Mowat's comment in PAC RG 10, vol. 3093, file 289, 300. Original is in file 186220, Indian Treaty #9, Ontario Ministry of Natural Resources, Toronto.

37 Long, *Treaty No. 9: The Half-Breed Question,* 7–9.

38 PAC, Stewart to McKenzie, January 29, 1910, RG 10, vol. 3093, file 289, 300. See also PAC RG 10, vol. 3105, file 309, 350–53.

39 PAC, McLean to Ramsden, May 2, 1906, RG 10, vol. 3097, file 297, 171; McLean to Ramsden, September 20, 1909 and Ramsden to McLean, December 15, 1909, RG 10, vol. 3093, file 289, 300; Louttit to McKenzie, November 28, 1909, RG 10, vol. 3093, file 289, 300. Biographical information on Ramsden can be found in *Toronto Municipal Handbooks* 1903–36, the Toronto *Globe,* August 20, 1932, and his obituary in the *Globe,* December 29, 1948. His personnel file (PAC RG 10, vol. 3097, file 297, 171) contains additional information.

40 Fred Bodsworth, *The Sparrow's Fall* (Garden City, N.Y.: Doubleday, 1967) 32–33; PAC, Dobie to McLean, October 20, 1912, RG 10, vol. 3105, file 309, 350–3.

41 HBCA, Groundplan of Moose Factory 1895, B.135/e/32; Gerald Hodge, "Moose Notes (II)," *Ministikok* (November 1970); a copy of the Deed of Surrender can be found on pp. 287–96 of Hartwell Bowsfield, ed., *The Letters of Charles John Brydges 1879–1882, Hudson's Bay Company Land Commissioner* (Winnipeg: Hudson's Bay Record Society, 1977).

42 PAC, Haythornthwaite to Department, January 5, 1914, RG 10, vol. 6203, file 467-1, part 1. Railway surveyors had visited the region after Treaty No. 9 was signed; see St. Thomas Anglican Church Preacher's Book, August 17, 1905.

43 From William McLeod's contract, copy made with the permission of his son, the late Herbert F. McLeod.

44 PAC, Holmes to McLean, February 11, 1907 and Secretary to Holmes, February 26, 1907, RG 10, vol. 467-1, part 1.

45 Bruno Carl Yurkowski, "Attitudes and Policies of Ontario Governments Toward Agricultural Colonization in the Clay Belt Districts 1892–1940" (M.A. thesis, University of Western Ontario, 1972); Peter A. Cumming and Neil H. Mickenberg, eds., *Native Rights in Canada* (Toronto: General Publishing Co., 1972), 2nd ed., 201; PAC, Indian Treaties – Treaty 9, Commutation and Enfranchisement, General Correspondence 1933–1951, RG 10, vol. 8595, file 1/1-11-14, vol. 1.

46 PAC, Ramsden to McLean, September 8, 1909, RG 10, vol. 3093, file 289, 300; conversation with Richard Neff, Moose Factory, June 15, 1981; conversations with Herbert F. McLeod and William E. Moore, Moose Factory and Moosonee respectively, 1981.

47 Moose Factory Anglican marriage register, June 14, 1886, September 24, 1886 and August 31, 1908; PAC, James Bay Treaty #9 (Consecutive no. 539), RG 10, vol. 1851. See PAC, Treaty 9 Paylists 1911, RG 10 vol. 9551 (Moose Band nos. 112 and 113 refused to enter treaty before due to "superstitious reasons.")

48 Morris Zaslow, *The Opening of the Canadian North 1870–1914* (Toronto: McClelland and Stewart, 1971) 225; PAC, Louttit to McKenzie, December 5, 1909, RG 10, vol. 3093, file 289, 300.

49 St. Thomas Anglican Church (Moose Factory), Register of Burials 1851–1906.

50 Conversations with William E. Moore, Moosonee, June 26, 1981; newspaper clippings, "Trapping Laws Forcing Indians to Ask Relief" and "James Bay's Twin Towns not Worried by Future," from Sam Waller Little Northern Museum, The Pas, Manitoba, were obtained courtesy of Dr. J. King, Keeper, Museum of Mankind, Burlington Gardens, London, England.

51 From William McLeod's contract; conversations with Herbert F. McLeod, Moose Factory, 1977–81.

52 HBCA, A. 16/24 Officers and Servants Ledger, Moose Factory, 1878–1909. See E.B. Borron's report in the Ontario *Sessional Papers* 87 (1890):84–85.

53 E.B. Borron's "Report" in Ontario *Sessional Papers* 87 (1890):84–85.

54 GSA, CMS, Bishop of Rupert's Land to Fenn, August 8, 1855, Fort Albany, mr A-79.

55 See my *"Born and Brought up in the Country": The Métis of Treaty No. 9,* unpublished report submitted to OMNSIA, March 16, 1979. Basic information on the claim was first distributed in Moose Factory in 1972–73, and was later published as part of "Tricentennial News," a feature of *Ministikok,* a mimeographed Moose Factory newspaper. It was republished in *Moosetalk* (a Moosonee-based newspaper) in November, 1977, and in pamphlet form by the Highway Book Shop, Cobalt, in 1978.

56 "Métis request on rights is rejected by Chretien," *The Globe and Mail* (Toronto) May 5, 1981, 9. On Chiltons, see K.G. Davies, ed., *Northern Quebec and Labrador Journals and Correspondence 1819–35* (London: Hudson's Bay Record Society, 1963), 6n ff.

57 Joanne Wetelainen, "New Organization for Treaty 9" *Wawatay News* 10 (May 1984)5:1; *Indian Self-Government in Canada* (Ottawa: Queen's Printer, 1983), 54–56.

58 *The Freighter* (a weekly Moosonee-based newspaper) vol. 1, no. 12, February 8, 1984.

59 Davies, *Northern Quebec and Labrador,* 4n ff.

60 See Shin Imai and Katherine Laird "The Indian Status Question: A Problem of Definitions" *Canadian Legal Aid Bulletin* 5 (January 1982)1:113–23.

61 Although *The James Bay and Northern Quebec Agreement* (Quebec: Editeur Officiel, 1976) did not discriminate against halfbreeds in defining beneficiaries, only Status Indians and Inuit were included as signatories to the agreement. See its section on eligibility, pp. 13–22. For information on MoCreeBec, contact Allan Jolly, director-chief, MoCreeBec, P.O. Box 4, Moose Factory, Ontario, P0L 1W0.

62 The Cree word, *wēmistikōsiw,* is usually translated as 'whiteman.' In a letter dated December 11, 1981, linguist C. Douglas Ellis suggested this word is likely derived from *omistikōsiw* 'he has a wooden boat.' The roots *ōš* (noun, inanimate, canoe or boat) and *mistik* (noun, inanimate, wood or timber) not to be confused with *mistik* (noun, animate, a tree), combine to form the compound *mistikōš* 'wooden boat.' Ellis goes on to state, "From the regular formation, *omistikōšiw* 'he has a wooden boat,' would be derived the noun, *wēmistikōšiw* 'one having a wooden boat,' by the regular mechanism of vowel change in the first syllable of the word. This term would likely have been used to describe seventeenth-century Europeans, who reached James Bay in wooden ships.

    The nominal affix *-ihkān* means a surrogate of some sort; see C. Douglas Ellis, "A Note on Okima.hka.n," *Anthropological Linguistics* (March 1960):1. The resulting word, *wēmistikōsihkān,* can be interpreted loosely as 'halfbreed,' 'métis,' 'made like a whiteman,' or 'not really a whiteman.'

63 Conversation with Earl Danyluk, March 14 1984; Cumming and Mickenberg, *Native Rights in Canada,* 5–9, 148. Although some might argue that terminology is unimportant, Earl Danyluk feels that it is important to emphasize "Indian" status under the *British North America Act of 1867* (not under the *Indian Act*). When Rupert's Land was transferred to Canada, it was done with the stipulation that "any claims of Indians to compensation for lands required for purposes of settlement shall be disposed of by the Canadian Government."

Grande Cache:
The historic development of
an indigenous Alberta métis population

Trudy Nicks and Kenneth Morgan

Grande Cache is a small métis community located on the eastern slopes of the Rocky Mountains, some eighty miles northwest of the resort town of Jasper, Alberta.[1] The population, which includes just over two hundred of the estimated seventy-five thousand métis in Alberta, is referred to as the Grande Cache métis. Although the community has been geographically isolated and its members have been non-literate until recent times, its development can be reconstructed from vital events and social and economic data found in records of the Roman Catholic Church, the Hudson's Bay Company, from a variety of federal and provincial government agencies, and from additional historical and demographic data gathered through fieldwork in the community.

The present population of Grande Cache is largely descended from free trappers who settled in the area in the early nineteenth century. The community is an indigenous development of subarctic west-central Alberta, with origins which were contemporary with, but quite independent of, the métis groups at Red River. Although the Grande Cache population has historical continuity in a demographic and genealogical sense, its members have not always been identified as métis by themselves or by outsiders. During the fur trade they were known as freemen; following Confederation they were commonly called halfbreeds or métis by outsiders. Their own adoption of the term *métis* appears to be related to the recent urban and industrial development of the Grande Cache area.

The Cree-speaking métis population came to the attention of the general public in the mid-1960s when extensive coal mining operations were begun along the Smoky River. With the mines came an instant town populated by nearly four thousand people, most of whom were skilled miners and their

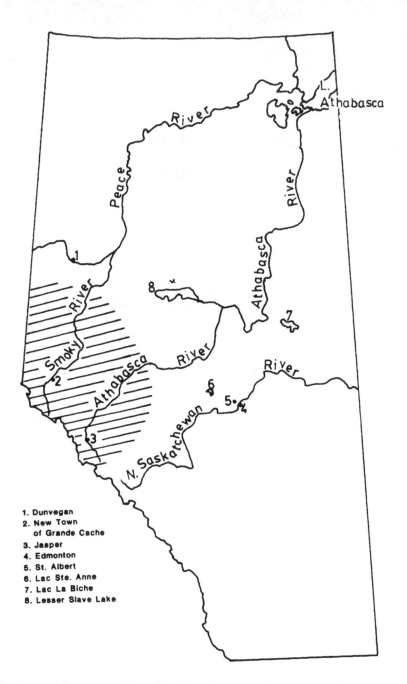

Province of Alberta, around 1970. Shaded area indicates estimated extent of hunting and trapping area used by Grande Cache métis.

families from Great Britain and the Maritime provinces of Canada. The métis had no forewarning of the urban and industrial development intended for their area; as squatters on crown land they had not been consulted before plans were drawn up for the mines, the town, and the railway, which was built in 1966 in anticipation of resource development.

Although legally squatters in the mid-1960s, the native people who watched the invasion of their homeland had roots in the area extending back for more than 150 years. The founders of the population included Iroquois freemen who had begun trapping fur-bearing animals along the Smoky River as early as 1803.[2] In 1819 the Hudson's Bay Company trader at Fort St. Mary's post near the confluence of the Peace and Smoky Rivers noted the presence of "a small band of free Iroquois, who are in the habit of killing a large quantity of furs" toward the foot of the Rocky Mountains.[3]

Iroquois males had come to the West both as fur company employees and as trappers without formal contracts.[4] They followed the westward expansion of the fur trade more by choice than necessity. As Alexander Mackenzie noted about a group which had settled on the Saskatchewan River in the 1790s, they came to escape the "improvements of civilization" in the East and to live the life of their forefathers.[5] Their services, as well as those of several Ojibwa bands, were much in demand during the years of rivalry for the rich Athabasca fur trade. While most of them ultimately returned to the East, a number preferred to remain permanently to hunt and trap as freemen.[6]

The Iroquois who moved up the Smoky River found a region rich in furs but not in game animals. Historic records suggest that they faced little or no competition for the region.[7] Local Indian groups, and indeed many freemen who were equally committed to fur trapping, preferred to work in regions where subsistence was less precarious. Of fifty-eight Lesser Slave Lake freemen (mostly French Canadian) whom the Hudson's Bay Company tried to convince to hunt in the region between the Athabasca and Smoky rivers in 1823, only five actually went to the area. The other fifty-three promised to do so, took the extra supplies of ammunition offered as inducements, and set their course either for Peace River or for Lac La Biche as soon as they were out of the Lesser Slave Lake postmaster's sight.[8]

Hunting and trapping bands in the subarctic have always faced the problem of seasonally and spatially variable resources. The solution to the problem is for the bands to be mobile over large tracts of land, a subsistence pattern resulting in a very low population density.[9] The Grande Cache people, in fact, used a wide area stretching north and south along the eastern slopes between the lower Smoky and Athabasca Rivers and eastward toward Lesser Slave Lake (see map 1). It was a pattern common across

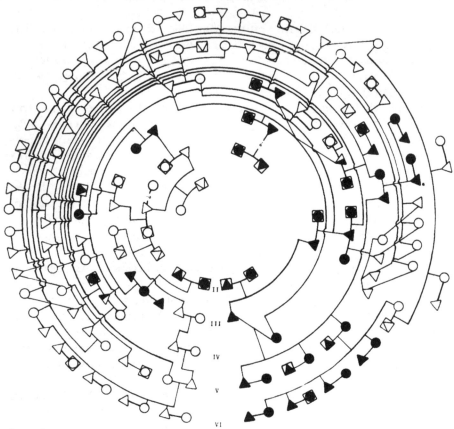

Legend

●▲   Reside at Jasper

○△   Reside at Grande Cache

◐▲   Reside in Peace River area

☐◪   Fur company employee or free-
      man, or descendant of same.

   △   Male

   ○   Female

A. Joachim family

B. Wanyande family

C. Delorme family

D. Moberly family

E. McDonald family

Figure 1
Marital alliances in contemporary and ancestral generations of the Grande Cache métis population.

northern Alberta: small mobile population units exploited areas large enough to contain the diversity of resources necessary to sustain life. The fur traders' journals and reports reveal something of the distribution of these populations. Regional bands of 150 to 500 people normally functioned as small extended family units or local bands interconnected by networks of kinship.[10]

During the fall and winter seasons, in particular, the population was distributed in small extended family groups. In spring and summer large groups might have come together in favourable locations, for example where fish or berries were plentiful, or at mission stations. Trading posts to some extent attracted ingatherings, but these were discouraged from continuing for any length of time by the traders who considered such groups to be unproductive and even a potential threat. The ingatherings facilitated socializing, arranging of marriages, and the establishment of new economic partnerships among kin for the coming fall and winter. The larger kinship network thus constituted a flexible system through which its members could be most effectively distributed in relation to the resources necessary for subsistence.

The historical pattern of marital alliances for the Grande Cache population reflects the wide geographical area which became home to the Iroquois trappers and their descendants (see figure 1). The pattern of extensive intermarriage in early generations is what would be expected with a widely dispersed small population in which marital alliances are formed between families who associate at spring and summer ingatherings.[11]

The five métis kin groups residing in the area in 1975 can be traced to men represented in the earliest fur trade records for the region. Ignace Nawanionthe had come to the Athabasca district by or before 1813.[12] In the 1818–1819 records he appeared as Ignace Waniante, a free trapper from the Smoky River area, and most probable founder, with a Sekani wife, of the Wanyande family whose contemporary members now live in the shadow of coal mines and tailing ponds.[13] Joachim Tonatanhan signed in Montreal in 1818 to work in the Athabasca district for the North West Company.[14] In 1853 Father Albert Lacombe formalized Tonatanhan's marriage of many years to a local native woman at Jasper.[15] Over the years his descendants have come to be known by his first name, Joachim.

The founders of the Delorme family were men employed by the Hudson's Bay Company in the Lesser Slave Lake district in the 1820s.[16] The McDonald and Moberly families were founded in the mid-nineteenth century when immigrants to the area married Findlay and Cardinal females, respectively, who were descendants of freemen who had come to the area

early in the century. Henry John Moberly, an Ontario-born postmaster at
Jasper House in the 1850s, was one founder who did not remain in the
area.[17] The family he founded, however, has become one of the largest
represented in the contemporary Grande Cache population.

From its founding, the Grande Cache métis population has been largely
endogamous, finding mates among fur company employees, or freemen, or
their descendants. Marriages outside the five named kin groups in figure 1
have been with mates from families founded by French Canadian and
European males carrying the surnames Findlay, Berland, Fraser, Cardinal,
Campbell, Gaucher, Chastellain, Gladu, Desjarlais and Plant.[18] Another
Iroquois freeman by the name of Karaconte is represented among the ancestors of the Grande Cache population.[19] Among the Indian groups
represented, primarily through female founders, are Sekani, Beaver, Cree
and Ojibwa.

The mobility of the population comprising the Grande Cache métis kinship network is further reflected in the patterns of movement over the
lifetimes of individual members of the group, as well as by a comparison of
birth and marriage locations for spouses.[20] Individuals have tended to
marry away from the place where they were born, and also to select a mate
from a birth locality different from their own. There has also been a greater
tendency for males than for females to change residence locality. This
would be consonant with a recorded tendency among native populations in
northern Alberta for males to move in with their wives' relations for a period of time after marriage.[21] This tendency has been reported for subarctic
hunting and trapping populations in other areas as well.[22]

Always off the beaten track in their eastern-slopes home, the Grande
Cache population can be glimpsed through the records kept by the traders
at whose posts they outfitted and sold furs, and by missionaries and government officials with whom they occasionally came in contact. The
missionaries in particular were welcomed, for the Iroquois and French
Canadian founders alike came from a strong Roman Catholic background
in Quebec.[23] It was the establishment of the Lac Ste. Anne mission in
1842, as much as the proximity of the major trading centre at Edmonton,
that drew members of the eastern-slopes group to the Edmonton area in the
summer months. A number of the visitors even opted to settle near the missionaries and in time signed an adhesion to Treaty 6 as the Michel Band.[24]
In the summer months of 1885 and 1886 the members of the North West
Half Breed Scrip Commission met many of the eastern-slopes group at the
missions around Edmonton and took their applications for scrip.[25]

The limitations of such external observations can be seen in a series of
population estimates given in table 1. The erratic pattern of growth proba-

TABLE 1
Casual estimates of population size for Grande Cache métis.

Year	Estimated population size
1820s	23 hunters regularly come into Jasper House[a]
1838	28 children from 16 nuclear families baptised[b]
1846	44 individuals baptised[c]
1856	200 Indians regularly trade at Jasper House[d]
1857	30 tents of "Iroquois half-breed Freemen" at Jasper or 150 people[e]
1879	6 families of Iroquois at Jasper House[f]
1882	13 families of Iroquois at Jasper House[g]
1889	6 families of Iroquois on south side of Peace River[h]
1935	150 "Halfbreeds" reside at Grande Cache[i]
1975	238 native people live at Grande Cache[j]

[a] HBCA B.115/a/6 Lesser Slave Lake Post Journals 1822–23.

[b] M.D.M. Warner and H.D. Munnick, *Catholic Church Records of the Pacific Northwest: Vancouver Volumes I and II and Stellamaris Mission*. St. Paul, Oregon: French Prairie Press, 1972.

[c] P. DeSmet, *Life, Letters and Travels of Father Pierre-Jean DeSmet, S.J. 1801–1873*. New York: Francis Harper, 1905.

[d] "Indian Population." Report from the Select Committee on the State of the British Possessions in North America which are under the Administration of the Hudson's Bay Company with Minutes of Evidence, Appendix and Index. British Parliamentary Papers. Colonies, Canada, 1857 (280 Sess. II) Vol. XV.

[e] Great Britain. "Journals and Reports relating to Captain Palliser's Exploration of British North America." British Parliamentary Papers. 1863 (3164) Vol. XXXIV (200).

[f] HBCA: B.60/b/3.

[g] HBCA: B.60/b/5.

[h] HBCA: B.56/e/3 Dunvegan Post Inspection Report, Peace River District. 1889.

[i] PAA.69.90 Letter of J.J. Soper to E.A. Braithwaite, Alberta Halfbreed Commission, 16 March, 1935. Papers relating to the Royal Commission on the Condition of Halfbreeds in Alberta. Provincial Archives of Alberta.

[j] Trudy Nicks, Grande Cache field notes.

bly reflects a tendency toward under-enumeration since the observers were seeing only a part of a widespread and mobile population.

The growth of the Grande Cache population is more accurately illustrated by the distribution of cohorts of 917 births ascertained from historical records and field data (table 2). After founding, population growth appears to be mainly the result of natural increase. Of the 917 births ascertained, 798 have been local, that is, they occurred within the geographical region identified by the kinship network already described. The decline in the fifth and sixth cohorts is explained by the 1918–1920 world-wide influenza epidemic which reached even this relatively isolated area. While no claim is made that

TABLE 2
Distribution of birth by 25-year cohorts for Grande Cache métis population (eleven ante-natal deaths excluded).

Cohort	1	2	3	4	5	6	7	
	Pre-	1825–	1850–	1875–	1900–	1925–	1950–	
Birth locality	1825	1849	1874	1899	1924	1949	1975	Total
Grande Cache			6	21	26	78	156	287
Jasper	14	80	84	81	63	19	50	391
Grande Cache/Jasper	18	22	21	27	14	12	6	120
Peace River		1	1	8	4	4	2	20
Edmonton	2	6	10	20	4	1	2	45
Lesser Slave Lake		1	3				1	5
Out of region	13	3	2	2	1	11	5	37
Unknown	4	3	4	1				12
TOTAL	51	116	131	160	112	125	222	917

Sources: Based on family reconstructions and linkage to archival data.

the 917 births represent a complete ascertainment of all people ever born or resident in the area, the births identified at least appear to be a representative sample insofar as they break down into a realistic sex ratio of 471 males to 437 females (table 3).

The beginning of the twentieth century brought the first major encroachment from the developing world beyond the eastern slopes. With the creation of Jasper National Park in 1907 all native squatters were evicted from homes and traplines inside its borders. Those evicted moved down the Athabasca River Valley to an area just beyond the eastern boundary of the park. In the years following 1907, many of them found seasonal employment on guiding and outfitting parties for tourists visiting the new park. In the summer of 1911 the Grand Trunk Pacific Railroad was moving toward Jasper and again native men found opportunities, if they wanted them, for wage labour on survey and construction crews.

Threats of eviction from the area north of Jasper Park came with the creation of the Athabasca Forest Reserve in 1916 and again with the planned land sales and leases of grazing areas by the provincial government in the 1930s. These threats, fortunately for the local people, were not carried through.

The 1930s also brought legislation requiring the registration of traplines and the establishment of the Royal Commission on the Condition of the

TABLE 3
Sex distribution by birth cohorts for population residing in Grande Cache neighbourhood.

Birth cohort	Males		Females		Unknown	Total	
Pre–1825	21	(13)	30	(2)		51	(15)
1825–49	51	(7)	61	(4)	4	116	(11)
1850–74	66	(10)	65	(6)		131	(16)
1875–99	87	(18)	73	(12)		160	(30)
1900–24	59	(3)	51	(6)	2	112	(9)
1925–49	60	(10)	64	(6)	1	125	(16)
1950–75	127	(6)	93	(4)	2	222	(10)
Total	471		437		9	917	

Note: Figures in parentheses indicate number of individuals in count who were born outside the referent area.
Sources: Based on family reconstructions and linkages to archival data.

Halfbreed Population of the Province of Alberta.[26] Trapline registration had the effect of stabilizing movement patterns to some degree as people gained legal licence to the use of specified areas. During the winters, the people were out on set traplines, while in spring and summer they congregated at campsites on the eastern slopes or at Lac Ste. Anne.

The Royal Commission of 1935 could have changed the course of history for the Grande Cache métis population. The Métis Association of Alberta recommended to the Commission that one of several proposed métis farming settlements be established in the Grande Cache area. The Commission recommended that the provincial government assist members of the proposed settlements to establish a firm economic base to alleviate the poverty then general among métis populations in the province. Under the Métis Population Betterment Act of 1938, which resulted from the work of the commission, métis people were required to set up a settlement association to govern the land which the government would set aside for them.

No settlement was ever established in the area of Grande Cache, for reasons which are not clear. Perhaps the people chose not to establish the required settlement association, even though some of them had initially shown interest in the idea of a settlement.[27] It has also been suggested that the government may have rejected the recommendation because too much land in the area had already been reserved for other purposes. By the time of the commission large tracts of land had already been set aside for Jasper National Park and the Athabasca Forest Reserve.[28]

By the mid-twentieth century the outside world had made significant further encroachments into the Grande Cache area. Old pack trails were replaced by oil and forestry roads in the 1940s and 1950s. As well as providing faster access to commercial centres to the north and south of Grande Cache, the roads have facilitated travel by outsiders into the region. A church and school were opened in the area in 1958. The school commenced full-time operations in 1961.

Hunting and trapping were still viable occupations despite these developments and the Upper Smoky River area still provided a refuge from "civilization" as the decade of the 1960s dawned. But the fact remained that the métis held no legal title to the area and thus were only able to watch the unfolding of plans for the industrialization of the area which had been concocted in government and company offices in cities hundreds of miles away.

A belated claim for aboriginal title, made with the assistance of white cultural brokers, won a provincial government grant of 4,150 acres of land in 1972.[29] This grant covered only the seven small settlement sites in the vicinity of the New Town of Grande Cache which were occupied by native people when the urban and industrial development began.[30] Certainly the land holdings granted to the métis are inadequate to support a hunting and trapping lifestyle, but such concerns are now largely academic. The construction and mining activities have destroyed many traplines and driven many of the game animals away from the region, effectively bringing to an end a lifestyle which had predominated for a century and a half.

As hunting and trapping resources disappeared in the 1960s and 1970s, the need for cash to pay for food, shelter, clothing and land taxes increased. Many members of the native population began to move into the local wage labour market on a full-time basis, rather than casually as had been the rule in previous decades. Grande Cache métis took above-ground jobs in the coal-mining industry, worked for a local small-scale logging company, or found service jobs in the New Town. A few individuals worked for the provincial government or attempted to set up their own outfitting businesses.

Because hunting and trapping have been replaced by wage labour as the basis of subsistence, the traditional pattern of seasonal mobility has all but disappeared. Trapping is now a secondary activity, usually done on days off from a regular job. The New Town now provides many of the goods and services which people previously travelled to outside communities to obtain. The annual pilgrimage to Lac Ste. Anne now lasts exactly the four days required primarily for travel and participation in the religious activities; in the past it had been part of a summer ingathering of social, economic, and religious significance spread out over an entire summer.

The urban and industrial development at Grande Cache has in the past attracted large numbers of British and Canadian immigrants. These newcomers are increasingly represented in marriages in the most recent generations (VI and VII on figure 1) of the métis population. The observed changes in mobility and marriage patterns suggest that the Grande Cache métis are losing their ties to the old kinship network which was once so integrated with their success as hunters and trappers.

The first years of adjusting to the development of their homeland have been marked by extensive social disruption in the Grande Cache métis community.[31] The task of re-orienting a lifestyle around the new developments has been made more difficult in the 1970s and 1980s by the instability of the coal market which has periodically resulted in mine shutdowns and the emigration of mining families from the town. Each time such events occur, the opportunities for wage labour are reduced.

The métis population now living in the Grande Cache area represents the most recent stage of an indigenous development of almost two centuries. Other studies published in this volume also trace local development of métis populations in several areas across North America.[32] It would thus appear that métis studies are already well on the way to overcoming the "Red River myopia" which has been characteristic in the past.

As an extant Alberta métis population which developed independently of Red River, Grande Cache may prove to be a typical rather than an exceptional case. On the basis of a preliminary analysis of migration patterns from data recorded in the applications made before the North West Half Breed Scrip Commission of the late-nineteenth century (tables 4 and 5) it appears that other métis communities across northern Alberta have had origins equally separate from Red River. People from Red River virtually colonized the adjacent areas of Saskatchewan and Assiniboia, but they appear to have settled far less frequently in the area which today comprises northern Alberta.

This conclusion may require some qualification, for Manitoba-born immigrants who had participated in the 1870 scrip issue in Manitoba would not have been eligible to apply for North West Half Breed scrip and thus would not be represented in the records on which the conclusion has been based. An independent source of information, however, suggests that the present results should not be far wrong. The Northern Engagement Registers of the Hudson's Bay Company show a progressive isolation of the area throughout the nineteenth century.[33] In the first half of the century

TABLE 4

Rank order of migration by birthplace into areas covered by North West Half Breed Scrip Commissions, 1885–1901. Sample of first marriages for males.

NWHB area	Birthplaces of people who married in an NWHB area															
	Lower Peace River	Upper Peace River	Smoky River/Jasper	Upper Athabasca	Lesser Slave Lake/Lac la Biche	Other Athabasca	Other Alberta	Saskatchewan	Assiniboia	North	Manitoba	British Columbia	East	United States	Other continents	Sample Size
Lower Peace River	2	1	5		6	9	7	8		[3]	4					48
Upper Peace River		2	1		5	8	[3]			6	4			7		80
Smoky River/Jasper		3	1		4		[2]									18
Upper Athabasca							[1]									1
Lesser Slave Lake/ Lac la Biche	11	7	6	9	[1]	8	2	4	10	5	3		13	14	12	379
Other Athabasca	6	4			7	[2]				1	3	5	8			55
Other Alberta	12	10	5	9	3	13	1	4	8	6	[2]		7	11		544
Saskatchewan		9	12		6	10	[4]	1	5	3	2		8	7	11	410
Assiniboia		7			6		5	4	2	8	[1]			3	9	175
North		8			5	7		3		[1]	2		6		4	149

Note: Absolute frequencies of these two events have been added and then converted to rank order of immigration sources for each NWHB area. The rank at which fifty percent of the sample size has been cumulated is enclosed by a square.

most of their employees came from outside the area and they commonly retired to Red River at the end of their careers. After 1850, most employees were local natives. Their employment with the Company was often intermittent, that is, employees would be under contract one year and free the next, over a period of several years. There were almost no retirements to Red River, and thus the ties of kinship which might have attracted immigration from that area were not maintained.

The Red River immigrants recognized in recent northern Alberta métis populations represent late-nineteenth-century migrations as new missions were established and independent trading companies moved in to compete

TABLE 5

Rank order of migration by birthplace into areas covered by North West Half Breed Scrip Commissions, 1885–1901. Sample of first marriages for females.

	Birthplaces of people who married or resided in an NWHB area														
NWHB area	Lower Peace River	Upper Peace River	Smoky River/Jasper	Upper Athabasca	Lesser Slave Lake/Lac la Biche	Other Athabasca	Other Alberta	Saskatchewan	Assiniboia	North	Manitoba	British Columbia	East	United States	Sample Size
Lower Peace River	1	[3]	8		4	5	6			2	7				63
Upper Peace River	5	1	[2]		4		3				6				91
Smoky River/Jasper		2	[1]		3										25
Upper Athabasca															0
Lesser Slave Lake/Lac la Biche	8	3	7	10	[1]		2	4	9	6	5	11			453
Other Athabasca	6				4	1	3	7		[2]	5				56
Other Alberta	12	8	5	13	2		[1]	4	6	7	3	10	11	9	774
Saskatchewan		8			6	10	3	[1]	5	4	2		7	9	756
Assiniboia		6	7		8		5	3	2	10	[1]		9	4	270
North		10	9		7	2	11	3	8	[1]	4	5	6		180

Note: Absolute frequencies of these two events have been added and then converted to rank order of immigration sources for each NWHB area. The rank at which fifty percent or more of the sample size has been cumulated is enclosed by a square.

with the Hudson's Bay Company.[34] These immigrants were an overlay to the métis populations which had been established in the early part of the century.

In the twentieth century, métis history in Alberta has been a phenomenon of the north. The sizeable métis population of southern Alberta in the 1880s has virtually disappeared through migration and loss of ethnic identity as a result of intermarriage with Euro-Canadian immigrants.[35] The Métis Association of Alberta, which estimates the 1981 métis population of the province at 75,000, has only ten out of eighty-four local organizations south of Edmonton. All of the métis settlements established under the 1938

Métis Betterment Act are in the northern part of the province. The 3,400 (in 1981) members of the settlements have their own organization, called the Alberta Federation of Métis Settlement Associations.

The historical study of the Grande Cache métis population serves as a reminder that questions concerning métis origins may have quite different answers depending on the sources consulted. The founding of the population can be well documented, but its identification as métis has historically been a perception of outside observers more often than it has of group members. From founding until the 1880s, members of the group were identified in terms of their Indian or European origins by observers, and, most probably, by members of the group themselves. They were among the freemen trading at Lesser Slave Lake in 1821–22 whom Hudson's Bay Company officer William Connolly identified as "Canadians, Halfbreeds, Iroquois, Sauteux [sic], Courteorielles and Nipisingues."[36] The freemen were a distinguishable social unit, endogamous in their marriage practices and receiving special recognition for their skill as fur trappers from the traders.[37]

With the North West Half Breed Scrip Commission of 1885, government officials recognized the descendants of the Iroquois as métis, or, to use the term then acceptable, halfbreeds. The objective of the scrip commission was political, to settle claims to aboriginal title in preparation for European colonization of the West. The main criterion for eligibility to receive scrip was racial admixture: one's parents had to be European and Indian or descendants of such a union. The biological criterion was a convenient way of identifying those eligible, but it was not an all-encompassing rule. People of racially mixed ancestry were not denied entry to treaty, as a study of virtually any reserve population would demonstrate. On the other hand, it was accepted that treaty "Indians" who could demonstrate biological admixture in their ancestry could renounce their treaty status and receive half-breed scrip. By 1892, 1,313 people in the North West Territories had withdrawn from treaty to take half-breed scrip.[38]

Half-breed scrip provided ready money without the restraints imposed by treaty status. It was therefore a preferable alternative for people who wished to continue an independent existence. The element of choice involved in opting for treaty or scrip irrespective of biological background is illustrated by the population presently considered. The hunters and trappers of Grande Cache chose scrip while their relatives who had taken up agriculture about the missions of Lac Ste. Anne and St. Albert signed Treaty 6. In 1885 Richard Hardisty, Hudson's Bay Company officer at Edmonton, commented on the latter group: "The halfbreed Iroquois settled halfway between Edmonton and Lac Ste. Anne under Michel Calehouis are retired servants and voyagers of the Hudson's Bay Company. They are classed here as Indians because they draw Treaty money. They will now probably accept Scrip, withdrawing from their position, and so become extinct."[39] Some members of the Michel band did withdraw from treaty, but a number opted to remain. After the band was enfranchised in 1958, some former members continued to farm in the area, while several families moved into the city of Edmonton. For the hunters and trappers it was the immediate economic benefit to be gained by applying for scrip that was of greatest interest, not the halfbreed identity implicit in this action.

Elderly informants in the 1970s, though quite conscious of the racial diversity in their background, generally did not dwell on the question of their identity vis-a-vis the outside world. When His Honour Ralph Steinhauer, Canada's first Indian Lieutenant Governor, visited Grande Cache early in the 1970s, he found the local people without a ready answer when he asked them if they were treaty Indians, non-status Indians, or métis.

Grande Cache people in the past had not found it necessary to use any of these labels, in part because of their geographic isolation, and in part because their interactions with Euro-Canadian society traditionally have been mediated by patrons. Using patrons as mediators allowed them the freedom to pursue their own lifestyle without having to become direct participants in another society. As free trappers they manipulated the patron-client relationship quite successfully by dealing with different fur companies or different districts according to the advantages to be gained.[40]

The patron-client system worked well until the urban and industrial development of the Grande Cache area. Contact with the outside world was intermittent, usually by choice, and a variety of patrons, including missionaries, outfitters, forestry officials, and store owners, were available to act on behalf of the native community. Modernization has forced the native community into virtually continuous face-to-face contact with Euro-Canadian society. Traditional patrons and strategies for dealing with external influences no longer served their needs and the Grande Cache people have begun to rely heavily on new patrons.

The first response to the stresses faced in the post-development period was the establishment, with the assistance of patrons with professional training in community development and anthropology, of a local organization, the Native Area Development Committee.[41] This organization enjoyed some early success, most notably in achieving the land settlement with the provincial government in 1972. It failed, however, after the daily leadership provided by the patrons was withdrawn.

The successor to the Native Area Development Committee in defending the interests of the first inhabitants of the Grande Cache area has been the Métis Association of Alberta. Although the Métis Association became active in the area soon after the town was built, it was generally not accepted by local people as long as their own committee functioned. Following the demise of the Native Area Development Committee, the Métis Association in effect stepped in as the new patron for the community.

No other patron with the singular interest in native concerns and the political strength of the province-wide organization has been available to assist the people of Grande Cache in coping with the social and economic difficulties brought about by the modernization of their homeland. With this patron, however, the client is required to become a member of the organization, and to assume its values and objectives. Adopting a new patron has meant adopting the patron's identity.

For the Grande Cache people, adopting a métis identity does not mean that they have lost sight of themselves as a distinct social group. Identifying themselves as métis achieves quite the opposite effect – it ensures their continued distinctiveness in a social, political and economic environment now dominated by Euro-Canadian immigrants. Of all possible identities, métis most closely fits the perceptions which outsiders have historically had of the group and thus is easily accepted by newcomers and government as a basis for interaction. It also perpetuates the distinctiveness from Indian social groups which characterized the freemen of the nineteenth century.

The Grande Cache example illustrates the importance of exploring métis society in terms of dynamic populations if we are interested in learning how it originates and how it is perpetuated. The adaptations which métis, or other social groups, make in order to maintain their identities may prove to be as important for understanding their roots as are those aspects of their culture that have remained unchanged over generations.

NOTES

1 This article is based in part on a doctoral dissertation by Trudy Nicks, "Demographic Anthropology of Native Populations in Western Canada, 1800–1975" (University of Alberta, 1980). Additional research was supported by Social Sciences and Humanities Research Council grant 410–78–0023.
2 Hugh A. Dempsey, "David Thompson on the Peace River, Part II," *Alberta Historical Review* 14(1966):19.
3 Hudson's Bay Company Archives (hereinafter cited as HBCA) B.190/a/2, Fort St. Mary's Peace River Journal, 1819–1820.
4 Iroquois in the western fur trade are discussed in Trudy Nicks, "The Iroquois and the Fur Trade in Western Canada," in C.M. Judd and A.J. Ray, eds., *Old Trails and New Directions:*

Papers of the Third North American Fur Trade Conference (Toronto: University of Toronto Press, 1980), 85–101,

5 W. Kaye Lamb, ed., *The Journals and Letters of Sir Alexander Mackenzie* (Cambridge: Cambridge University Press, 1970), 411.

6 The merger of the XY Company and the North West Company in 1804 resulted in the release of employees inland. Many of these men probably became freemen (Nicks, "The Iroquois").

7 Fur trade records suggest that the freemen who ventured into the eastern slopes area about the upper Athabasca and the Smoky rivers at the beginning of the nineteenth century were entering an uninhabited area. Local legends exist concerning Snare Indians about Jasper who were massacred by Assiniboine Indians early in the contact period. Other Indians frequenting the area were most likely Shuswap from west of the mountains. Members of the Shuswap tribe did come into Jasper House to trade well into the nineteenth century, and it may well have been members of this tribe who met with the Assiniboine, if the local legend is to be credited.

8 HBCA, B.115/a/6, Lesser Slave Lake Post Journal, 1822–1823.

9 In the late nineteenth century the population density for northern Alberta is estimated to have been one person per hundred square miles compared to an estimated density of ten to fourteen people per hundred square miles on the northern plains. Nicks, "Demographic Anthropology," 76.

10 The analysis is presented in Nicks, "Demographic Anthropology," chap. 2.

11 The kinship terminology recorded at Grande Cache in the 1970s is virtually identical with that for Plains Cree cited by David G. Mandelbaum in *The Plains Cree,* Anthropological Papers of the American Museum of Natural History, vol. 37, no. 2. Like the Plains Cree of Mandelbaum's study, the Grande Cache métis were never rigorous in the application of the cross-cousin marriage rule inherent in the terminology. The Cree language appears to have been adopted at an early point in the development of the population. Dr. James Hector of the Palliser expedition noted its use when he visited the Jasper area in the winter of 1858–59 (Great Britain, Journals and Reports relating to Captain Palliser's Exploration of British North America 39 [1863]:124).

12 HBCA, F.4/32, North West Company Ledger 1811–1821.

13 HBCA, B.190/a/1, Fort St. Mary's Peace River Journal 1818–1819.

14 HBCA, F.4/32, North West Company Ledger 1811–1821.

15 Provincial Archives of Alberta, Oblate Records, PAA.71.220.3, "Baptèmes et Mariages faits dans les Missions des Fort des Prairies 1824–1859."

16 HBCA, B.115/d/9, Lesser Slave Lake Account Books, 1823–1824.

17 For a description of his career, see H.J. Moberly, *When Fur Was King* (Toronto: J.M. Dent and Sons, 1929).

18 The earliest reference for each name found in fur trade records from northern Alberta is indicated below.

FINDLAY: brothers, freemen. Recorded in Jasper House post journal for 1827–28 (HBCA, B.94/a/1).

BERLAND: recorded in Jasper House post journals for 1827–28, 1829–30, and 1830–1831 (at Smoky River) (HBCA, B.94/a/1-3).

FRASER: Clerk at Lesser Slave Lake 1821–1822 (HBCA, B.115/d/6).

CARDINAL: in Smoky River area 1818–1819 according to Lesser Slave Lake post journal (HBCA, B.115/a/2).

CAMPBELL: recorded in Edmonton District Report for 1818–19 (HBCA, B.60/e/3).

CHASTELLAIN: a Canadian hired by the Hudson's Bay Company in 1816. Between 1818 and

1820 he was at Fort St. Mary's on Peace River (E.E. Rich, ed., *Journal of Occurrences in the Athabasca Department by George Simpson, 1820 and 1821, and Report* [London: HBRS, 1938]).

GLADU: several men in family, in Smoky River area in 1818–19 according to Lesser Slave Lake post journal (HBCA, B.115/a/2).

GAUCHER or GAUTHIER: Hyacinthe Gauthier listed in Northern Department Engagement Register for 1823 to 1851 as a labourer hired at Lachine in April, 1850 (HBCA, B.239/u/1).

DESJARLAIS: several men in family, interpreter, freemen, identified at Fort St. Mary's on upper Peace River in 1819–1820 in Lesser Slave Lake District Report (HBCA, B.115/e/1).

PLANT or LAPLANTE: François Plante, a Canadian, worked at Lesser Slave Lake and the Rocky Mountains in 1821–22 (HBCA, B.115/d/5).

19 Louis Karaquienthe traded with the North West Company at Dunvegan in 1818–1819 (HBCA, F.4/32).

20 These analyses are presented in Nicks, "Demographic Anthropology," 154–60.

21 An analysis of the composition of bands identified in fur trade journals indicated that they tended to be made up of a man and his sons-in-law or of brothers-in-law (Nicks, "Demographic Anthropology," 40). The Lesser Slave Lake Journal entry for November 13, 1825 illustrates the former instance: "The Petit Gris eldest Son arr'd in the evening from the Gigiers Lodge to Join his Father at the Smoky River Having parted with the Gigiers Daughter who he had for a wife" (HBCA, B.115/a/7).

22 See, for example, studies cited in Charles A. Bishop and Shepard Krech III, "Matriorganization: The Basis of Aboriginal Subarctic Social Organization," *Arctic Anthropology* 17(1980)2:34–45.

23 The Iroquois were from mission villages in Quebec, particularly Caughnawaga near Montreal.

24 They entered Treaty 6 under adhesion no. 157G on September 18, 1878 (Canada, *Indian Treaties and Surrenders From 1680–1902: Treaty Numbers 140–280* [Ottawa: Queen's Printer, 1891. Facsimile edition reprinted by Coles Publishing Company, Toronto, 1971], 2:48).

25 Further information on the North West Half Breed Scrip Commissions can be found in: D.J. Hall, "The Half-breed Claims Commission," *Alberta History* 25(1977):1–8; Trudy Nicks, "Demographic Anthropology," chap. 3; and The Métis Association of Alberta, with Joe Sawchuk, Patricia Sawchuk and Theresa Ferguson, *Métis Land Rights in Alberta: A Political History* (Edmonton: Métis Association of Alberta, 1981).

26 Provincial Archives of Alberta, Report of the Royal Commission on the Condition of the Halfbreed Population of the Province of Alberta, Sessional Paper No. 72, PAA.72.242. This commission is also referred to as the Ewing Commission after one of the members, the Honourable A.R. Ewing, a justice of the Supreme Court of Alberta.

27 Métis Association of Alberta, *Métis Land Rights,* 218.

28 Ibid.

29 See Bruce Morrison, "Stress and Socio-cultural Change in a New Town" (Ph.D. dissertation, University of Alberta, 1977).

30 In Alberta, urban centres experiencing very rapid growth due to industrialization may acquire "new town" status and thereby become eligible for special financial and planning assistance from the provincial government.

31 The early period of adjustment is described in detail in Morrison, "Stress and Socio-cultural Change."

32 See, for example, the articles by Peterson, Dickason, Long and Brown in this volume, and Jacqueline Peterson, "Prelude to Red River: A Social Portrait of the Great Lakes Métis," in *Ethnohistory* 25(Winter 1978)1:41–67.
33 HBCA, B.239/u/1-3, Hudson's Bay Company Engagement Registers, Northern Department, 1823–1851.
34 One such population is described in Patrick C. Douaud, "Métis: A Case of Triadic Linguistic Economy," *Anthropological Linguistics* (December 1980):392–414.
35 Theresa Ferguson, "Métis, Land and Scrip in Southwestern Alberta," *The Métis and the Land in Alberta: Land Claims Research Project* (Edmonton: Métis Association of Alberta, 1980), 57.
36 HBCA, B.115/e/3, Lesser Slave Lake Report on District 1821–1822.
37 The special recognition was particularly true of the pre-1821 period of competition. Connolly went on to say in his 1821–1822 report that the freemen "were, during the late opposition, accustomed to get good[s] to any amount they pleased, and at very reduced prices" (HBCA, B.115/e/3). After 1821, Connolly attempted to withdraw many of the privileges formerly allowed the freemen, with the result that many of them went on strike, preferring to spend their winters along good fishing lakes, troubling themselves "but little about paying their Debts" (HBCA, B.115/e/4). At this time also the freemen began dealing with posts in other districts to obtain supplies refused them by Connolly (HBCA, B.115/e/4).
38 Public Archives of Canada, Department of Interior Records, "List of Halfbreeds withdrawn from Treaty to June 1, 1892," RG10. vol. 3888, file 83, 93.
39 HBCA, B.60/b/3, Edmonton Correspondence Book, 1878–1886. Richard Hardisty to Joseph Wrigley, Commissioner, HB Winnipeg, August 17, 1885.
40 In the late nineteenth century the Hudson's Bay Company records contain several complaints that the Jasper Iroquois and other freemen were in the habit of frequenting posts in different districts, making it difficult to control the trade with them (HBCA, B.60/b/3; B.60/e/13, 14; and B.297/e/1 [Edmonton Correspondence Book 1878–1886]; Saskatchewan [Edmonton] District Reports for 1887 and 1888; and Inspection Report for Lac Ste. Anne's Post, 1889, respectively).
41 Morrison, in "Stress and Socio-cultural Change" (pp. 113–16) discusses patron-client relationships for the Grande Cache population in general and the role of the Native Area Development Committee in particular.

Diasporas and Questions of Identity

III

"Unacquainted with the laws of the civilized world": American attitudes toward the métis communities in the Old Northwest

R. David Edmunds

During the first two decades of the nineteenth century, federal officials in the United States actively pursued a policy of forced acculturation toward the Indian and métis peoples of the Old Northwest. Subscribing to Jeffersonian concepts of the agrarian myth, bureaucrats in Washington and in many of the Indian agencies strongly encouraged tribal people to relinquish their current lifestyles and to become small yeoman farmers. At first, the bureaucrats seemed to achieve some success. In the years preceding the War of 1812, Moravian and Quaker missionaries worked among the tribes of Ohio and Indiana. Sponsored by the government, these evangelists attempted to both convert the souls and alter the lifestyles of the people, baptizing Indians and métis alike, and teaching their followers the precepts of frontier agriculture. Among some communities of Shawnees, Delawares, Miamis and Potawatomi, the missionaries were successful, and by 1808 some of these people had cleared small fields, planted crops of corn, wheat and barley, and were living in log cabins resembling those of their white neighbours. But the changes did not last. The emergence of the Shawnee Prophet and the displacement caused by the War of 1812 did much to undermine the missionaries' influence, and after 1815 the small communities of "civilized" Indians shrank in size and importance. Isaac McCoy, Johnston Lykins and other missionaries continued to encourage agriculture, but their followers were few and, by the mid-1820s, even McCoy admitted that the members of tribal communities in northern Indiana and southern Michigan were not becoming small yeoman farmers.[1]

Other agents echoed his views. In 1830 Lewis Cass reported to officials in Washington that "so far as respects the three great tribes of the Northwest, the Chippewas, Ottawas, and Pottawatomies, I am not aware that any improvement has taken place in their condition within the last eight years . . . On the Contrary, I believe every year adds to the moral and physical evils which surround them." Meanwhile, Superintendent of Indian Affairs Thomas L. McKenney, a former champion of assimilation, toured the Old Northwest and also concluded that the government's "civilization" programs had failed. The Indian and métis people had not become small farmers. Indeed, according to McKenney, their way of life remained the same as that of their forebears. He lamented that the tribal peoples "pretend to do nothing more than to maintain all the characteristic traits of their race. They catch fish and plant patches of corn; dance, paint, hunt, get drunk, when they can get liquor, fight, and often starve."[2]

McKenney and other officials viewed the tribal people as being in a state of cultural stagnation. Although the métis and Indians had adopted a few of the technological advantages of European culture (such as firearms and clothing) and had fallen victim to some of its vices (alcoholism), McKenney and many other Americans believed that Native American culture in the region remained in a static state. Some officials asserted that Indians were incapable of desirable change. Others argued that the "traditional" Indian lifestyle might be altered in the future, but any desirable modification would require the isolation of the Native Americans under the concentrated supervision of government personnel and programs.

Such views, coupled with the western states' hunger for Indian lands, led to the Indian removal policies championed during the administration of Andrew Jackson. During the 1830s most of the tribal peoples in the Old Northwest were removed from their lands to new homes in the trans-Mississippi west, or were pushed into the northernmost regions of Michigan and Wisconsin. Others fled to Canada. This new isolation, according to government spokesmen, would permit this "poor, degraded set of human beings" to follow the ways of their fathers until they finally became capable of making those changes desired by the government. Otherwise, their extinction was assured.[3]

The Anglo-Americans were not the first Europeans to encounter the Indian peoples of the Old Northwest. Early in the 1600s French explorers and voyageurs had penetrated the Western Great Lakes and, in the centuries that followed, other Frenchmen had followed the waterways into the Illinois and Wabash Valleys. By the late eighteenth century the vast majority of Europeans living in the region were of French descent and the creole dialects (dialects spoken by people born in North America, but of French ancestry) of the area had literally become the "lingua franca" of the Great Lakes and Upper Mississippi Valley. As late as the War of 1812, frontier settlements

such as Vincennes, Peoria, Cahokia, Fort Wayne, Prairie du Chien and
Detroit held predominantly French-speaking populations, and in 1816
Lewis Cass estimated that "four fifths" of the white population of Michigan
territory "are that class of population."[4]

Unquestionably, the French-speaking population maintained a close re-
lationship with the Indians. In the colonial period most of the tribes of the
Western Great Lakes had assisted Onontio[5] against the British, and
Howard Peckham has illustrated that disgruntled French creoles near
Detroit encouraged the Indians to rise in Pontiac's rebellion. During the
American Revolution the French from Illinois and Indiana rallied many of
the western tribes against King George, and Siggenauk, a Potawatomi chief
from the Milwaukee region, risked his life to assist the Long Knives
(Americans). Meeting with George Rogers Clark at Cahokia, the
Potawatomi leader impressed Clark with his command of the French language and his adherence to the manners of a French gentleman. Following
the Revolution, traders of French descent remained active among the tribes,
although American officials suspected that some of these individuals now
were using their influence against the United States. In 1814, Benjamin
Parke, in a letter to Thomas Posey, complained that "the descendants of the
Ancient Canadian French . . . are to be found at every village or camp from
our frontier settlements to the Slave Lake, and the Mountains, and by their
employment only, the Northwest Company were enabled to extend their
trade and obtain the Control they now possess over the Indians."[6]

For their part, most of the Indians held only fond memories of their long
association with the French. John Johnston, an Indian agent among the
Shawnees and Miamis in Ohio and Indiana admitted: "I have seen Indians
burst into tears in speaking of the time when their French father had dominion over them"; and when Volney (a French agent) visited the post at
Vincennes, on the Wabash, the Indians, hearing there was a man arriving
from their French father, came in such multitudes to see him that Major
Thomas Pasteur, the commanding officer, became alarmed for the safety of
the fort, sent for Volney and forbade his communicating with the Indians.
And in 1809 William Henry Harrison echoed the same thought: "The hap-
piness they [the Indians] enjoyed from their intercourse with the French is
their perpetual theme – it is their golden age. Those who are old enough to
remember it, speak of it with rapture, and the young ones are taught to ven-
erate it as the Ancients did the reign of Saturn."[7]

By the early nineteenth century the close association between the French
and the Indians created a culture based upon values extracted from both
groups. The new people, the métis, dominated both the French creole and

Indian communities, combining much of the rich heritage from both ancestries. Intermarriage between the two peoples had become common. Tribes
such as the Kaskaskias, Peorias, Miamis, Potawatomis, Ottawas and
Chippewas held large biracial populations, and frontier settlements
throughout the Old Northwest contained significant numbers of métis. At
Detroit, Cass reported that "many of the traders and a great many of the
agents and clerks employed by the companies have Indian or half-breed
wives and the mixed offspring they produce has become extremely numerous." Nicolas Boilvin described the population of Prairie du Chien
(Wisconsin) in similar terms, as did William Keating, who visited Fort
Wayne (Indiana) in 1820. According to Keating, "the inhabitants [of Fort
Wayne] are chiefly of Canadian origin, all more or less imbued with Indian
blood . . . it is almost impossible to fancy ourselves still within the same territorial limits [of the United States]."[8]

Yet the métis had ties to their French ancestors other than those of
blood. In contrast to the agriculturally oriented British settlers, the early
French inhabitants of the Old Northwest had been coureurs de bois, voyageurs and engagés: traders, not farmers. Not surprisingly, by the early
nineteenth century most of the métis men were following in their fathers'
footsteps. The fur trade held many attractions. Traders were men of wealth
who enjoyed economic and political influence, yet were not tied down to
farms and the back-breaking labour required to maintain them. Moreover,
the close ties of the métis to the Indian communities gave them access to and
certain advantages in dealing with the providers of furs. As cultural brokers, the métis spoke the tribal languages and were welcome in the Indian
camps. At the same time, because many of them had the rudiments of a
European education, they were able to function in the world of frontier
commerce. Indeed, many métis were so adept at the trade that British and
American firms attempted to hire them as agents. Most, however, continued to remain self-employed. Of particular note was Jean Baptiste
Richardville, of Miami and French extraction, who kept a trading house at
Fort Wayne. Richardville was so successful that in 1816, when Indiana entered the union, he was reputed to be the richest man in the state.[9]

Métis participation in this commerce spanned the entire region. On the
Mississippi, Judge John Lucas reported that almost all the French and métis
inhabitants "of St. Louis, St. Charles, and other french [sic] settlements,
have derived their chief support either Mediately or Immediately from that
trade . . . as their principal means of support; agriculture was a secondary
object." Cass reported similar economic activity at Detroit, while other observers described métis communities dominating the trade at Vincennes,
Fort Wayne, Chicago, Green Bay, and Michilimackinac.[10]

Meanwhile, the acculturation process, which had begun centuries earlier, continued. Just as the creole French once had served as acculturation models for their biracial descendants, the métis in turn were prototypes for many of the remaining Indians. Not only did métis hire Indian tribesmen as agents in the latters' home communities, but some of the Indians were employed as seasonal labourers around the trading posts while others, in true engagé fashion, served as porters, transporting merchandise over the portages between rivers.[11]

Early American ideas of the métis people of the Old Northwest are contradictory. On one hand the métis were seen as a people who had adopted many of the traits of their French forebears. Most spoke French, answered to French surnames, and followed a lifestyle reminiscent of the creole population that had settled in the region during the seventeenth and eighteenth centuries. Although few métis lived lavishly, most were comfortable by frontier standards, and a significant minority had become wealthy through the Indian trade. Unquestionably, they served as important instruments in the commerce of the Great Lakes and the Upper Mississippi Valley. They were an important minority group rapidly adapting to European ways, who played a major role in the economic development of the region.

Why then were the métis forced out by the Americans? Why did American officials urge that the métis people and the Indian emulating them be removed to new lands beyond the Mississippi? How could McKenney, Cass, and others argue that these people remained in a cultural limbo and were incapable of taking their place in nineteenth century America?

The answer lies in the ethnocentric viewpoint of the Americans and in their vision of the future development of the United States. Admittedly, the métis differed from the Anglo-American frontier population which was pouring into the Old Northwest. And these differences, coupled with the métis' close association with the Indian communities, made them objects of suspicion. Although many métis spoke French in addition to several Indian languages and were able to maintain extensive trading ventures, the Americans considered them ignorant because many spoke no English. Americans new to Indiana complained that their contacts with the métis had "a surprising, and to say the least, an unpleasant effect; for the first twenty-four hours the traveller fancies himself in a real Babel." Reflecting their English heritage, American pioneers also took a dim view of the interracial marriages that had produced the métis in the first place. Captain Jonathan Fulton described the biracial inhabitants of Green Bay as being of "mongrel" descent, while William Keating complained that Fort Wayne "contains a mixed and apparently very worthless population. The inhabitants are chiefly of Canadian origin, all more or less imbued with Indian blood." At

Detroit, Cass echoed such views charging that the métis settlers possessed the vices of both races while failing to inherit their virtues.[12]

What shocked other Americans was the métis' adherence to certain material aspects of Indian culture. Although such complaints seem strange in a region where almost everyone wore some leather clothing, Adam Walker, a member of the Fourth Regiment of the United States Army who passed through Vincennes, Indiana, in 1811, objected strongly to the métis' buckskin garments. When métis militia helped to pull his boat ashore, he described them as a "rabble whose appearance caused us to doubt whether we had not actually landed among the savages themselves." According to Walker, "many of these militia spoke the French language; their dress was a short frock of deer-skin, a belt around their bodies, with a tomahawk and a scalping knife attached to it, and (they) were nearly as destitute of discipline as the savages." At Fort Wayne, Keating was also shocked that métis traders dressed similarly to their Indian kinsmen:

To see a being whom, from his complexion and features, we should expect to find the same feelings which swell in the bosom of every refined man, throwing off his civilized habits to assume the garb of the savage, has something which partakes of the ridiculous, as well as the disgusting. The awkward and constraining appearance of those Frenchmen [Métis] who had exchanged their usual dress for the breech-cloth and blanket, was as risible as that of the Indian who assumes the tight-bodied coat of the white man. The feelings which we experienced while beholding a little Canadian stooping down to pack up and weigh the hides which an Indian had brought for sale, while the latter stood in erect and commanding posture, were of mixed and certainly not of a favorable nature.

At Detroit, William Hull also complained that the métis had adopted many aspects of Indian culture. Worst of all, they openly fraternized with the Indians. "From their infancy they have been in the habit of friendship with the Indians – and in a variety of respects there is a great similarity and connection between them. The Indians are as familiar and as much at home in the homes of these people, as the people themselves."[13]

Yet for the Americans, the métis' greatest shortcoming was that they had no interest in becoming small yeoman farmers. To the American settlers flocking into the Old Northwest, this lack of interest was the worst sacrilege imaginable. The settlers believed that because the métis and their Indian kinsmen were not farming the region, they were wasting it. Indeed, the métis position as a role model for the Indian people made them doubly undesirable, for if the Indians ever became as self-sufficient as the métis were, they might never be removed. And, of course, the tribes still held legal title to large acreages of potentially good farmland, land that might remain un-cultivated.

Charges of agricultural ignorance were rampant in the Americans' de-nunciations of their métis neighbours. At St. Louis, John Lucas complained that the creole and métis populations had been so lax in their claims and ag-ricultural practices that Anglo-Americans had difficulty in ascertaining just which lands remained unclaimed. In Michigan, William Hull denounced the métis farms as being no better than those of the Indians. But it was Lewis Cass, later to become a cabinet member and presidential candidate, who was most critical of all. Cass charged that "as traders . . . they spend one half of the year in labor, want and exposure, and the other in indolence and amusements. Associated with the Indians, they contracted their man-ners, and gained their confidence. As a necessary consequence their farms were neglected and the agricultural products of the Country formed a small proportion of the subsistence of its inhabitants." Indeed, their farms "shew the extreme defect of agricultural knowledge," for the métis farmers threw manure into the river rather than spreading it upon their fields, and refused to raise sheep to supply themselves with wool garments. Cass complained that métis women, unlike the sturdy wives of Anglo-Saxon settlers, refused to spin or weave their families' clothing, for "a pound of wool is not manu-factured in the Territory by any person of Canadian descent." The only possible solution, according to Cass, was a migration into the region, of American settlers, who might teach the métis new ways, or more probably, the removal of the métis population from the territory, otherwise "we shall have a number of indigent, helpless people, the supply of whose wants will exceed any means which the Government should raise from the people of this Country."[14]

It is obvious that the métis people and many of the Indians had made great strides toward accepting certain European values. Although American leaders complained that they were indigent, many métis main-tained a standard of living comparable to that of American settlers. But, to the Americans, they had accepted the *wrong* European culture, that of the creole French. Moreover, their close ties with the remaining Indian com-munities made them doubly undesirable. Therefore, the onrushing Americans deemed them "unacquainted with the laws of the civilized world,"[15] and urged that they be removed along with the rest of the tribal people. Although the new United States prided itself upon becoming a melt-ing pot, settlers demanded that the crucible forge models in their own image. The métis were made of a different substance. They were not farmers, so ac-cording to the settlers, they had no place in the future of the Old Northwest.

NOTES

1   A good discussion of American Indian policy during this period can be found in Francis
    Paul Prucha, *American Indian Policy in the Formative Years: The Indian Trade and Intercourse
    Acts, 1790–1834* (Lincoln: University of Nebraska Press, 1970), and in Bernard Sheehan,
    Seeds of Extinction: Jeffersonian Philanthropy and the American Indian (Chapel Hill: Univer-
    sity of North Carolina Press, 1973). Also see: Joseph A. Parsons, "Civilizing the Indians of
    the Old Northwest, 1800–1810," *Indiana Magazine of History* 61 (September 1960):195–216;
    R. David Edmunds, "Redefining Red Patriotism: Five Medals of the Potawatomis," *Red
    River Valley Historical Review* 5 (Spring 1980):13–24; and George A. Schultz, *An Indian
    Canaan: Isaac McCoy and the Vision of an Indian State* (Norman: University of Oklahoma
    Press, 1972).
2   Lewis Cass to Thomas McKenney, February 11, 1830, U.S. Congress, Senate, 21st Congress,
    first Session, Senate Document 110, 14; Report by McKenney, March 22, 1830, U.S.
    Congress, Senate Document 110.
3   John Tipton to McKenney, January 31, 1830, U.S. Congress, Senate Document 110, 13–14.
    See also: Herman J. Viola, "Thomas L. McKenney," in Herman J. Viola and Robert
    Kvasnicka, eds., *The Commissioners of Indian Affairs, 1824–1977* (Lincoln: University of
    Nebraska Press, 1979), 5; Ronald N. Satz, *American Indian Policy in the Jacksonian Era*
    (Lincoln: University of Nebraska Press, 1975), chap. 1.
4   Petition by the Inhabitants of Michigan, January 23, 1809, Clarence E. Carter, ed., *The
    Territorial Papers of the United States, 27 vols. (Washington: Government Printing Office,
    1934–), 10:226–28; Memorial to Congress by the Inhabitants of Peoria, December 20, 1813,
    Carter, *Territorial Papers,* 16:379–83; Isaac Darnielle to John Breckinridge, October 22,
    1803, Carter, *Territorial Papers,* 7:133–34; William H. Keating, *Narrative of an Expedition to
    the Source of the St. Peter River,* 2 vols. (London: George P. Whittaker, 1825), 1:79; Nicolas
    Boilvin to the Secretary of War, March 5, 1811, Carter, *Territorial Papers,* 14:154–57; Lewis
    Cass to the Secretary of War, May 31, 1816, Carter, *Territorial Papers,* 10:642–45.
5   Onontio was the term that the Algonkian-speaking tribes of the Old Northwest used in
    referring to the governor of New France.
6   Benjamin Parke to Thomas Posey, November 18, 1814, Letters Received by the Secretary of
    War, Main Series, Record Group 107, National Archives M221, Roll 65, 8346–8348. See
    also: R. David Edmunds, *The Potawatomis: Keepers of the Fire* (Norman: University of
    Oklahoma Press, 1978), 39–58; Howard H. Peckham, *Pontiac and the Indian Uprising*
    (Princeton: Princeton University Press, 1947), 95–97; George Rogers Clark to John Brown,
    1791, *Collections of the Illinois State Historical Society,* 34 vols. (Springfield: Illinois State
    Historical Library, 1903–), 8:252–55.
7   John Johnston's Recollections, Frank J. Jones Collection, Cincinnati Historical Society;
    William Henry Harrison to the Secretary of War, July 5, 1809, Logan Esarey, ed., *Messages
    and Letters of William Henry Harrison* 2 vols. (Indianapolis: Indiana Historical Commission,
    1922), 1:349–55.
8   "Extracts from Franklin's Narrative," Lewis Cass Papers, William L. Clements Library,
    University of Michigan, Ann Arbor; Boilvin to the Secretary of War, March 5, 1811, Carter,
    Territorial Papers, 14:154–57; Keating, *Expedition,* 1:79. Also see: Parke to Posey, November
    18, 1811, M221, Roll 65, 8346–8348; and "On the Prophet," George Winter Papers,
    Tippecanoe County Historical Society, Lafayette, Indiana.
9   Bert Anson, *The Miami Indians* (Norman: University of Oklahoma Press, 1970), 188–90;
    Wallace Brice, *History of Fort Wayne* (Fort Wayne: D.W. Jones and Son, 1868), 293–94;

Edmunds, *The Potawatomis,* 226–27; Cass to William Crawford, May 31, 1816, M221, Roll 68, 1376–1380; Harrison to Dearborn, March 3, 1803, in Esarey, *Harrison Letters,* 1:77–84; Cass to Noah Noble, January 5, 1826, Office of Indian Affairs, Letters Received, Record Group 75, National Archives M234, Roll 300, 28–29.

10 John Lucas to Henry Dearborn, February 9, 1807, Carter, *Territorial Papers,* 14:93–97; Cass to George Graham, July 19, 1817, *Collections of the Michigan Pioneer and Historical Society,* 40 vols. (Lansing: Thorp and Godfrey, and others, 1874-1929), 36:340 – 43; Jonathan Fulton to Richard Johnston, October 8, 1816, Records of the Secretary of War Relating to Indian Affairs, Letters Received, Record Group 75, National Archives M271, Roll 1, 1275-1285; Cass to Crawford, May 31, 1816, M221, Roll 68, 1376-1380; Park to Posey, November 18, 1814, M221, Roll 65, 8346-8348; Noah Dashney to John Calhoun, June 15, 1824, M234, Roll 747, 136.

11 Gerrard Hopkins, *A Mission to the Indians From the Indian Committee of Baltimore Meeting to Fort Wayne in 1804* (Philadelphia: T. Elwood Zell, 1862), 62, 88; C.C. Trowbridge to Cass, January 22, 1825, Trowbridge Papers, Burton Historical Collection, Detroit Public Library; Thomas Dean, *Journal of Thomas Dean* (Indianapolis: C.E. Pauley Co., 1918), passim; Ernest E. East, "Contributions to Chicago History from Peoria County Records," *Journal of the Illinois State Historical Society,* 31 (April 1938):341–42; E. Reed to Cass, Potawatomi File, Great Lakes-Ohio Valley Indian Archives, Glenn A. Black Laboratory of Archaeology, Indiana University, Bloomington; Gurdon S. Hubbard, *The Autobiography of Gurdon Saltonstall Hubbard* (Chicago: Lakeside Press, 1911), 146–47.

12 Keating, *Expedition,* 1:79; "Extracts from Franklin's Narrative," Cass Papers, Clements Library; Fulton to Johnston, October 8, 1816, M271, Roll 1, 1275–1285; Keating, *Expedition,* 1:79; Lewis Cass, "Indian Treaties and Laws and Regulations," Cass Papers, Clements Library.

13 Adam Walker, "A Journal of Two Campaigns of the Fourth Regiment of U.S. Infantry," in Esarey, *Harrison Letters,* 1:697; Keating, *Expedition,* 1:79–80; Hull to Eustis, July 20, 1810, Ottawa File, Great Lakes-Ohio Valley Indian Archives.

14 John Lucas to Henry Dearborn, February 9, 1807, Carter, *Territorial Papers,* 14:93–97; Hull to Eustis, July 20, 1810, Ottawa File, Great Lakes-Ohio Valley Indian Archives; Cass to the Secretary of War, May 31, 1816, M271, Roll 68, 1376–1380.

15 "Extracts from Franklin's Narrative," Cass Papers, Clements Library.

Diverging identities:
The Presbyterian métis
of St. Gabriel Street, Montreal

Jennifer S.H. Brown

In North America of the late twentieth century, it has become fashionable and even normal to wear, more or less visibly, some label of ethnic identity and to display it by various symbolic means. Whether involuntarily or by choice, most of us become ethnics; for censuses, or with a diversity of political, economic, or psychological motives, we check ourselves into one or another ethnic pigeonhole, no matter how varied or undocumented our ancestors may have been. Ethnicity, as Karen Blu noted in her study of the Lumbee Indians of North Carolina,[1] has not only gained ground as a means of classifying people; it is also the foundation for both personal and expressive declarations about one's "roots," and for a variety of interest groups who seek power and legitimacy and need members and converts – people who elect an ethnic identity that they had formerly rejected, concealed or had been unaware of.

Ethnic movements exhibit strong tendencies to redefine the past – or better, a multiplicity of pasts – in terms provided or actively promoted in the present. The growth and cultivation of ethnic identity may be seen as a centripetal process; of the varied strands of individual and group histories, certain ones are sorted, drawn together and interwoven to form a strong core, a heart or centre that gives integrity (in all its senses) to people's lives and personalities. The Newberry Library Conference on the Métis in North America was, among other things, an expression of our times – of a dynamic present in which concerns about ethnic roots, history, survival and political and economic rights are vigorous and widely shared. Among the métis of the Canadian West, Montana, Ontario and elsewhere, such concerns have recently gained a momentum that is demonstrated in the current intensity of political, organizational and publishing activity.[2]

Métissage, or the process by which this population arose, is a term that has been used with two meanings which need to be carefully distinguished. Biologically, it is the creation of persons of mixed Indian-white parentage and the mingling of groups characterized by distinctive traits such as blood group gene O, so widely distributed in New World aboriginal populations.[3] For the purposes of this discussion, however, it is the social, cultural and political creation of persons who accept or decide to affirm that "we are métis," taking that dual aspect of their ancestry and affiliation as a central fact of life.

An effort has been made to avoid the term *mixed-blood* because of its connotations for English speakers. Although blood cannot "mix," English folk biology, reflected in language usages, suggests that it can, and uses the word as a gloss for shared genetic substance ("blood" relatives are closest and most real; "blood" is thicker than water; "blood lines" are lines of descent; a purebred animal is also a "pureblood").[4] These unconscious and rather insidious linguistic habits tighten their hold upon us when we translate the etymologically neutral French term, *métis,* by using a term emphasizing blood, in the absence of good English alternatives.

The centripetal processes by which modern métis identities are being constructed and maintained have proved richly productive of research and synthesis, stimulating the mining of untapped sources of information, the devising of new analytical approaches, and the study of communities long neglected or misunderstood. Some of the new work has vital legal implications as it uncovers past governmental abuses and neglect, and as it attempts to chart a better course for the future under Canada's new Constitution. Data recently assembled by the Native Council of Canada, the newly founded Métis National Council and the Manitoba Métis Federation, for example, have reopened questions about the handling of "halfbreed" claims in the making of Canada's numbered Indian treaties, and about the abuses that followed upon the Manitoba Act of 1870 which specified that 1,400,000 acres were to be allotted to the children of the "halfbreeds" in that new province.[5] The great range and variety of recent writing in other social, cultural, literary and linguistic domains are reflected in a rapidly expanding number of other publications,[6] as well as in this volume.

There is always some risk, however, that historical work done in response to the perspectives and pressing concerns and needs of the present may distract us from understanding people of the past on their own terms, in all their complexity and variability. The viewpoints and interests of the living are readily projected onto the dead, who regrettably refuse to answer our queries and questionnaires or to dispute our interpretations. We cannot, for example, ask the nineteenth-century Atkinson or Richards families of James

Bay or the Anglican clergyman James Settee of Manitoba (all of Hudson's Bay Company [HBC] and Cree descent), or the Connolly, Rowand or Barnston offspring in Montreal (all North West Company native families) how they felt about their mixed ancestry. We can only infer their opinions (or lack thereof) from the incomplete records that they and others have left, and try to avoid co-opting them into groups or categories that were absent from or irrelevant to their own lives and communities. One thing we have been learning, after all, is that the northern fur trade of the seventeenth to nineteenth centuries was a multiplicity of social settings, too shifting and variable to allow unitary categorization of all the biracial individuals born in its midst.[7]

In fact, in counterpoise to the understandably centripetal tendencies of much modern ethnic historiography, the fur trade is better viewed as centrifuge, that is, spawning a diversity of persons and groups who were spun off, so to speak, into numerous different niches and categories in the period from the mid-eighteenth to mid-nineteenth centuries. Rather than a unified, bounded society, the fur trade was the meeting ground of many Indian communites and two major groups of specialized, relatively transient European traders – the English HBC men with their royal charter, remote directorship, and salaried "servant" status, and the Montreal-based Scottish and French entrepreneurs who coalesced into the dominantly Scottish North West Company after 1784. Given their trade and fur-extraction orientation, neither company aimed to build a stable new society in the Northwest; there was no sponsorship of settlement and colonization by company personnel until the HBC support of efforts to found Red River in 1811–12 and thereafter. This meant that traders, whatever their degree of commitment to their native wives and children acquired during their careers, were given no option for permanent, secure retirement in the places where they had worked. HBC men were shipped back to England with an occasional family member, perhaps a son, in tow, unless they found their way to the Montreal region to retire, as a few did between 1810 and 1820. Among the old Nor'Westers of the Canadian-based trade, in contrast, low-ranked employees, usually of French descent, might become "freemen" and form their own homes and ties with métis and Indian kin and friends, away from the posts where they had worked. The Scottish Nor'Westers who were typically the higher-ranked partners and clerks sooner or later withdrew to eastern Canada, perhaps with some of their children, but usually without the native mothers.

The effects of these centrifugal forces on fur-trade families were considerable. No strong company sanctions kept parents and children together in long-term co-residential units. Often, in fact, the demands of fur-trade life imposed considerable pressures against their maintenance, as for HBC men whose familial ties violated company rules in the first place, and for men travelling to different points far inland. Marriages "according to the custom of the country" were widely accepted, but the seriousness with which these ties were treated varied with individual traders' moral stances, as did the priority they were granted when conflicting with business and practical considerations.[8]

Given these varied circumstances, mixed-descent offspring of white traders and native women found and were assigned a variety of social positions and identities. Numerous eighteenth- and early-nineteenth-century HBC descendants were absorbed into the "homeguard" bands that took shape around the major HBC posts, and were classed as Indian. Others who took countless low-level jobs around the posts became known at times as "natives of Hudson's Bay," a category of persons who, although possessing close, interlocking familial ties, did not coalesce as a political force in their early days and lacked (or were spared) distinguishing labels such as métis (or halfbreed) to give focus to their uniqueness. Still others, in much smaller numbers, faded into white society outside the Indian country.

A comparable diversity of destinies awaited the progeny of the Montreal Nor'Westers and Indian women. Some disappeared into Indian societies, and some into white. Most distinctive was a third population whose members, like their French predecessors, found a semi-independent life with freemen and métis already settled in the Indian country.[9] In this particular group, more or less connected with the North West Company as the context of its most rapid growth and maturation (both demographic and political) lay the genesis of the mid-nineteenth-century métis (or in older English translation, halfbreed) sense of identity and pride, the ramifications of which are still spreading among modern métis, and among collateral biracial groups whose ancestors would have found the concept of métis identity unfamiliar and foreign.

The registers of the St. Gabriel Street Presbyterian Church in Montreal provide a core of data for the study of a group of Nor'Westers' progeny – potentially métis – who experienced the fur trade as centrifuge, finding themselves cast at young ages into a new urban world remote, in most instances, from the sites of their early childhoods. For the first forty years of its existence, from 1796 to 1835, the St. Gabriel Street Church witnessed a relatively small but distinctive and continuing influx of strangers of mixed descent. During these years, the clergy of the church baptized and/or buried eighty-nine children whose parents were connected with the North West Company (or after 1821, the HBC with which it merged in that year), and had lived or were still living in what Canadian traders called the Indian country – areas west and north of the Great Lakes. A further ten baptisms were of native descendants of old (pre-1821) HBC employees who arrived in the Montreal area between 1812 and 1820.[10]

These individuals had several traits in common. With one or two exceptions, all were of partly Indian descent, given the almost complete absence of white women in the Indian country before the 1820s.[11] All were born to parents whose unions either were never regularized in accord with British law or Christian ritual, or else received only belated church and legal recognition. Although the fathers' names were invariably entered in the registers, mothers' names were lacking in the great majority (over eighty-five percent) of cases (see table 1), with the exception of the pre-1821 HBC entries which, as we shall see, must be treated separately. The absence of maternal names (most were described simply as "a woman of the Indian Country") reflected both these women's lack of standing and the fact that most were themselves not present at the baptismal or burial rites of these offspring; enduring co-residence with both parents was not a typical attribute of most of these children's lives, particularly during their Montreal sojourns.

The register data show a pattern of temporal variation. The numbers of fur-trade offspring appearing in baptismal and burial entries rose during the 1796–1805 decade, peaked in the years between 1806 and 1815, declined somewhat between 1816 and 1825, and fell sharply between 1826 and 1835, probably for several reasons. From the late 1700s to the early 1800s, there was a tendency for traders of both Montreal and the HBC to become more committed to and open about their family ties in the Indian country and to acknowledge paternity of their native children; and, beginning in 1796, the St. Gabriel Street Church gave Presbyterian Nor'Westers their own setting for such acknowledgement. In the years after 1820, however, several developments probably contributed to the decline in entries. Missionaries became active at Red River (Manitoba) and beyond, and some children who might otherwise have joined their siblings in the Montreal registers were instead baptized in the Northwest (for example, offspring of John George McTavish, Alexander McKay, Angus Bethune, and John Dougald Cameron: Red River Anglican entires 215, 294, 582, 285, 392 and 580, respectively). The schools that opened in Red River may also have kept more offspring there – although British Nor'Westers themselves did not favour settling in that place and remained oriented toward eastern Canada where they had roots, social standing, and kin and friends. Additionally, the rising trend of company officers to seek white wives around 1830[12] may have made some traders less anxious to acknowledge their native offspring, par-

TABLE 1

Baptismal and burial entries, fur trade offspring*, St. Gabriel Street Presbyterian Church, 1796–1835.

Years	Baptismal Entries					Burial Entries		
	Father present	Mother present and/or named	M	F	Total	M	F	Total
1796–1805	13 (of possible 17; 1 deceased)	1	15	10	25	2	0	2
1806–1815	9 (of possible 27; 1 deceased)	5[†]	27	11	38	3	3	6
1816–1825	5 (of possible 15; 1 deceased)	1	11	5	16	6	1	7
1826–1835	0 (of possible 2)	2	1	1	2	2	1	3
Total	27	9[†]	54	27	81	13	5	18

* Excludes entries concerning pre-1821 Hudson's Bay Company families.
† Three of these entries concern David Thompson's wife.

Note: Because more than one child at a time were sometimes presented for baptism, the total of possible occasions on which a father might have been present is lower than the total number of children baptized. Ten burials were of individuals who had been previously baptized in the church.

ticularly in an eastern urban setting. And the constituency of the St. Gabriel Street Church parish itself was also changing and growing; entries after 1820 indicate a membership active in a variety of trades, with a large component of new immigrants and relatively fewer old fur-trade families, white or of mixed descent.

Who were the St. Gabriel Street fur-trade offspring of 1796 to 1835, both individually and as a category of persons assuming and being assigned identities in the changing contexts in which they matured? Names, statistics, and information regarding their fathers' occupational and company ties provide some answers. Close to three-quarters were fathered by men bearing

Scottish surnames or of known Scottish ancestry – a proportion not surprising in a Presbyterian church founded in good part by the Scottish families who after the British conquest of New France had taken over leadership of the Canadian fur trade. The other fathers were of English, French or other European backgrounds (for example, Willard F. Wentzel, Charles O. Ermatinger, Peter W. Dease).

Ages at baptism ranged from one year and under (notably, three children of explorer David Thompson born after his retirement to Terrebonne) to thirteen, averaging about six years. The burial register indicates that they were a vulnerable population, doubtless reflecting the fact that so many were separated from one or both parents to be sent at early ages on long journeys from various parts of the Indian country to the foreign setting of Montreal. Close to one out of every eight children baptized at the church was buried there within a few days to three or four years later, and the deaths of a further eight fur-trade children not baptized there are also on record in the years from 1796 to 1835.

The ratio of males to females baptized and buried is worthy of note (see table 1). Twice as many boys as girls were baptized, and the proportion of male to female burials was still higher. This evidence, along with data from other sources, indicates that, without doubt, sons were sent down to Montreal more commonly than were daughters. Trader fathers were more willing and anxious to invest their energies and funds in the placing and advancement of boys than of girls; the father-son bond took priority over those of father to mother or father to daughter.

For numerous of the Scottish Nor'Westers, this tie between males was also integrated at their sons' baptisms with other male-dominated kinship or friendship ties; brothers or other male associates were persuaded to take young strangers from the Indian country into their charge and witness their baptisms. On October 17, 1815, Alexander McKenzie and Roderick Mackenzie of Terrebonne were among the baptismal witnesses for four boys aged six or seven, the sons of their associates Alexander McKay (deceased), Robert Henry, Edward Smith and Thomas McMurray by women "of the Indian Country." Duncan McDougall fathered a son and daughter in the James Bay area between 1804 and 1807. On October 26, 1812, when McDougall was at Fort Astoria on the Pacific coast, Alexander McDougall presented the son, George, for baptism; the daughter remained in James Bay. On November 7, 1798, James, son of Cuthbert Grant, was baptized, the witnesses being merchants James Laing and James Grant, and on October 12, 1801, his younger brother Cuthbert was presented by Nor'Westers William McGillivray and Roderick Mackenzie, the father having died in 1799. The boys' three sisters remained unbaptized in the Indian country.[13]

For the Grant boys, as for other such offspring, the trip to Montreal was not made solely to be baptized; that rite of recognition was a prelude to being educated, particularly, as some fathers and patrons hoped, for a career in the upper echelons of the fur trade. Such hopes were usually in vain or only partially fulfilled. Cuthbert Grant, having attended school for several years, probably in Scotland, returned to the Indian country as a nineteen-year-old clerk in 1812; he was later kept on, as Governor George Simpson put it in 1832, "intirely [sic] from political motives" for "the benefit of his great influence over the half breeds and Indians of the neighbourhood" [Red River].[14]

Roderick, son of Daniel McKenzie, was baptized at age six in 1804 and entered the North West Company in 1818; in 1832, he was said by Simpson to be "tolerably steady considering his breed, but a man of poor abilities and of very limited education." Alexander William, son of William McKay, was baptized at age seven in 1809 (witnesses being his uncle Alexander McKay and Simon and Catharine Fraser), and acquired sufficient education to serve the HBC as a low-level clerk from 1823 to 1843. Simpson in 1832 had "a very poor opinion" of him, although admitting that he "manages a small Trading Post satisfactorily." Benjamin, son of Chief Factor Roderick McKenzie, was baptized at age ten in 1815, witnesses being Daniel and Roderick McKenzie. He joined the company in 1827, became a clerk in 1833, and died in 1837. Simpson, less dyspeptic on his character than on that of other "halfbreed" employees, admitted that he had "had the benefits of a tolerably good Education and had made a good use of the advantages he has had. . . . Promises to become a useful Man."[15]

Not much is known about many of the other offspring named in the registers. Most sons and daughters disappeared into various niches in eastern Canadian society; unlike the fur-trade clerks and postmasters just mentioned, their names do not recur in records of the Indian country.

Yet the fur trade as centrifuge did not necessarily destroy the fragile unity of its families; Nor'Westers John Thomson, John Dougald Cameron, and a few others who visited St. Gabriel Street retained their native wives. Nor'Wester and former HBC man David Thompson in fact married Charlotte Small in the church, as well as baptizing six children there. And another fur-trade cluster, the retired HBC families of Robert Longmoor and his son-in-law, James Halcro, occupied ten spaces in the baptismal register upon settling in Vaudreuil in 1813. Longmoor brought with him his wife, Sally Pink, aged about forty, from Hudson Bay; she was baptized on July 1,

1813. The Longmoor daughters, Catharine, Jane and Phoebe, were baptized earlier that year, as were Catharine's and James Halcro's four children. And on the same day that her mother was baptized, Catharine and James Halcro were married; if Robert Longmoor had not died by that time, he and Sally Pink probably would have done likewise. The unity of this family and the presence of both parents contrast, as does David Thompson's family configuration, with the residential fragmentation along sex lines that was typical of most Nor'Westers' families represented in the registers.

The St. Gabriel Street Church records, then, provide one view in microcosm of some of the varied and uncertain destinies that awaited fur-trade progeny of mixed descent. The fact of their shared Indian-white parentage and birth in the Northwest by no means cast them into a single social group or category; the differing circumstances in which they matured steered them in several different directions.

Yet amid the diversified experiences of individuals, some patterns emerged. Gender differences carried significance, as already remarked. The tendency, suggested in both the St. Gabriel Street Church and other data, of more daughters than sons to remain in the Indian country rather increased the proportion of mixed-descent women to mixed-descent men around the posts, and may have been one factor urging the North West Company partners to rule in 1806 that their employees should marry daughters of white men rather than Indians.[16] Another effect of this pattern would have been to maintain mother-daughter bonds; and the effect of these linkages as a basis for family-building and identity-formation may have been considerable in the métis communities that grew up in the nineteenth-century Northwest (see Louis Riel's statement, "It is true that our savage origin is humble, but it is meet that we honor our mothers as well as our fathers.")[17] Additionally, where maternal ties between Indian and mixed-descent women bonded them to Indian communities as well as to white communities, such women could act as important informal intermediaries in dealings with the white man's world. Some recent research has called attention to the wide distribution of what is termed *matriorganization* in subarctic Indian societies. This feature could have allowed mixed-descent women an extra degree of influence among their Indian kin – and may also have carried over into related métis communities, reinforced by the other factors noted above.[18]

While strong Indian maternal ties were a factor in the genesis of a métis identity among fur-trade children, they were not in themselves a sufficient force. Most offspring who experienced lasting bonds only with maternal kin and whose fathers or other white male associates played no role in their lives tended to be reintegrated into Indian societies, just as the relatively few children whose fathers intervened actively and consistently in their upbringing and career placement could become assimilated into white society.

Between these two poles, however, lay a large and fertile ground in which métis identity-building and activism could flourish, particularly in the cases of the numerous North West Company sons who combined roots in the Indian country with a limited and perhaps frustrating exposure to life in eastern Canada or Europe. It is of interest that nineteenth-century métis political activity and self-conciousness arose in good part from men who were in a tension between two worlds – Cuthbert Grant, Jr., the North West Company sons involved in the Dickson Liberating Army on the Great Lakes in 1837,[19] and Louis Riel himself, schooled as a youth in Montreal. In the Canadian Northwest, as elsewhere, a recipe for ethnic political awareness was to be cast between worlds, having had enough experience of each to realize that life could be different and better. Fur-trade sons who visited Montreal but lacked enduring paternal ties and returned to the Indian country experienced a distinct back-and-forthness in their lives – abrupt removals from maternal bonds, along with intermittent or lasting isolation from fathers whose attempts to replace themselves with relatives or friends were likely to be unsuccessful. Such familial fragmentation would have spawned alienation and disillusionment. And it was particularly a North West Company phenomenon; far fewer sons of the old HBC, given its policies and travel restrictions, could travel to London and then return, to interact and combine with others of similar experience.

In conclusion, the familial data gleaned from the St. Gabriel Street registers and elsewhere suggest the uses of looking for the genesis of métis identity-building, or lack thereof, first in the microcosm of parental, parent-child, and gender roles and relationships. Métis consciousness and commitment, or their absence, were of course much affected by the political and economic conditions of fur-trade children's adult lives. But the early years of growth were formative. The relative importance and consistency of paternal and maternal ties, and the nature and strength of their attachments to the broader communities in which they were enmeshed, determined the various trajectories these children would follow, moving outward from the variable contexts of their fur-trade origins. The full story of métissage as a sociocultural and political phenomenon in northern North America involves the study and understanding of a wide range of individual and group experiences – both those that led to *la nation métisse* and those in which métissage was a potentiality denied, unrecognized, or left unfulfilled, perhaps to be discovered some generations later.

NOTES

1 Karen I. Blu, *The Lumbee Problem: The Making of an American Indian People* (Cambridge: Cambridge University Press, 1980), 212–14.

2 Expressions of this momentum are to be found in, for example, Duke Redbird, *We Are Métis: A Métis View of the Development of a Native Canadian People* (Willowdale, Ont.: Ontario Métis and Non Status Indian Association, 1980) which lists on p. 31 the many métis organizations founded in Canada since 1900; Joe Sawchuk, *The Métis of Manitoba: Reformulation of an Ethnic Identity* (Toronto: Peter Martin Associates, 1978); and Alberta Federation of Métis Settlement Associations, *Métisism: A Canadian Identity* (Edmonton: 1982).

3 Alfred W. Crosby, Jr., *The Columbian Exchange: Biological and Cultural Consequences of 1492* (Westport, Conn.: Greenwood Press, 1972), 28–29.

4 For discussion of this point, see David M. Schneider, *American Kinship: A Cultural Account* (Englewood Cliffs, N.J.: Prentice-Hall, 1968).

5 Native Council of Canada, *A Statement of Claim Based on Aboriginal Title of Métis and Non-Status Indians* (Ottawa: 1980); Métis National Council, *Report on Historical Research* (typescript for the federal–provincial meeting of officials on aboriginal constitutional matters, Ottawa, 1983); Manitoba Métis Federation, *Métis Anoutch: Manitoba Métis Rights Constitutional Consultations* (Winnipeg: 1983). See also: Douglas N. Sprague, "Government Lawlessness in the Administration of Manitoba Land Claims, 1870–1887" (*Manitoba Law Journal* 10[1979–80]:415–41); and Douglas N. Sprague and R.P. Frye, *The Genealogy of the First Métis Nation* (Winnipeg: Pemmican Publications, 1983).

6 For another sampling besides this volume, see the thirteen papers in the 1983 special issue of the *Canadian Journal of Native Studies,* vol. 3, no. 1, on the métis since 1870, edited by Antoine S. Lussier.

7 Daniel Francis and Toby Morantz, *Partners in Furs: A History of the Fur Trade in Eastern James Bay, 1600–1870* (Kingston and Montreal: McGill-Queen's University Press, 1983) offers important background on this point. For a wide range of other recent literature, see the annotated listings in Jacqueline Peterson and John Anfinson, "The Indian and the Fur Trade: A Review of Recent Literature" in W.R. Swagerty, ed., *Scholars and the Indian Experience: Critical Reviews of Recent Writing in the Social Sciences* (Bloomington: Indiana University Press, 1984).

8 For detailed discussion of Company patterns and the familial patterns therein, see Jennifer S.H. Brown, *Strangers in Blood: Fur Trade Company Families in Indian Country* (Vancouver: University of British Columbia Press, 1980).

9 See Jacqueline Peterson, this volume.

10 St. Gabriel Street Presbyterian Church registers. Archives of Ontario, Toronto. Microfilm.

11 The exceptions in question were Frederick (baptized 1818), son of Nor'Wester Charles Grant and Lizette or Elizabeth Landry who had the unique distinction of being herself a former engagée in the Company; and Ann, whose mother, Ann Foster, presented her for baptism in 1828 and whose naming of Governor George Simpson as the father was accepted without question, he being absent. The stories of some of the first white women in the Canadian Northwest are recounted and placed in context by Sylvia Van Kirk in *"Many Tender Ties": Women in Fur-Trade Society, 1670–1870* (Winnipeg: Watson and Dwyer, 1980), 175–81.

12 Van Kirk, *"Many Tender Ties,"* chap. 8.

13 Margaret MacLeod and W.L. Morton, *Cuthbert Grant of Grantown* (Toronto: McClelland and Stewart, 1974), 2. See also Jennifer S.H. Brown, "Duncan McDougall," *Dictionary of*

   Canadian Biography, ed. Francess G. Halpenny and Jean Hamlin, 11 vols. (Toronto: University of Toronto Press, 1983)5:525–27.

14 MacLeod and Morton, *Cuthbert Grant,* 7; Glyndwr Williams, ed., *Hudson's Bay Miscellany, 1670–1870* (Winnipeg: Hudson's Bay Record Society, 1975), 30:210.

15 Williams, *Hudson's Bay Miscellany,* 219–33.

16 W.S. Wallace, ed., *Documents Relating to the North West Company* (Toronto: Champlain Society, 1934), 22:211.

17 Joseph Kinsey Howard, *The Strange Empire of Louis Riel* (Toronto: Swan Publishing, 1965), 46.

18 Charles A. Bishop and Shepard Krech, III, "Matriorganization: The Basis of Aboriginal Subarctic Social Organization," *Arctic Anthropology* 17(1979)2:34–45; Jennifer S.H. Brown, "Woman as Centre and Symbol in the Emergence of Métis Communities," *Canadian Journal of Native Studies* 3(1983)l:39–46.

19 Brown, *Strangers in Blood,* 190–92.

"What if Mama is an Indian?":
The cultural ambivalence of
the Alexander Ross family

Sylvia Van Kirk

Recent historical studies of the mixed-blood people of western Canada have concluded that within this broad category there were specific groups which can be differentiated on the basis of ethnicity, religion and class. In the period before 1870, there was a discernible Anglophone mixed-blood group, sometimes known as the "country-born."[1] These people exhibited a cultural orientation quite distinct from that of the larger Francophone mixed-blood group, or métis. There is considerable truth to Frits Pannekoek's assertion that the principal aspiration of these "country-born" people was assimilation into the British, Protestant world of their fathers.[2] As Jennifer Brown has emphasized, this was due in large measure to the active and pervasive paternal influence evident in many of these British-Indian families.[3] Much work remains to be done, however, in analyzing the actual effect of this process of enculturation on the children of these families.

In one of the few studies which focuses on a particular family, Elizabeth Arthur has argued that, for the children of Chief Factor Roderick McKenzie and his Ojibwa wife Angèlique, the pressures to succeed in their father's world resulted in severe psychological distress, especially for the sons.[4] In determining the success of the program of enculturation that British fathers, aided by church and school, mapped out for their children, it is useful to focus on mixed-blood families who were part of the old colonial elite. Their heads (usually retired officers of the Hudson's Bay Company [HBC or the Company]) had the desire, along with sufficient rank, wealth and education, to secure the enculturation of their children as members of the British Protestant community in spite of their birth in a distant and isolated part of the Empire.

The Alexander Ross family of Red River appears to have been one of the most successfully enculturated British-Indian families in Rupert's Land. Yet, ultimately, an outstanding younger son, James, suffered an "identity crisis" so profound that it destroyed him. The tragedy of his life is suggestive for the fate of the Anglophone mixed-blood group as a whole. Unlike the métis, this group was not permitted to build a cultural identity based on the recognition of their dual racial heritage. British-Indian children were taught to deny and increasingly felt the need to suppress the Indian part of their heritage, but racist attitudes could nevertheless deny them the positions in white society to which they aspired.[5]

The young Scot Alexander Ross first emigrated to the Canadas in 1804. After several unremunerative years as a schoolteacher, he decided to try his fortune in the fur trade. As a clerk with the Pacific Fur Company, he helped to establish trade with the Okanagan Indians of the Upper Columbia River. Shortly after, around 1813, he wed, à la façon du pays (in the fashion of the country), an Okanagan chief's young daughter whom he called Sally. Their first child, Alexander, was born in 1815, followed by three girls, Margaret (born 1819), Isabella (born 1820), and Mary (born 1823). Although Ross had a high regard for the Okanagans, he felt it best, as his family grew, to remove them from the world of fur-trade post and Indian camp. In 1825, he retired from the trade and settled his wife and children on an extensive land grant in the Red River colony. There he hoped they would be able to receive "the Christian education" that he considered the best portion in life that he could give them.[6]

In time, the Ross family comprised twelve children – four boys and eight girls. For the eight youngest children, Red River was the only home they had ever known; they never had any contact with their mother's kin across the Rocky Mountains. We don't know what Sally Ross felt on taking leave of her people for the last time, but there is certainly evidence that her loving maternal presence considerably strengthened the Ross children's sense of family. Yet, as a Christianized Indian, the extent to which she transmitted her native heritage to her children appears to have been limited. That Sally Ross spoke her native tongue in the family circle is illustrated by the little endearments James penned to his mother in later years, and the older girls were proficient in crafts such as making moccasins.[7] But such attributes were almost completely overshadowed by the Scots Presbyterian influence of the father.

As the patriarch of the family home, known as Colony Gardens, Alexander Ross shaped the upbringing of his half-Indian children. It was Ross who determined their religious and secular education and who later gave land to his sons to establish their own households or provided succour for widowed daughters.[8] Ross's most ardent desire was that his family be imbued with the precepts of Christianity. Although deeply disappointed that there was no Presbyterian clergyman in the settlement, Ross initially accepted the official ministrations of the Anglican Church. Sally Ross and her children were all baptized by the Reverend William Cockran, who also formally married the Rosses in 1828. But while religious observances had to be made at the Anglican church, Ross kept his staunch Presbyterianism alive through regular family gatherings for Bible reading and prayers. All the while he campaigned to bring a Presbyterian minister to Red River, which was at last achieved in the person of the Reverend John Black, who arrived in 1851. Religion was one of the most formative influences in the lives of the Ross children. Their sincere conviction gave them a sense of purpose; they subscribed to the Presbyterian view that God had put them on this earth to be instruments of His purpose and that He would reward those who diligently applied their talents.[9]

The application of the benefits of secular education seems to have been somewhat more uneven than those of their religious education. With the exception of two of the younger ones, little formal education was bestowed upon the girls, most of whom married in their teens. But the sons, who were to carry on the family name, received the best education that Red River had to offer. William (born 1825) was a very creditable graduate of the Red River Academy, while his younger brother James (born 1835) was such an outstanding pupil of Bishop Anderson's that he was sent to further his education at the University of Toronto in 1853. The education of the youngest Ross children was taken over by the Presbyterian minister, John Black. Sandy (Alexander, who was named in memory of his eldest brother, who had died in 1835) was one of a class of six young scholars. Privately, Black tutored Henrietta (born 1830), who later became his wife, and undertook to improve upon the superficial schooling for "young ladies" that her younger sister Jemima (born 1837) had received.

For the Ross daughters, marriage would be the key to their continued assimilation. Significantly, four out of the six girls who reached adulthood married white men. In 1831, Margaret Ross married Hugh Matheson of Kildonan, and she was eventually listed in the Red River census as white. Henrietta's marriage to the Reverend John Black, while it helped to seal the family's identification with the Scots Kildonan community, emphasized the family's orientation toward newcomers, for Black had but recently come from the Canadas. (The Canadas comprised Canada West and Canada East, today contained within the provinces of Ontario and Quebec. United in 1840, they were entirely separate from Rupert's Land.) Isabella Ross's second husband was James Stewart Green, an American free trader who arrived in the settlement in the 1840s. Finally in 1860, the Canadian connection was further extended when the youngest Ross girl, Jemima, married William Coldwell, who had arrived the year before to start the colony's first newspaper.

These marriages to white men not only underscore the Ross family's desire to be viewed as "British," but also symbolize the way in which the family identified with the forces of "progress" in Red River. It was a measure of the family's success that its sons were equipped and ready to play leadership roles in the colony, to bring about a new order based on the benefits of civilization. Old Alexander Ross had every reason to be proud of his son William. By the early 1850s, William had succeeded to all his father's public offices, which included councillor of Assiniboia, sheriff, and keeper of the jail. "Is it not very pleasing to see a son step into the shoes of his father and do ample justice to all of these offices?" the old patriarch enthused.[10] William, who could not have been unaware that his station in the colony depended in large measure on the good will of the old Company establishment, did not publicly criticize the rule of the HBC; yet, like many of his peers, he chafed under the old regime. He wrote to his brother James in 1856:

You know the fact that Red River is half a century behind the age – no stirring events to give life and vigour to our debilitated political life – The incubus of the Company's monopoly – the peculiar government under which we *vegetate* . . . ; all hang like a nightmare on our political and social existence. . . . Such a state of things cannot last forever, sooner or later the whole fabric must be swept away. . . . We ought to have a flood of immigration to infuse new life, new ideas, and destroy all our old associations with the past, i.e. in so far as it hinders our progress for the future – a regular transformation will sharpen our intellects, fill our minds with new projects and give life and vigour to our thoughts, words, and action – when that day comes along you may rest assured that there will be no complaint.[11]

Just what role William Ross would have played in the turbulent years that followed must remain a matter of speculation, for a few months after he wrote these words, at the age of thirty-one, he was dead.

James Ross, however, emerged as an ardent champion of the cause of Canada in Rupert's Land. It is scarcely surprising that from young James's point of view, Canada was the land of opportunity. He performed brilliantly at Knox College, winning an impressive array of scholarships and prizes. His father, highly gratified, exclaimed, "What will they say of the Brûlés now?"[12] Socially, James's acceptance also seemed to be complete, for in

1858 he married Margaret Smith, the daughter of a respected Scots Presbyterian family in Toronto. To marry a white woman represented a considerable achievement for a British-Indian man and was almost unheard of in Red River. Both of James's brothers, for example, had married well-connected Anglophone mixed-bloods.[13]

On the surface, the children of Alexander Ross were extremely successful in terms of criteria derived from their father's world; yet they were not immune to racial prejudice. This was evident in the Kildonan community's reaction to Henrietta's marriage to the Reverend John Black. It was intimated that his marriage to a native would prove detrimental to his ministry.[14] Indeed, at least some members of the predominantly white congregation resented the prominent position of this "halfbreed" family – in the church, they occupied three out of the six prestigious square pews. The ears of young Jemima Ross were stung by remarks that Mr. Black must feel rather ashamed to look down on all his "black" relations when he stepped into the pulpit.[15] Although she tried to make light of the situation, it is evident that Jemima was wounded and began to feel ambivalent about having an Indian mother. Although privately she might have been quite devoted to her mother, she became increasingly embarrassed to be seen in public with her. Ambivalence toward their native mothers, which was in essence an ambivalence toward their own Indian blood and heritage, was apparently not uncommon among British-Indian children. James Ross himself lamented that "halfbreed" children often did not show enough respect to their Indian mothers. It was his fear that some of his brothers and sisters might succumb to this temptation, especially after the death of their father, which prompted his anguished admonition to them, "What if Mama is an Indian?"[16] While James loved his mother, it is difficult to interpret this statement as a positive defence of his mother's Indianness. What the statement does signify is that, *even* if their mother was an Indian, she was a most exemplary mother and for that reason was entitled to the love and respect of her children. Her simple Christian virtue, he argued, was far more worthy of esteem than were the superficial accomplishments of some of the white ladies who were held in such high regard in Red River. But the fact that he felt moved to make such a comparison indicates the social strains to which the younger members of the family in particular were exposed.

James's own response to racial prejudice, to which he appears to have been quite sensitive, was to work diligently to prove that one could rise above the derogatory stereotypes of mixed-blood people perpetrated in non-native circles in nineteenth century Red River. Indeed, these stereotypes were uncomfortably close to home. On reading his father's book, *The Fur*

Hunters of the Far West, James was disconcerted to find that his own father made unflattering generalizations about halfbreeds, characterizing them as "fickle" and "destitute of steady purpose." "I think some of your statements about Halfbreeds unnecessarily harsh," James could not help telling him, and he vowed that his father would never be able to accuse him of such behaviour.[17]

In fact, James Ross seems to have been almost obsessed with the desire to make his father proud of him. He must not fail. The pressure on him increased unexpectedly when in 1856 not only his elder brother but also his father died. Within a few short months, the Ross family had suffered a double blow – they had lost not only their guiding head, but also the one who had been groomed to take his place. In a British-Indian family where the family's welfare and status was so dependent upon the father, his demise could be catastrophic. Again James Ross acknowledged that "halfbreed" families generally dwindled into insignificance after their patriarchs died.[18] He fervently believed that the same must not happen to the Ross family. In a moving letter to his siblings, he exhorted them to a standard of conduct that would ensure the family's standing and respectability within the community.

After completing his bachelor of arts degree at the University of Toronto, James Ross returned to Red River with his Canadian bride in the summer of 1858. In assuming the mantle of family leadership, he was proud to be chosen to follow in the footsteps of his father and brother by being appointed sheriff and postmaster. Unlike his brother, however, James Ross felt compelled to speak out against the HBC. In the late 1850s, agitation for a Canadian takeover was growing and there was considerable support in the Anglophone mixed-blood community. In 1857, for example, the sons of the late Chief Factor Alexander Kennedy and his Cree wife had obtained hundreds of signatures to a petition appealing to the Legislature of the Province of Canada for annexation.[19] James Ross was ideally placed to continue this campaign and he found his vehicle for expression in *The Nor'Wester,* of which he became co-editor in 1860. But Ross was to learn that although the Company might be weakened, it had not yet lost all power. In 1862, after publishing a petition which ran counter to the one being promoted by the HBC on the question of defence for Red River, Ross found himself summarily divested of his appointed offices. Shortly afterward, he became heavily involved in the sordid Corbett case; along with a significant number of Anglophone mixed-bloods, he seemed to feel that the unhappy minister was being persecuted because of his anti-Company stance.[20] By 1864, with his prospects tarnished, Ross, perhaps at his wife's urging, decided to return to Canada.

Canada seemed so promising that James urged other members of the family to emigrate. William and Jemima Coldwell and young Sandy Ross with his mixed-blood wife Catherine Murray arrived in Toronto in 1865. It was not a happy interlude. Although Sandy had previously spent some years at Knox College, he and his wife were so homesick that they returned to Red River within twelve months. Jemima Coldwell also did not adapt well to her new surroundings. Although she had a fine house, she may have shared her sister Henrietta's apprehension that a "dark halfbreed" such as herself would never really be acceptable in Canadian society.[21] In any event, Jemima grew increasingly melancholy, especially after the death of her eldest daughter, and she herself died in Toronto in 1867.

Only James seemed to thrive; his list of accomplishments was increasingly impressive. He completed his master of arts degree and articled at law, coming first in the class when he was admitted to the bar. He quickly attracted the attention of George Brown, and later became a lead writer and reporter for *The Globe*. As Jennifer Brown has pointed out, Canada could absorb a few talented native sons, isolated as they were from their fellows.[22] Doubtless, James Ross would have prospered had he stayed in Canada. Instead he returned to Red River on the eve of momentous change. He had been encouraged by the lieutenant-governor-to-be, William McDougall, who advised him that the new Canadian possession would need leaders like himself. Indeed, few could match his credentials. A man of striking mien and persuasive speech, he was fluent in both English and French, devoted to Red River, but had influential and sympathetic ties to Canada. Ross had always felt that his destiny was somehow bound up with the colony. Here was the golden opportunity – the longed-for time that his brother had not lived to see. The Anglophone mixed-blood community was apparently ready to secure the promise of their British Protestant heritage through union with Canada, and Ross intended to lead them to it.

For James Ross, however, the Red River Resistance proved to be not only a political but also a personal crisis of great magnitude. It essentially destroyed him. Instead of providing consistent leadership, Ross vacillated. At first the ardent champion of the Canadian cause, he ended up as Chief Justice of Riel's provisional government. Ross was won over by Riel's appeal to racial unity; the métis were fighting not solely for their own rights, but also for the rights of all the indigenous people of Red River. The bond of their native ancestry made Ross anxious to avoid taking up arms against the métis. Nothing was worth a civil war against "brothers and kindred."[23] At a fundamental level, the crisis must also have forced Ross, anglicized as he might be, to face the Indian dimension of his origins; indeed, genetically, he was far more Indian than was Riel. The racist attitudes of the

Canadians undoubtedly accentuated Ross's crisis of identity. He would have been deeply hurt when even his beloved *Globe* printed disparaging remarks about renegade half-breeds, tarring the entire mixed-blood community with the same brush.

His course was a tortured one; as the darling of the Canadian cause, it was not easy for him to be allied with Riel. Friends and relatives in Canada suspected Ross of treasonous conduct and British-Indian compatriots who remained opposed to Riel accused Ross of being a self-seeking rogue.[24] During the course of the resistance, Ross actively counselled restraint, trying desperately to prevent a violent clash between the Canadians and the métis. He interceded with Riel to spare Major Boulton and his men, and was shocked to learn of the subsequent execution of Thomas Scott.[25] This event led to Ross's estrangement from the provisional government, but the vengeful reaction of the Canadians brought further despair. Indeed the Anglophone mixed-blood community in general experienced a real sense of disillusionment as a result of the violent excesses perpetrated by the Canadian troops, being apprehensive that they too would fall victim to racist attacks.[26]

As he found himself torn between the two communities – Canadian and métis – Ross's own feelings of ambivalence and guilt must have been profound. In his turmoil, he turned to drink and seriously undermined his health. In the summer of 1870, however, Ross tried to pull himself together. A business trip to Toronto provided the opportunity for him to regain some of the idealism of his student days, to feel that he had been strengthened by the trials through which he had passed. He returned to Red River with renewed purpose, hoping to escape the stigma of his association with Riel and to be called upon to serve in the new administration of Governor Archibald. Instead, he suffered the mortification of seeing himself passed over in favour of Canadian newcomers.[27] This further crisis likely contributed to his premature death in September 1871.

After James's death, the youngest son, Sandy, did not take over as head of the Ross family. Although not much else is known about him, he was the most insecure of all the sons and never found his niche. Death claimed him early, too, at the age of thirty-one. The leadership of the Ross family passed to the white sons-in-law, the Reverend John Black, who remained concerned for the family's welfare even after the death of Henrietta in 1873, and especially William Coldwell, who married Jemima, the widow of William Ross, in 1875.

In spite of their great promise, an air of tragedy hung over the children of Alexander Ross. By 1874, all the children except one daughter were dead, most having died in their thirties. They seem to have been particularly susceptible to lung diseases, but one wonders to what extent psychological stress contributed to their poor health. The degree of psychological dislocation which they suffered appears to have been proportional to the degree to which they attempted to assimilate, accompanied as this was by the hazards of personal ambivalence and the threat of rejection.

The ones who fared best were the daughters, perhaps partly because there was less pressure on them to succeed. Yet even the most well-adjusted of the daughters seem to have been those who were not forced to suppress their Indian heritage completely. An elder daughter, Mary, for example, who married the mixed-blood Orkneyman George Flett, eventually helped her husband establish a Presbyterian mission among the Riding Mountain "Chippewas" or Saulteaux. There, her familiarity with Indian language and customs was an advantage, not a detriment.[28] Her younger sisters who married prominent whites had to confront prejudice more directly. Henrietta was able to weather the racial jibes of the Kildonan community, being assisted by a loving and supportive husband, but Jemima, who was the youngest and most upwardly mobile, had a great deal of trouble coping with her situation.

The sons suffered most. Their fate is important, for in the 1850s and '60s, talented young Anglophone mixed-bloods such as themselves were emerging in leadership roles in Red River.[29] In 1861, according to compatriot A.K. Isbister, British-Indians occupied nearly all the significant and intellectual offices in the colony. Most prominent among them had been James Ross.[30]

Indeed, the pressure on Ross must have been enormous, for he was upheld as an example to all. Yet James Ross's crisis in 1869–70 is really symbolic of an inherent tension in the enculturation process to which Anglophone mixed-blood children were subjected. The Red River Resistance polarized the settlement into two elements – white and métis. British-Indian leaders such as James Ross suffered their own personal agony when they were brought face to face with the fact that they were really neither, and that increasingly their place in Rupert's Land was being threatened. Ultimately, the biases of the newcomers, often racist in nature, would deny to the Anglophone mixed-bloods the successful integration into white society that they desired.[31] Significantly, the new elite of Winnipeg soon bore little resemblance to the old Red River elite that had given Isbister so much satisfaction. Yet, leaders such as James Ross could not be métis, even though they might have felt a bond of kinship with the French-Indian community. Unlike the métis, the Anglophone mixed-bloods lacked a distinct cultural identity based on the duality of their heritage, and this made it difficult for them to build upon their uniqueness as a people of mixed racial ancestry. In 1869–70, the métis were secure enough in their own identity to champion native rights and would produce the foremost leaders in promoting this cause. Significantly, after 1870 the Anglophone mixed-bloods rapidly ceased to be recognized as a separate indigenous group, and *métis* has become the label which has tended to subsume all of the mixed-blood people of Western Canada.

NOTES

The original version of this article was published in *The Developing West: Essays on Canadian History in Honor of Lewis H. Thomas,* edited by John E. Foster, The University of Alberta Press, 1983.

1 The term *country-born* was first used in modern scholarship by John E. Foster in his Ph.D. dissertation "The Country-Born in the Red River Settlement, 1820–1850" (University of Alberta, 1972). Although occasionally used by the Anglophone mixed-bloods of Red River, it is significant that they most commonly used the term *half-breed* to refer to themselves (*The Nor'Wester,* 1862). Unfortunately, this term is unacceptable today because of the pejorative connotations it has taken on. The term *mixed-blood* seems to me most satisfactory and I am grateful to Irene Spry for suggesting the designations Anglophone and Francophone.

2 See Frits Pannekoek, "The Churches and the Social Structure in the Red River Area 1818–1870" (Ph.D. dissertation, Queen's University, 1973).

3 Jennifer S.H. Brown, *Strangers in Blood: Fur Trade Company Families in Indian Country* (Vancouver: University of British Columbia Press, 1980), 216–20.

4 Elizabeth Arthur, "Angeliqué and her Children," Thunder Bay Historical Museum Society, *Papers and Records* 6:30–40.

5 For a discussion of the racial attitudes of the Hudson's Bay Company which denied advancement to well-qualified Anglophone mixed-bloods in the period after the union, see Brown, *Strangers in Blood,* chaps. 8 and 9. See also John Long, "Archdeacon Thomas Vincent of Moosonee and the Handicap of 'Métis' Racial Status," *Canadian Journal of Native Studies* 3(1983):95–116.

6 Alexander Ross, *The Fur Hunters of the Far West,* 2 vols. (London: Smith, Elder and Co., 1855) 2:233.

7 Provincial Archives of Manitoba (hereinafter cited as PAM), Alexander Ross Family Papers, James to father, December 31, 1853; father to James, June 11, 1854; James to father, July 1, 1854.

8 The Ross family seems to have conformed to the patriarchal household type described by Frits Pannekoek in his article, "The Demographic Structure of Nineteenth Century Red River" in L.G. Thomas, ed., *Essays in Western History* (Edmonton: University of Alberta Press, 1976), 83–95.

9 PAM, Ross Family Papers, James to father, July 1, 1854.

10 Ibid., father to James, August 25, 1854.

11 Ibid., William to James, February 9, 1856.

12 Ibid., John Black to James, February 9, 1854. *Bois Brûlé* was a term originally applied to the métis.

13 William Ross married Jemima McKenzie, a daughter of former Hudson's Bay Company officer Roderick McKenzie, and a granddaughter of Chief Factor James Sutherland. The youngest son, Sandy, married Catherine, the daughter of prosperous Kildonan settler Donald Murray and his mixed-blood wife Catherine Swain.

14 Hudson's Bay Company Archives, D. 5/38, Jas. Sinclair to Simpson, December 11, 1853, f.342 and John Bunn to Simpson, December 16, 1853, f.372d–373.

15 PAM, Ross Family Papers, Jemima to James, November 9, 1854.

16 Ibid., James Ross to siblings, December 25, 1865.

17 PAM, Ross Family Papers, James to father, October, 1856. James may well have thought that his father was ashamed of his half-Indian family. Significantly, their existence is never mentioned in Alexander Ross's later volume, *The Red River Settlement* (London: Smith, Elder and Co., 1856).

18 PAM, James Ross to siblings, December 25, 1856.

19 "Petition of Inhabitants" in L.G. Thomas, ed., *The Prairie West to 1905* (Toronto: Oxford University Press, 1975), 59–61.

20 For a discussion of this episode, see Frits Pannekoek, "The Rev. Griffiths Owen Corbett and the Red River Civil War of 1869–1870," *Canadian Historical Review*, 57 (1976):133–49.

21 PAM, Ross Family Papers, Henrietta to James, early 1854.

22 Jennifer S.H. Brown, "Ultimate Respectability: Fur Trade Children in the 'Civilized World,' " *The Beaver* (Spring 1978):48–55.

23 W.L. Morton, ed., *Alexander Begg's Red River Journal* (Toronto: Champlain Society, 1956), 422.

24 Morton, *Red River Journal*, 351; PAM, Ross Family Papers, James Smith to Maggy, November 30, 1869; Rev. John Laing to Ross, February, 1870.

25 PAM, Ross Family Papers, James to wife, September 24, 1870.

26 PAM, James to wife, September 29, 1870; Matthew Cook to James Ross, November 22, 1870.

27 Ibid., James to Governor Archibald, March 11, 1871.

28 PAM, William Coldwell Papers, draft notes about Mary Ross Flett.

29 Frits Pannekoek has suggested in his thesis (cited above) that the "country-born" or British-Indian community was not able to produce its own leaders. The evidence does not support this view. Men such as William Hallett, James Sinclair and the Kennedy brothers, in addition to the Ross brothers, were leaders and more attention needs to be given to their roles.

30 W.L. Morton, *Manitoba, A History* (Toronto: University of Toronto Press, 1967), 90.

31 Consider the fate of William Hallett, for example. An ambitious man, his attempts to secure acceptance in white society were hindered by racial prejudice. He committed suicide after the failure of the "Canadian party" to overthrow Riel (Pannekoek, "Churches and the Social Structure," 250).

Cultural Life

IV

In search of métis art

Ted J. Brasser

If a particular group of people in a particular period is shown to have acquired an ethnic and cultural identity of its own, then we may assume that
these people also expressed their identity in a distinctive style of arts and
crafts. In the case of the Red River métis it took some dogged foolhardiness
to maintain this assumption, since little craftwork besides the Red River cart
was documented as being of métis origin. Yet, the search for evidence has
resulted in a considerable amount of data, odds and ends found in the printed literature, in archives and in museum collections. This evidence led me to
publish preliminary statements in 1975 and 1976[1] which have since stimulated similar research by others.[2]

Honour should be given to Burton Thayer and Frederick Douglas, who
were the first scholars to identify the métis as producers of a distinctive art
style.[3] Apparently, however, the conclusions of these scholars fell on deaf
ears. No museum has felt the need to review its collections and, in fact, all
Indian-looking artifacts are still being identified as originating from one or
another tribal community. Marius Barbeau faced this well-established assumption when he found that many early pieces of quillwork on birchbark
were not made by Maritime Indians but by the nuns in French-Canadian
convents.[4] If we accept the lack of well-documented métis art collections
as evidence that there was no such thing as métis art, then we should be consistent and accept, for the same reason, that the Saulteaux, Cree and
Assiniboine living in and around the Red River Colony produced no arts
and crafts either.

The fact is that Red River métis culture and its artistic expressions flowered and withered before the ethnologists began their systematic collections
of documented artifacts. As a result of historical research, the latest edition

of George P. Murdock's bibliography of North American Indians includes a separate list of publications relating to these métis but, in museum collections, most of their arts and craft products have been ascribed to the Cree, Ojibwa, Assiniboine, Eastern Sioux and a variety of northern Athapascan tribes.[5]

It is clear then that problems arise when we try to distinguish métis art from that of neighbouring – and related – tribal groups. Literature about the widespread and culturally far-from-homogeneous bands of Cree is lumped together under one heading by Murdock and the same is true for the Ojibwa and Assiniboine-Stoney. A similar lack of differentiation exists in the catalogue systems of most ethnographic museums. These collections provide a fair, though highly generalized, idea of, say, "Cree" material culture in the recent ethnographic period, but we cannot yet present a detailed review of the art and art history of the Red River Saulteaux, Rocky Cree, or any other regional band of these widespread groups. Obviously, we will not be able to define Red River métis art until we know what their Indian neighbours were producing in the early nineteenth century.

What we do know of these Indian communities is not conducive to easy art identification. Both archaeological research and the historical record clearly indicate that the native population of southern Manitoba was heterogeneous in its makeup long before the métis concentrated there. Particular bands were defined as Cree or Saulteaux depending on their nucleus or dominant population segment; however, Cree, Saulteaux, Ottawa, Assiniboine and métis families and individuals could be found in any of these bands. Thus the regional situation was different from that in which each tribal unit, Blackfoot or Crow, for example, carried a distinctive art tradition.

When, in the early nineteenth century, the métis concentrated on the Red River, they were what sociologists call marginal people, originating from earlier fur-trade frontiers primarily around and north of the Great Lakes where they were referred to as "French Indians" or "Homeguard Indians," depending on their trade affiliations. In these locations women were employed by the traders in the manufacture of such necessities as clothing, snowshoes and guncases.[6] Long moose-skin winter coats were also produced in such contexts in the region northwest of Lake Superior, their elaborately painted and quillworked decoration showing a merging of northern Cree and Ojibwa art styles (plate 2). Undoubtedly, Indian women were employed, but the growing numbers of métis permanently residing around the posts provided a more reliable workforce. We may assume that the arts and crafts of these métis were derived indeed from Swampy Cree and Ojibwa traditions, but were modified by a considerable influence from the French mission stations during the eighteenth century.

Barely aware of a distinct ethnic identity as yet, these widespread and early métis neither recognized nor manipulated socially discriminating mechanisms. In common with the regional Indian bands, their society was of a heterogeneous composition, shading off into Indian and Canadian societies at its margins.[7] On the Red River, since the early nineteenth century, this nucleus was enriched by regional intermarriage, particularly with the Pembina Saulteaux. Whereas the Saulteaux reinforced the Great Lakes tradition, Plains Cree, Assiniboine and Eastern Sioux relatives expanded the range of artistic expression. However, by 1830 the sheer size of the Red River métis population was already promoting an endogamous marriage preference and, as a result, the emergence of a distinctive métis art style.

Allied with the westward-expanding fur trade, these métis derived part of their income from the manufacture of garments and implements for the trading posts as well as for their own trading expeditions. On the plains, they became involved in a large-scale production of horse gear. In 1800, a trader noted that saddles were made by personnel of the North West Company.[8] The widespread trade in these saddles was implied by François Larocque in 1805, who found the Crow Indians using saddles "such as the Canadians make in the North-West Country."[9] Who these North West Company men and Canadians were becomes clear from pictures made by Paul Kane in 1846, showing "Halfbreeds running buffalo," all of them using identical saddles.[10] Even more convincing is the field sketch made by Frank Mayer in 1851 entitled "Red River saddle."[11] In the same year, Friederich Kurz was on the Upper Missouri, where he met Red River métis and made a sketch entitled "Halfbreed bridle and saddle."[12]

All of these pictures show a pad saddle of Northern Plains Indian type, identically decorated at the four corners with a rosette-and-lozenge design (plate 16). While on the Red River in 1841, the Earl of Caledon had a pad saddle with the same decoration.[13] Many pad saddles preserved in museums carry this particular decorative pattern, pointing to a single source of origin which was clearly identified by Paul Kane, Frank Mayer and Friederich Kurz. These data raise questions about John Ewers's conclusion in 1955 that "tribal differences in construction and decoration of the pad saddle among the Upper Missouri tribes were negligible."[14] Ewers, however, shared the conclusions of ethnographic museums, which have ascribed these saddles to a variety of Indian tribes, never to "halfbreeds." Similar arguments concerning Indian versus métis origins can be brought forward with regard to a particular type of horse headstall and crupper, both decorated in quillwork (plate 14).

The beginnings of a distinctive métis art style are not surprisingly linked to the rise of an ethnic identity in the early decades of the nineteenth century.

Among the forces which contributed to this new identity was the decision made in 1806 by the North West Company to restrict its traders to marriage with native women of mixed parentage instead of to Indian women.[15] Soon thereafter, pictures made by Peter Rindisbacher on the Red River in the 1820s showed métis dressed in blue summer capotes (coats) held together with an Assumption sash, decorated leggings and moccasins, with a colourful shotpouch hanging on the breast (plate 13). Some of these métis wore top hats wrapped in ribbons and in which plumes were stuck. In wintertime, two-peaked caps called wide-awakes were worn, as well as leather coats which were painted, quillworked and trimmed with fur. Adopted by the voyageurs in the mid-eighteenth century, this costume remained distinctively métis until the late 1860s.

Paul Kane has also left us a portrait of a métis, his quillworked shotpouch and powderhorn attached to beadworked straps (plate 1).[16] A shotpouch of this type, acquired on the Red River before 1840, is in the collections of the National Museum of Man in Ottawa (plate 9).[17] Friederich Kurz met a group of Red River métis on the Upper Missouri in 1851 and left this description: "All were dressed in bright colors, semi-European, semi-Indian in style – tobacco pouches, girdles, knife cases, saddles, shoes, and whips were elaborately decorated with glass beads, porcupine quills, feather quills, etc., in artistic work done by their wives and sweethearts, but their clothes were of European rather than western cut."[18] Kurz's portrait in writing was echoed in sketches made the same year by Frank Mayer at the Treaty of Traverse des Sioux in present-day Minnesota which are in the Edward Everett Ayer collection at the Newberry Library in Chicago.

Rindisbacher's and Kane's paintings also reveal other métis creations, such as richly ornamented blankets covering the dogs that pulled the métis carioles (sleds). Métis in the North West Territories were still making and using such tuppies, as the blankets were called, in the early decades of the twentieth century.[19] Dog blankets of this type can be seen in the McCord Museum in Montreal (plate 3).

We are able to follow the development of several forms of métis decorative art from native prototypes and to trace their popularity among the métis throughout the history of these people. Veritable trace elements are the so-called octopus pouch with the lower half cut into four double tabs and a rectangular tobacco pouch with an ornamental flap of loomed beadwork along the bottom (plates 6, 7, 10, 11 and 15). These pouches were used to carry pipe, tobacco and flint-and-steel.

Neither métis art nor any other art style was ever born mature, without revealing its roots. The métis artisan is detected in creations combining the

PLATE 1 While on the northern plains in 1846, Paul Kane painted this portrait entitled "François Lucie, a Cree halfbreed" (Stark Foundation, Orange, Texas).

PLATE 2 Some fifteen long skin coats dating back to the last decades of the eighteenth century have been preserved. Their painted and quillworked decoration reveals a mixture of Swampy Cree and Northern Ojibwa art styles and techniques. Their documentation is meagre but indicates an origin somewhere northwest of Lake Superior, at a time when both Indian and métis women of that region manufactured skin garments to be used as merchandise in the fur trade (National Museum of Man, Ottawa, No. III-X-229).

PLATE 3 Dog blanket, decorated with beadwork and bells. One of a series acquired in the Mackenzie District (McCord Museum, Montreal).

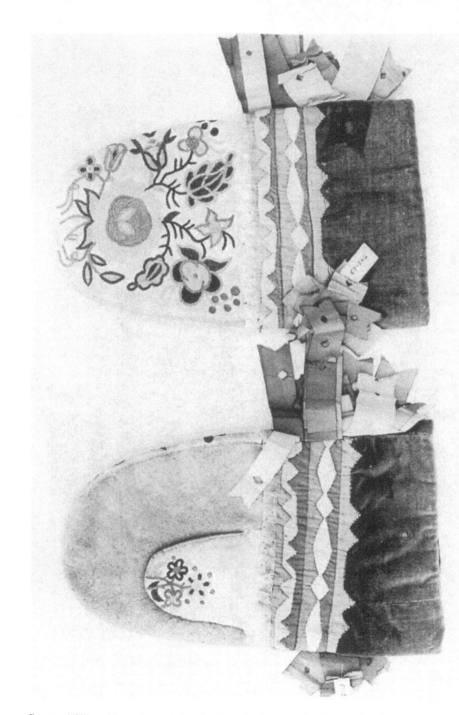

PLATE 4 Skin mittens, decorated with silk embroidery and ribbon appliqué, made by métis at Fort McMurray in the 1880s (Haffenreffer Museum, Brown University, Bristol, R.I.).

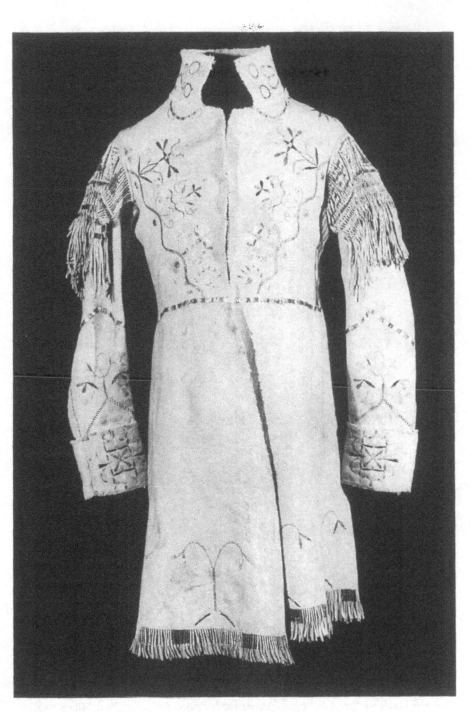

PLATE 5 A quillworked skin coat with quillwork decoration, representative of the work done by Sioux métis at Fort Pierre in the 1840s (National Museum of Man, Ottawa, No. V-E-299).

PLATE 6 Joseph Rolette represented the Pembina métis in the Minnesota Territorial legislature during the 1850s. In this picture he is dressed in classic métis fashion, including a tobacco pouch with woven beadwork flap at the bottom (Minnesota Historical Society, St. Paul, Minnesota).

PLATE 7 Frank Mayer met this Red River métis in Minnesota in 1851. The man wears a beadworked skin coat, now in the Museum of the American Indian, New York. From his belt hangs a tobacco pouch with a decorative beadwoven flap at the bottom (F.B. Mayer sketchbook, #44, Edward Everett Ayer Collection, Newberry Library, Chicago).

PLATE 8 Flora Loutit at Fort Chipewyan made this jacket in 1904. It is made of skin and decorated with silk embroidery, quill-wrapped fringes and fur trimming (National Museum of Man, Ottawa, No. VI-Z-249).

PLATE 9 Acquired on the Red River before 1840, this quillworked shot pouch is similar to the one shown in Kane's portrait of François Lucie (plate 1). Geometric designs in loomed quillwork, a technique inherited from northern Cree ancestors, were very popular among the Red River métis.

PLATE 10 A beadworked octopus pouch from the Mackenzie River region around 1900 (National Museum of Man, Ottawa, No. V-X-131).

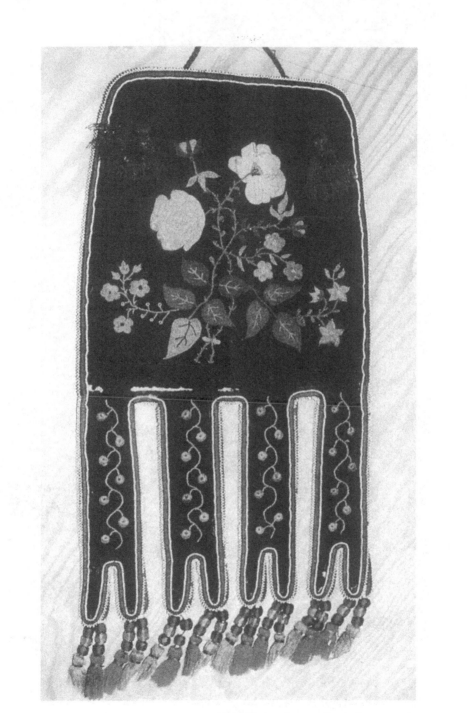

PLATE 11 Of black cloth decorated with silk embroidery, this octopus pouch belonged to Peter W. Bell, a Hudson's Bay Company trader in the 1860s (National Museum of Man, Ottawa, No. III-X-293).

PLATE 12 Baptiste Garnier, a métis living among the Sioux, late nineteenth century. His elaborately beadworked dress was typical for the regional métis (Amon Carter Museum, Fort Worth, Texas).

PLATE 13 While in the Red River Colony in the 1820s, the Swiss artist Peter Rindisbacher made several pictures of métis. This one, entitled "A Halfcaste and his two Wives," is in the collection of M. Knoedler and Co., New York City.

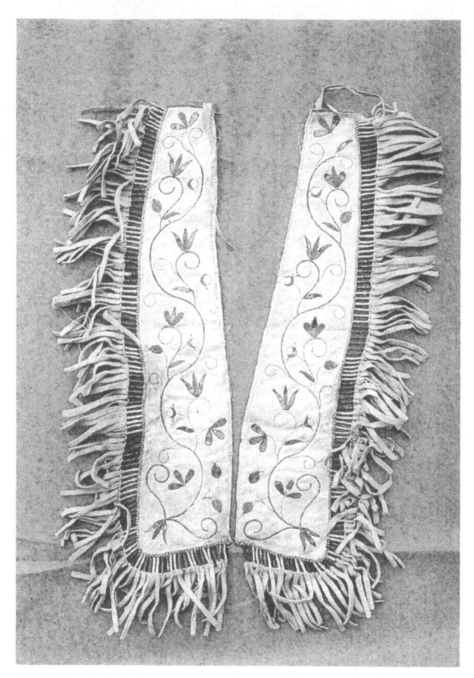

PLATE 14 Nearly identical horse cruppers to these are visible in one of Paul Kane's paintings. The cruppers shown here were acquired together with the illustrated saddle on the Lower Red River in 1841 (plate 16). The quillworked pattern is representative of the early semi-floral work of the Red River métis (National Museum of Man, Ottawa, No. V-X-290).

PLATE 15 A tobacco bag of red cloth with a flap of woven beadwork at the bottom. These bags were very popular among the Red River métis in the 1850s (National Museum of Man, Ottawa, No. V-E-230).

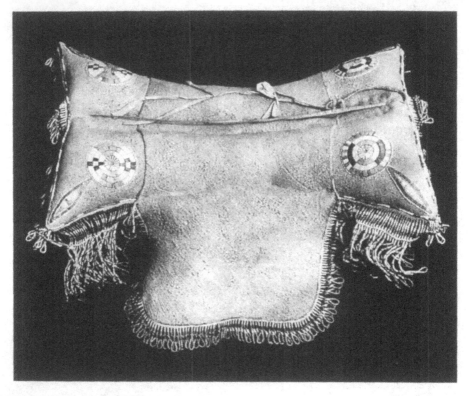

PLATE 16 Rosette-and-lozenge designs decorate a large number of pad saddles originating from the northern plains around the mid-nineteenth century. They were produced, used and traded by the Red River métis (National Museum of Man, Ottawa, No. V-X-300).

heritage of all regional traditions. Though poorly documented, much of the early ethnographic material originating from the Red River region indicates an experimentation with the fusion of diverse art traditions. In quillwork, beads and silk embroidery, a decorative art style emerged that made an elaborate use of a large number of small design elements in a wide range of colours. In the early stages, that is, up to the 1840s, rigidly geometric design elements of aboriginal origin predominated, but a floral style became increasingly popular thereafter.

According to Alfred G. Bailey, "the floral designs preponderate along the line of what was the main route of the fur trade."[20] However, there is no evidence that the traders were instrumental in the introduction of this European folk art derivative. Instead, it can be demonstrated that the correct connection is with the Roman Catholic missions, beginning on the St. Lawrence River and moving west through the Great Lakes region. Small and stylized semi-floral designs were used by the French métis who came from the Great Lakes missions. Increasingly naturalistic and flamboyant floral designs become noticeable on métis products by the 1830s, shortly after the establishment of Roman Catholic mission schools at Pembina, St. Boniface and Baie St. Paul in the Red River country. Jan Morier identified recurrences of the French embroidery patterns used by the Grey Nuns in their mission schools.[21] Representative of this style is a beadworked shotpouch made by a métis woman at Norway House about 1890.[22]

The study of Red River métis art requires a wide focus, since this art expression did not remain an exclusive hallmark of métis culture. Due to the very nature of métis society, the wide distribution of métis crafts in trade, and the subsequent migrations of Red River métis groups into the most remote corners of the greater Northwest, the métis art style put its stamp on the art of practically every tribal group of the northern plains and the North West Territories. Indian statements from various parts of these regions confirm the effect upon tribal arts exercised by the "flower beadwork people," as the métis were referred to by the Sioux.[23] Particularly in the North, a break with aboriginal traditions followed the introduction of the métis art style. Métis-style octopus pouches became popular as far away as the Tlingit region of coastal Alaska.

It is significant, however, that métis art patterns adopted by tribal artisans were used almost exclusively to decorate the types of garments, pouches and horse gear introduced by métis traders. Many of these "tribal" artisans were probably métis who had joined Indian communities. Many métis underwent such assimilation and a large proportion of the people now living on and around Indian reserves are descended from them. Beginning in the 1830s, very productive métis colonies grew up among the Eastern Sioux in Minnesota and among the Sisseton at Fort Totten, as well as among the Sioux along the Missouri River. Their presence can be detected, for example, in the Jarvis Collection in the Brooklyn Museum in New York.[24] Documented métis beadwork from Fort Totten is in the Smithsonian Institution in Washington, D.C.[25] The Yankton Sioux incorporated the Fort Totten métis as a tribal subdivision.[26] There is evidence that a high percentage of the geometric designs in recent Sioux beadwork were based upon floral prototypes. Knee-length leather cuffs decorated with semi-floral beadwork and worn over cloth trousers were particularly popular among these Sioux métis (plate 12).

Apparently, then, métis art represents a regional climax within a cultural continuum. Almost unnoticed, it made its appearance among the Indian art styles to be submerged again by them when the métis lost visibility as a distinct population. In its "classic" period, during the mid-nineteenth century, a multi-ethnic continuum can be detected as well, ranging from the Assiniboine at the most aboriginal extremity, via Sioux, Cree and Saulteaux métis, to the French Canadians at the most European extremity. Their arts and crafts blended into each other, frequently making it difficult, if not impossible, to draw a sharp line. Métis art in the North West Territories formed a late nineteenth-century extension of this base. Of course, métis employees of the fur-trade companies had penetrated the North long before that time. Yet, it required an influx of Red River métis, disenchanted with developments in their homeland, to introduce métis art production in the North West Territories.

Many visitors to the North West Territories were aware of the métis origin of this artwork. While travelling in the Mackenzie River region in 1894, Frank Russell noted the following métis manufactures: "Hunting frocks . . . decorated with porcupine quills, ribbons, beads, and silk embroidery. . . . Mittens . . . ornamented with ribbons, silk, and beads, besides fur trimming and cords of variegated worsted. . . . Carrying straps . . . made by métis women and are more elaborately ornamented than those used by the Indians. . . . Dog whips . . . have a large bunch of worsted on the handle to prevent the whip from sinking from sight when dropped in soft snow."[27] Documented as métis, such a whip is preserved in the Royal Ontario Museum in Toronto.[28] Métis mittens as described here were acquired at Fort McMurray in the 1880s and are now in the Haffenreffer Museum in Bristol, Rhode Island (plate 4).[29]

Around 1900, a métis woman named Flora Loutit lived at Fort Chipewyan; her silk embroidery and quillwork "[set] the fashion for the whole North."[30] A jacket made by her is in the collections of the National Museum of Man in Ottawa (plate 8).[31]

In 1913, anthropologist Edward Sapir reported from the Great Slave Lake area: "In practically every line the work done by half-blood women and by native girls in the mission schools is far superior to purely aboriginal work, and the influence of civilized art is such that it is difficult to isolate the native basis from the modern complex. . . . Bead and silkwork are the principal methods of decoration. In both, floral designs are the only ones used and the better work is not done by 'bush' Indians."[32] Cornelius Osgood's 1932 record is more detailed:

There has been a considerable introduction of art work by the métis population of the Mackenzie. It takes the form of silk work on moccasins, gloves, mittens, and other articles of dress, of painted and tasseled snowshoes, of elaborately decorated carioles, of carved wooden whip handles with whorls and varied designs, of carved draw-knife handles with animal heads at the ends, of tuppies (dog-blankets) elaborately embroidered with silk or wool on stroud, of standing irons of dog collars decorated with the tails of fur-bearing animals or with wollen [sic] tassels, and of ingeniously designed hat bands. Most of this métis art is disappearing; the decorated carioles are entirely gone. A few carved whip handles are seen among the Satudene today and also a few with coloured wool. Tuppies are used to some extent, especially when visiting a trading post at Easter or Christmas. Canoe paddles were also carved by the métis, but none was seen on Great Bear Lake. The silk work takes the form of flower patterns, realistic when made by the women who have been to the schools or lived much in the forts, and tending toward the conventional when made by women with fewer white contacts.[33]

Obviously, there is no lack of documentation for this northern postscript on métis art. In recent decades these métis have developed the art of moose hair bristle decoration and the only people still making woven quillwork are some métis women at Fort Providence.

More than in any of its formal characteristics, Red River métis art may be distinguished from tribal art expressions in its strong market orientation. Métis art was strictly decorative, ignoring the symbolism so frequently present in tribal art. In 1851, Frank Mayer referred to this phenomenon when he noted that the métis at Pembina

produce the most beautiful garnished work of beads, porcupine quills and silk with which they adorn leather coats, moccasins, pouches, saddles, etc. Until within a few years they have been entirely dependent on the Hudson's Bay Company for their supplies and trade, but of late have directed their attention to the settlements here, and have found it greatly to their advantage to do so, for their caravans or trains have annually increased in number, and now two hundred carts make the yearly pilgrimage across the prairies, six hundred and fifty miles, to St. Paul. They are laden with buffalo hides, pemmican, . . . peltries, fur, embroidered leather coats, moccasins, saddles, etc. These they sell or exchange at St. Paul and return again to their secluded homes.[34]

Throughout the history of métis artistic development, this market orientation was constantly present, yet the market itself can be divided into three partially overlapping foci. Artistic production began in the late eighteenth century as métis artisans in the employ of the trading companies explored and experimented with various tribal and mission arts. During the nineteenth century, métis artistic production matured and at the same time provided the merchandise for métis trading expeditions to Indian consumers all over the northern plains. During this classic period, métis artisans appear to have established local workshops, such as at Fort Pierre on the Missouri, where elaborately quillworked costumes were produced for white travellers and mountain men.[35] Ultimately, as the buffalo herds dwindled and as the pressures of eastern "civilization" and white settlement intensified, the focus upon the early tourist trade came to dominate production. At the end of this art's history, métis artisans catered to aristocratic sport hunters, government officials, and the like. A fine example of this final phase is the large set of silk-embroidered deerskin table mats made by métis of the Winnipeg region in the 1870s, now found in the Royal Ontario Museum in Toronto.[36]

NOTES

1 T.J. Brasser, "Métis Artisans," *The Beaver* (Autumn 1975); "*Bo'jou Neejee!*," *Profiles of Canadian Indian Art* (Ottawa: National Museum of Man, 1976).

2 J. Morier, "Métis Decorative Art and Its Inspiration," *Dawson and Hind,* Publication of the Association of Manitoba Museums, vol. 8 (October 1979); K.C. Duncan, "The Métis and Production of Embroidery in the Subarctic," *The Museum of the Fur Trade Quarterly* 17 (Fall 1981)3:1–8.

3 B. Thayer, "Some Examples of Red River Half-Breed Art," *The Minnesota Archaeologist* 8 (April 1941).

4 M. Barbeau, "Saintes Artisanes," *Cahiers d'Art Arca* 2–3 (Montreal: Editions Fide, 1945).

5 G.P. Murdock and T.J. O'Leary, *Ethnographic Bibliography of North America,* 4th ed. (New Haven, Connecticut: Human Relations Area Files Press, 1975).

6 Charles A. Bishop, *The Northern Ojibwa and the Fur Trade* (Toronto: Holt, Rinehart and Winston, 1974), 233.

7 On the early concentration and number of métis see: Marcel Giraud, *Le Métis canadien: son rôle dans l'histoire des provinces de l'Ouest* (Paris: Institut d'Ethnologie, 1945), 766; Daniel W. Harmon, *A Journal of Voyages and Travels in the Interior of North America* (Andover, Massachusetts: 1820), xiv (introduction by Daniel Haskel).

8 Charles M. Gates, ed., *Five Fur Traders of the Northwest* (Minneapolis: University of Minnesota Press, 1933), 143.

9 L.J. Burpee, ed., *Journal of Larocque* (Ottawa: Government Printing Bureau, 1910), 64.

10 J.R. Harper, ed., *Paul Kane's Frontier* (Austin, Texas: University of Texas Press, 1971), fig. 67.

11 Edward Everett Ayer Collection, Newberry Library, Chicago, Illinois.

12 J.N.B. Hewitt, ed., *Journal of Rudolph Friederick Kurz,* Bureau of American Ethnology Bulletin 115 (Washington: Government Printing Office, 1937), plate 24.

13 Collections of the National Museum of Man, Ottawa, Ontario, no. V–X300.

14 John C. Ewers, *The Horse in Blackfoot Indian Culture,* Bureau of American Ethnology Bulletin 159 (Washington: Government Printing Office, 1955), 84.

15 Harmon, *A Journal of Voyages and Travels,* xiv.

16 Harper, ed., *Paul Kane's Frontier,* plate 27.

17 Collection of the National Museum of Man, Ottawa, Ontario, no. VZ6.

18 Hewitt, ed., *Journal of Rudolph Friederick Kurz,* 82.

19 C. Whitney, *On Snowshoes to the Barren Grounds* (New York: Harper and Brothers, 1896), 106.

20 Alfred G. Bailey, *The Conflict of European and Eastern Algonkian Cultures, 1504–1700,* 2nd ed. (Toronto: University of Toronto Press, 1969), second edition 151.

21 Morier, "Métis Decorative Art and Its Inspiration."

22 Collections of the Iowa Museum of National History, Iowa City, Iowa.

23 John C. Ewers, *Blackfeet Crafts,* Indian Handicraft Series No. 9 (Lawrence, Kansas: U.S. Indian Service, 1944), 38; J.H. Howard, *The Plains Ojibwa or Bungi,* Anthropology Paper No. 1, South Dakota Museum (Vermillion: University of South Dakota, 1965), 55.

24 Norman Feder, *Art of the Eastern Plains Indians* (New York: The Brooklyn Museum, 1964).

25 Smithsonian Institution, Office of Anthropology, Catalog no. L27–35.

26 J.H. Howard, "The Wiciyela or Middle Dakota," *South Dakota Museum Notes* 27 (1966)7–8:7.

27 F. Russell, *Explorations in the Far North* (Iowa City: University of Iowa, 1898), 169–80.

28 Collections of the Royal Ontario Museum, Toronto, Ontario, no. HK 233.

29 Collections of the Haffenreffer Museum, Bristol, Rhode Island, no. 57–542.

30 A. Cameron, *The New North* (New York: Appleton and Cy., 1912), 321.

31 Collections of the National Museum of Man, Ottawa, Ontario, no. V1–Z–249.

32 Quoted in J. Alden Mason, *Notes on the Indians of the Great Slave Lake Area,* Yale University Publications in Anthropology 34 (New Haven: 1946), 21.

33 Cornelius Osgood, *The Ethnography of the Great Bear Lake Indians,* National Museum of Canada Bulletin 70 (Ottawa: 1932), 65.

34 B.L. Heilbron, "Mayer and the Treaty of 1851," *Minnesota History* 22 (1941) 2:148.

35 Hewitt, ed., *Journal of Rudolph Friederich Kurz,* 134.

36 Collections of the Royal Ontario Museum, Toronto, Ontario, no. HK 528–559.

What is Michif?:
Language in the métis tradition

John C. Crawford

> Aykwa weet eur en mée kawtakoushihk weekeewawhk,
> en lamp keewawpahtum, en pchit lamp.
> (He went) akouta, keepakamahaim la port.
> "Rawptree!"[1]

At least four different opinions have been expressed about the origin and nature of what is commonly, although not always, popularly referred to as Michif: it is nothing worthy of note; it is a creole language; it is a dialect of Cree; and it is a mixture of languages. For each of these opinions there is cause, although the validity varies among them.

Defining Michif as language in the métis tradition is not meant to imply that it is the only linguistic development worthy of note among métis people. The large number of métis who have apparently spoken French since the early days of French-Indian contact constitute a linguistic group whose language is certainly worth studying.[2] The fact that most métis in the United States (and probably Canada as well) now speak English as their first language is also a topic worthy of linguistic and sociolinguistic study.

Michif is nonetheless significant in itself for three reasons: it is an important part of the development of language in the métis tradition; in its nature and by implication in its development it is unusual if not unique among the world's languages; and in the range of métis linguistic phenomena it is near the Indian end of a continuum ranging from most clearly Indian to simply French.

MICHIF IS NOTHING WORTHY OF NOTE

Perhaps the most remarkable fact about Michif is its apparent tendency to be ignored. People who speak it often do not wish to be recognized as

Michif-speakers; non-speakers on the reservation often look down on it. Efforts to promote its study in local schools have met opposition, not just because of variations in the way it is spoken, but also because opponents question its basic identity and insist that Ojibwa and Cree should be taught in their pure or pre-European-influenced forms, not in mixtures like Michif. In a language use and attitude survey conducted in 1972,[3] the following answers (among others) to the question "Do you consider Michif to be a language?" were given:

"Yes, a slang language."

"No, too much mixture."

"No, because French and Cree are mixed."

"No, it's a jargon."

"No, it's not understandable."

"No. Have heard it called a bunch of jumble."

"A mixed jumble or a little of each."

"There is no such language."

"Michif is not a language, it's just a word that's been used by a lot of people when one is calling another half-breed."

"A name for people, not a language."

"No, because the word 'Michif' is not in the dictionary."

Only about thirty percent of the answers were so negative; some of the positive responses were equally expressive in their support of Michif. Nonetheless, the negative opinions do represent a significant and vocal minority.

A similar attitude grants that Michif is a language but would assign it a different name, such as Turtle Mountain Chippewa (which it definitely is not), Turtle Mountain Cree, or French-Cree, as though a stigma attaches to the word *Michif* itself. Mary Peske, in a recent study of the French origins of Michif, uses the term "French-Cree,"[4] and a movement in that direction is likely, at least on the Turtle Mountain Reservation, although Michif is the label most used and most commonly known.

Part of the reason for the negative attitudes can be easily understood. To many speakers of French, whether European or Canadian, exposure to a language in which Canadian French is a major component but which at the same time is dominated by another language, and an Indian one at that, brings a feeling of shock and despair about the "deterioration" of language. Similar responses are to be expected from speakers of Cree. The combination of French and Cree is felt to be less legitimate or natural than the Cree on which it is based. These ethnocentric reactions – natural manifestations of ethnic pride – are reinforced by institutions in France, Canada and the United States (schools, churches, media) which place great value on "pure" or standard forms of language, in the process degrading Canadian French to a low status, and Michif to an even lower one. This pressure parallels social classifications which tend to portray (more in the United States than in Canada to be sure) "half-breeds" as neither legitimately Indian nor clearly "white."

Defenders of this attitude frequently claim that Michif is unorganized, a hodge-podge, spoken completely at personal whim, or mixed up at random from whatever language sources the speaker has at hand. They would hold that it varies so much from speaker to speaker and from family to family, if not from occasion to occasion, that it makes no sense to talk of "Michif" as a single entity. There is, to be sure, considerable variation in the way the language is spoken, a variation great enough that when Michif is taught to children in schools, someone inevitably complains that the materials are in error because they differ from those used or remembered in the family of the child being taught. Dialect distinctions are in fact great enough that it would be reasonable to investigate their distribution along both geographical and family lines.

It is also true that one dimension of difference is the extent to which French is involved. Although there is a practically fixed lower limit – there is a great deal of French in all Michif – some individuals and families use more French than others do. On the surface, this information seems to support the opinion that Michif is a haphazard mixture, not sufficiently organized or regular enough to warrant serious consideration.

However, there is a great deal of regularity in Michif. Indeed, the nature of its regularity makes it of special linguistic interest, and the range of dialect variation is minor in comparison with its core uniformity. The extraordinary characteristic of Michif is the manner in which French and Cree components combine: the noun phrase is a French domain; verb structure is clearly and thoroughly Cree, and syntax is Cree with French and probably English influence. Minor word classes seem to split, some words being French and some Cree.

234 John C. Crawford

Of these characteristics, perhaps the most striking is the noun phrase. Almost all Cree nouns have been replaced by French ones, and not only nouns but articles and adjectives have been absorbed with them. In the process, French phonology and the French gender system have been maintained, as illustrated by examples like:

en pchit fee   'a little girl'   (une petite fille)
aiɲ pchi garsouɲ   'a little boy'   (un petit garçon)

So pervasive is the domination of French in the noun phrase that when English words are borrowed, they occur with French articles, as in *aiɲ [un] bus* 'a bus.' Some words of Cree origin even appear with French markings: *li [le] shikak* 'the skunk,' or *li skunk*.

At the same time a Cree system of demonstrative pronouns operates in conjunction with the noun phrase. This system preserves the Algonquian animate-inanimate gender distinction and produces sequences like the following:

Kaykwy ouma?   'What is this (inanimate)?'
En taib ouma.   'This is a table.'

Kaykwy awa?   'What is this (animate)?'
Aiɲ zhwal awa.   'This is a horse.'

Aiɲ shawr ouma.   'This is a car.'
En fawm awa.   'This is a woman.'

Taib 'table' is inanimate and feminine, *zhwal* 'horse' (cheval) animate and masculine, *fawm* 'woman' (femme) animate and feminine, *shawr* 'car' (char) inanimate and masculine. The distinction between animate and inanimate is further supported by differences in person and number markings on transitive verbs. Since these characteristics are common to the language of all speakers of Michif, they strongly indicate that Michif, far from being haphazard, is extremely regularized in the manner in which the two languages have combined.

Attitudinal as well as linguistic evidence challenges the view that Michif is not worthy of serious consideration. Growing numbers of people affirm the distinctive values of métis culture and accept and promote the term *Michif* as applicable to the Turtle Mountain Reservation. Among the increasing efforts to raise local consciousness and pride in ethnic origins, in both specifically Native American and métis aspects, the strongest voice to date is the one promoting Michif identity, despite certain efforts not to use the term. Attempts at language survival programs were initiated at least by 1974, and, although there has been some protest that Chippewa should be taught as the language of the Turtle Mountain Band of Chippewa, all the materials prepared so far have been in Michif.

There are indications that linguistically as well as socially the métis constituency and the Michif language have been dominant and increasing influences on the reservation for a considerable period. Many people report that their parents or grandparents spoke Ojibwa, but that they are speakers of Michif. One elderly woman said that her grandfather, an Ojibwa or full-blood, was angry with her and called her a "white woman" because she spoke Michif rather than his language. I have not heard of any cases in which offspring of Michif-speaking people have changed to Ojibwa.

Perhaps even more remarkable than Michif's recognition and anti-recognition on the reservation has been the slowness on the part of the scholarly community to take Michif seriously. At the time that I began studying Michif in 1972, no one had made a formal study of it. There seemed to be an unwillingness to look at languages in other than "pure" form, and so the Michif of North Dakota and western and central Canada went largely unreported. Recently this situation has changed. With increased attention to sociolinguistics and to language contact, and the recognition by established Algonquianists that Michif is sufficiently and interestingly enough Algonquian to merit study, initial studies have appeared by Boteler, Crawford, Rhodes, Pentland and Peske.[5]

MICHIF IS A CREOLE LANGUAGE

Because Michif is a mixture coming out of contact between languages, and because it has been a first language for a sizeable number of speakers, it is natural to suggest that Michif is a creole language. Recent developments in the study of language contact seem to be leading toward a broader definition of what may be considered a creole, and thus the determination of whether Michif is to be classified as a pidgin or creole is not a simple matter. However, relatively traditional definitions of pidgins and creoles, despite their shortcomings, offer useful comparisons to Michif.

A *pidgin* is a marginal language which arises to fulfill certain restricted communication needs among people who have no common language. In the initial stages of contact the communication is often limited to transactions where a detailed exchange of ideas is not required and where a small vocabulary, drawn almost exclusively from one language suffices. The syntactic structure of the pidgin is less complex and less flexible than the structures of the languages which were in contact, and though many pidgin features clearly reflect usages in the contact languages others are unique to the pidgin.

A *creole* arises when a pidgin becomes the mother tongue of a speech community. The simple structure that characterized the pidgin is carried over into the creole but since a creole, as a mother tongue, must be capable of expressing the whole range of human experience, the lexicon is expanded and frequently a more elaborate syntactic system evolves.[6]

In several respects, Michif does not seem to fit this characterization of creole languages. For one thing, its vocabulary does not come principally from one language. The relatively even and carefully categorized division between French and Cree grammatical and lexical domains is quite different from the situations described for the best-known pidgin and creole developments.

Secondly, from modern evidence, it is difficult to see how the language can be viewed as having gone through a period of syntactic simplification. Since both French and Cree are present in relative complexity (although it may be that the overall complexity for Cree is greater than for French), it does not seem reasonable to suggest that the combination could have gone to a simple syntax and then redeveloped toward full complexity in both languages, especially since the movement toward complexity characteristic of creole languages is usually accomplished under the predominant cultural impact of one of the languages. Perhaps such an argument could be made with Cree as the dominating language (see the discussion of Michif as a dialect of Cree), but it would be intricate, and would in any case have to explain the syntactic complexity of the French component. The simple and important observation is that the complexity of Michif suggests a different path of development from that usually ascribed to creole languages.

The forces which produced Michif have been in operation in one form or another since the beginnings of French-Indian contact. It is not unreasonable to suggest that something like modern-day Michif began to develop early in that contact, and that something like the present situation has been in existence for a considerable period. And yet there seem to be few historical records of Michif development: the evidence known to me comes from the behaviour of contemporary speakers.[7] What can be said about its development must therefore be limited by lack of direct evidence and is conjectural. Nevertheless, two suggestions seem relevant.

First, the development of Michif must have required a relatively long period in which a population was bilingual in French and Cree. It seems unlikely that the complex representations of both languages could have been maintained unless both cultures remained healthy, in a relationship in which the domination of one group over the other was not extreme. Perhaps the métis situation was more amenable to that sort of contact between Europeans and indigenous peoples than were the contact histories which have produced the more typical pidgin-creole developments.

Second, the early and strong development of métis culture as sharply distinct from both European and Indian groups must have been important in the development of Michif. It is true, of course, that within the total métis community today, and probably during its entire history, not all people with strong cultural ties to the tradition are or were speakers of Michif. In fact, if the Turtle Mountain situation may be taken as typical, those métis most closely tied to the Native American communities are the people most likely to be speakers of Michif. Yet, modern speakers of Michif do show a strong identification with the métis culture, in spite of some detractors and strong pressures at Turtle Mountain in the 1970s and early 1980s to identify more strongly with the specifically Indian part of the cultural tradition. This strong identification evidences a cultural strength which must be considered a central factor in the development of Michif in the cultural space between French and Cree.

My comments so far suggest problems for considering Michif as a creole. Still, the obvious and wide range of Michif dialect differences within a small geographical area is typical of language development where change is rapid, as in creole situations.[8] Moreover, it is difficult to define the boundaries between Michif and French, and Michif and Cree. Most speakers on conscious reflection make their language more Cree than it in effect seems to be in conversation. Even when they do so, however, it is rare for additional Cree nouns to be introduced, showing that the French noun phrase is extremely well established in Michif. And speakers vary in the amount of French they use, probably depending on the extent of their listeners' understanding of Cree.

In summary, although Michif does not fit simple definitions of creoles, perhaps the most important consideration to keep in mind is that, whether or not we call it a creole, it is a result of language contact and therefore relevant to the study of pidgins and creoles.

MICHIF IS A DIALECT OF CREE

Richard Rhodes suggests that Michif should be considered a dialect of Cree, specifically Plains Cree, and he illustrates quite clearly that the Cree of Michif is Plains Cree with only minor changes.[9] He gives no further evidence for considering it as a dialect with extensive borrowing rather than as a creole or some other product of language contact, although his demonstration of the predominance of Cree over French in basic grammatical structure might be considered an argument. Mary Peske provides similar documentation for the French of Michif, demonstrating its relationship to Canadian French and to specific sources in France.[10] Showing the legitimacy of linguistic antecedents or dialect connections does not of course answer the basic questions about the nature of Michif.

Nonetheless, there is syntactic evidence to support the notion that Michif is best viewed as a dialect of Cree. Although it is not at present possible to evaluate the relative complexity of languages, let alone the relative complexity of the two parts in a mixture like Michif, and although the impressive word structure of Cree tends to awe English speakers, making objectivity difficult, still the balance between Cree and French seems to be as Rhodes presents it, with more emphasis on Cree. The syntax of Michif is basically Cree syntax.

Important sociolinguistic considerations support the centrality of Cree in Michif. It is common for the terms *Cree* and *Michif* to be used as synonyms, so that *Awp Cree beekishkwawn,* literally "I speak in Cree" means "I speak Michif." (Note the French preposition *awp* [en] occurring with the word *Cree.*) Speakers are sometimes apologetic about the amount of French in their speech and self-consciously revert toward Cree, particularly when there are clear alternative ways of saying common things. For example, a Michif speaker may say:

Kaykwy tou nou?   'What is your name?'

in which the noun phrase tou nou (ton nom) is French, and the answer is phrased completely in French words:

Mou nou si Bachis.   'My name is John.'

The same content may also be expressed in a Cree format:

Tawnshi eshinihkawshouyen?   'What is your name?'
Bachis zhinihkawshoun.   'My name is John.'

There is some cultural pressure to prefer the second alternative, since it is real Cree, not French.

This sort of evidence lends credence to the suggestion that Michif has developed predominantly under the influence of Cree rather than French, although the importance of French in the societies where it was and is spoken cannot be questioned. Considering Michif a dialect of Cree explains the Algonquian syntactic complexity simply by suggesting that Cree is the continuing and controlling cultural context in which change has occurred. It is concordant with speakers' responses which make the words *Michif* and *Cree* synonymous.

Overall, I think the arguments for Michif being a dialect of Cree are the strongest ones. Still, further evidence is needed to make a clear case, and the lack of direct historical evidence is a severe limitation. A great deal of information may be derived from studying, for example, the distribution of Michif speakers, especially in relation to Cree-speaking and French-speaking communities, as well as from searching the historical record for allusions to or illustrations of early Michif language.[11] Evaluations of speakers' attitudes and memories, investigation of the freedom with which speakers move from Michif to Cree and to French, and studies of bilingualism in areas where non-Michif Cree is spoken could all aid our understandings of the processes of borrowing that were involved in this unusual dialect.

Whether Michif is considered a creole or a dialect of Cree, its strong identification with a cultural structure which is neither completely Indian nor European has made it behave in some ways like an independent language. The fact that it has cultural dominance on a reservation which is legally Chippewa, plus the movement of speakers away from Cree and Ojibwa to Michif, and the prevailing opinion among Turtle Mountain Reservation residents that Michif is a language – their language – all point to its linguistic importance and a degree of autonomy, as well as to the complexity of the relationship between dialect and language.

MICHIF IS A MIXTURE

Little needs to be said about Michif as a mixture. It has been popularly believed, for example, that English is a mixed language because a large part of its vocabulary comes from other languages. Scholars have generally rejected this view, pointing out that in all periods of its development English has been clearly and continuously Germanic. The heavy influx of Latinate borrowing, even the threat for a time that French might replace English as the language of England, did not affect the status or genetic affiliation of English as a language, and certainly should not suggest that English be looked at as a Romance language. More broadly, scholars recognize that languages do not mix randomly. Social factors are always operative in the process; one language borrows heavily from another, usually a politically or economically dominant one, or is absorbed by it, allowing for some special processes like pidginization and creolization.

Language contact is now being examined more carefully, and scholars are suggesting that something like creolization may have operated in the formation of languages like French.[12] Regardless of the final outcome or characteristics of the population at large, language contact phenomena of some complexity must have been present in situations such as that of English during the period of French political domination. With reference to these studies, Michif seems to furnish a known language situation, one which can be directly studied, where it does make sense to talk about language mixture, leaving the definition of the term somewhat open. Its highly unusual nature, in which whole blocks of lexicon, syntax and phonology are replaced by those of another language, does not seem to fit very well with established descriptions of either borrowing or creolization. Thus, mixture may not be a poor choice of term after all.

CONCLUSION

Except for eliminating the first alternative, that Michif "is nothing worthy of note," which served merely to clarify the importance of Michif, firm and final conclusions about the nature of Michif have not been reached. However, whatever classificatory labels are used, they should not divert us from making serious and continuing study of the highly unusual data which Michif comprises. None of the last three alternatives should be eliminated at this point: Michif is clearly a product of language contact and clearly worth studying in relationship to creoles and pidgins. Its patterns of vocabulary and syntax, and even its phonology, suggest that if they are to be treated as borrowing, they represent a most unusual case of it. Michif looks like a dialect of Cree, albeit an unusual one because of its special language contact characteristics. Its study as a dialect has relevance to our understanding of general characteristics of language and dialect, and perhaps points the way to distinguishing pidgins, creoles and other neo-linguistic constructions (like mixed languages) from the relatively straightforward development of distinctive dialects of a language.

NOTES

The data on which this study is based were collected almost exclusively on the Turtle Mountain Reservation in North Dakota. Although Michif is spoken extensively in other areas, the material presented here applies directly only to that reservation.

1 "Then about eight-thirty arriving home he saw a light, a little lamp. He went there, knocked on the door. 'Come in!' " The orthography of these examples was developed by me and others for use in practical programs on the reservation. It basically follows English spelling practice rather than international phonetic convention. See Patline Laverdure and Ida Rose Allard, *The Michif Dictionary: Turtle Mountain Chippewa Cree,* ed. John Crawford (Winnipeg: Pemmican Publications 1983), 364.

2 For a case in point, see Patrick C. Douaud, "Métis: A Case of Triadic Linguistic Economy," *Anthropological Linguistics* (December 1980) 9:392–414.

3 John Crawford, unpublished.

4 Mary Peske, "The French of the French-Cree (Michif) Language" (M.A. thesis, University of North Dakota, 1981).

5 Bette Boteler, "The Relationship between Conceptual Outlooks and the Linguistic Description of Disease and Its Treatment Among the Chippewa and/or Cree Indians of the Turtle Mountain Reservation" (M.A. thesis, University of North Dakota, 1971); John C. Crawford, "Some Sociolinguistic Observations about Michif," *Proceedings of the Linguistic Circle of Manitoba and North Dakota* 13 (1973), 18–22 and "Michif: A New Language," *North Dakota English* 1 (1976) 4:3–10; Richard Rhodes, "French Cree: A Case of Borrowing," *Actes du huitième Congrès des Algonquinistes* (1977), 6–25; David Pentland, "A Historical Overview of Cree Dialects," *Actes du neuvième Congrès des Algonquinistes* (1978), 104–26; Peske, "The French of the French-Cree (Michif) Language."

6 Loreto Todd, *Pidgins and Creoles* (London: Routledge and Kegan Paul, 1974), 1, 3.

7 For some evidence of a French-Ojibwa language mixture in the Upper Great Lakes in the nineteenth century, see Jacqueline Peterson, "The People In Between: Indian-White Marriage and the Genesis of a Métis Society and Culture in the Great Lakes Region, 1680–1830" (Ph.D. dissertation, University of Illinois at Chicago, 1981), 178–79.

8 Derek Bickerton, *Dynamics of a Creole System* (London: Cambridge University Press, 1976).

9 Rhodes, "A Case of Borrowing."

10 Peske, "The French of the French-Cree (Michif) Language."

11 John Crawford, "Speaking Michif in Four Métis Communities," *The Canadian Journal of Native Studies* (1983) 1:47–55.

12 Todd, *Pidgins and Creoles.*

Afterword

Very early in my life I became aware of the complexities of group identity. During the 1920s and 1930s, as I was being raised in eastern Oklahoma, there appeared to the casual observer to be three societies in that part of the country: whites, blacks, and Cherokee Indians (my own people). But the situation was not nearly as simple as that. For instance, many of the blacks there were referred to as "freedmen" and were descendants of former Cherokee slaves. A number of them spoke the Cherokee language and, in fact, these black Cherokee-speakers were the majority in some black settlements. Among the whites, there were people of my father's and grandfather's generations who were "Cherokees"; not Indians or Cherokee Indians, but "Cherokees." They were usually prestigious and influential members of white society for whom "Cherokee," to a large degree, had come to mean original settlers. Although these "Cherokees" were largely white by "blood," culture, and language, they were very proud of their former citizen status in the old Cherokee Nation which had preceded the state of Oklahoma in our area. However, their children, those people of my generation, thought of themselves simply as whites who were part-Cherokee or part-Indian.

An understanding of these distinctions was part of my upbringing, but I was not prepared for my first contact with the métis! I came out of the armed services early in World War II, and in the summer of 1944 I found myself working as a horse wrangler at a lodge on a Chippewa Indian reservation in the Great Lakes area. This reservation was sharply divided socially into full-bloods and mixed-bloods, as they were called locally. Many of the mixed-blood Chippewas had French names and seemed to be psychologically uncomfortable with their designation as Chippewa Indians.

(I was to learn much later that most of these families had originally lived as members of fur trade settlements established in the seventeenth and eighteenth centuries, rather than as members of Chippewa society.)

That summer I became acquainted with a young man of my own age who was visiting from Manitoba. He had a French name and was obviously an Indian physically. I assumed that he was a mixed-blood Chippewa. He informed me that he was not an Indian at all, that although he had some remote Indian ancestors and was a North American native (as we term it in these days) he was a Red River halfbreed. I was confused and wondered, a halfbreed what? When I asked him what was "his language," he told me "halfbreed." The local Chippewa confirmed his statements and I was left with a profound puzzlement and an intellectual drive to unravel the mystery.

After ten years of reading and two visits to métis settlements east of Winnipeg, I found that my friend from Manitoba had informed me correctly, that he was indeed a member of a new North American *people,* a people who had formed on the western Canadian frontier as a result of the contact between Indian and white. The Red River métis are probably the classic example of such cases in the western hemisphere, more clearly distinct as a people than even the Mexicanos of northern Mexico or the *cabalco* of Brazil. It is not surprising, therefore, that they have served as the type case for the more broadly based studies of racially mixed North American groups presented at the 1981 Newberry Library conference and reflected in this volume.

My interest in the métis has grown over the years and I have attempted to encourage my fellow scholars to undertake research in this area. Nonetheless, I am somewhat embarrassed to find myself in the position of having the last word in this volume, of being the summarizer, particularly among so many historians. I am an anthropologist, not an historian, and I make no claim to particular expertise in métis history. I do think, however, that the contributors to this volume are delving into a social and cultural arena with which anthropologists and social psychologists have concerned themselves for a number of years now. Perhaps I can profitably pass along some ideas and concepts about the dynamics of identity, as they may apply to the métis.

There first may be a need to distinguish between identification and identity. The word *identity* has been used in this collection in both senses. But very simply, the question of identification is only as the term implies: that is, with whom or what does one identify? The question of identity, on the other hand, is a much "deeper" notion. As identity is used in anthropology and social psychology, it means in a very broad and simplistic sense, the answer to the question, "Who am I?", or, on the level of the group, the answer to the question, "Who are we?" When one looks at tribal groups in North America the answers to the questions, "Who am I?" and "Who are we?" become virtually the same and I suspect that to some degree this is true with the métis as well.

At first glance, such "working" definitions may seem rather offhand and over-simplified, but if one ponders the enormity of the answers to those questions one can see that he or she has stepped into a profound sphere of human life. Individuals, no matter how sophisticated, cannot explicitly answer those questions about themselves and that of their "people." Such questions are too all-encompassing. No human being is that self-aware. Rarely are we able to examine our own basic assumptions about ourselves and our world. Thus, as social scientists, we have to rely not only on explicit verbal answers to the above questions but also on observations of behaviour which bear on those questions – behaviour of which most of us are unaware which may be preconscious or unconscious in origin. Fortunately, historians are able to explore the behavioural and recorded answers to such questions over time, and thus to compensate for many of the inherent difficulties.

The essays in this collection are concerned with the very question, "Who are we?" In other words, they examine, in very broad terms, the nature of the métis as a people or peoples. In recent years, some major focuses of social science research have been on such questions as peoplehood, ethnicity, social cohesion, assimilation, pluralism and religous nationalism. Many of the contributors to this volume have built upon the work of previous scholars in these areas, particularly that of the anthropologist Fredrik Barth, who pointed our attention to the significance of the membership and boundaries of a people. In addition, several of the contributors grapple with two other important dimensions of a peoplehood. The first has to do with the content, the "what" of the "we" – that which anthropologists generally call culture. The second concerns the more abstract dimension of collective identity, the question of nationality, that sense of common origin and common destiny felt even between strangers who live many miles apart.

However, there is another question which follows on the heels of, "Who are we?" That question pertains to the strength of the "we." For not only do a people have membership and boundaries and content, but their sense of peoplehood can be powerful, or it can be problematic. This variation in the sense of the "we" becomes extremely important in looking at the métis. In some métis groups, we get the feeling of a strong sense of peoplehood. In other groups called métis, the sense of peoplehood seems questionable. In fact, these essays cause one to think that as métis acquire more contact with education and more sophistication about the Canadian-American scene, their sense of identity as a people becomes more problematic and questions of group rank within the general society become important. At the same time, however, there is a striving on the part of some educated métis for the legitimization of the métis as a people by the outside society, either as a "native" people or as a group apart with a unique history and national consciousness.

Generalizations, if one can judge by the case studies presented at the 1981 Newberry Library Conference and in this volume, are hazardous. In fact, the tremendous variation from one social situation to another is striking. Lionel Demontigny told us in his conference paper, "In-Between Man," that the métis' sense of peoplehood is intimately associated with their historical middle position vis-a-vis Indian groups and that métis collective identity and métis culture fare best when métis still retain this mediator role. Other essays here point our attention to how autonomous and local the sense of peoplehood is among many groups which are called métis.

Trudy Nicks has presented the case of a loosely structured and not very cohesive group of people in Alberta, usually referred to as métis by outsiders, who have little sense of the "we" and hardly consider themselves a separate group. If they attach any label to themselves at all it is the label of "our people." Neither do they see themselves as related to other "métis" groups. And as Antoine Lussier explained at the conference, even in the older métis areas such as southern Manitoba, although some sense of nationality exists, local definitions of peoplehood are much more significant than is any abstract concept of métis nationality.

One point made by Jennifer Brown deserves repeating at this point. She warns that scientific concepts, if applied too heavily, can distort our data and, given the modern métis situation, can be socially destructive as well. As an old hand in the "identity business," I want to echo her sentiments and urge that scholars interested in the métis develop their concepts as they go along and, in fact, that they should apply the very concepts which I am advocating with a light brush.

I am not suggesting, however, that we turn our whole attention toward the development of concepts as they apply to different sets of data in different métis communities. I am too intrigued by the data themselves to counsel caution. I think that the conference from which this volume emanates (and I saw this in almost every paper) dealt with a very exciting phenomenon – not simply the examination of a particular people's notion of themselves as a people, but the whole question of how a new people come into being. And we have been offered a great many ideas about the origin of the métis!

Jacqueline Peterson has suggested that the seeds of a métis identity began to mature in the Great Lakes area during the seventeenth and eighteenth centuries in response to the fur trade as an activity or style of life. John Elgin Foster, on the other hand, while accepting the concept of a nascent métis identity in the Great Lakes region after the conquest of New France, argues that it was in the Winnipeg vicinity – when métis were caught up in a caste-like occupational ranking order imposed by the Hudson's Bay Company – that the métis emerged as a self-conscious people.

Lionel Demontigny posed just the opposite notion at the conference. He believes that the lines distinguishing métis and Indian and French Canadian from one another remained very fluid until the Red River métis began to deal with American and Canadian officialdom in the second half of the nineteenth century. In the West especially, nineteenth-century Canadian and American governments in some instances treated the Red River métis as a separate category of people and in the course of this experience – the result of a group response to official actions – the métis coalesced as a people (and as a "nation") in the 1870s and 1880s.

Many of the data presented here raise other questions about the timing or the "when" of métis ethnogenesis. For instance, are métis groups with a problematic identity simply incomplete peoples who did not have the time to develop a strong sense of themselves as métis, or have they been eroded by external definitions imposed by official and lay sections of the general society? In Canada, the legal definition and status of métis are ambiguous, at best. In the United States, the courts do not at present even recognize the existence of the métis in law. Moreover, most North Americans do not have a conceptual place for the métis in their view of the world. Thus, we need to zero in on the role of legal definitions and ethnic relationships, particularly since 1890, in the development of métis consciousness.

We must also consider the *context* of a peoplehood. A new people can hardly come into being or continue to exist without some degree of cultural uniqueness and perhaps the recognition of certain cultural symbols. Ted J. Brasser's article makes a convincing case for the appearance of a distinctive métis art which developed in the early 1800s and flowered in the middle years of that century. The appearance of a recognizably métis art must mean that other aspects of métis life and culture on the Red River were assuming a uniquely métis form as well. Brasser's article may also give us some insight into what may be a more general process in métis culture, that is, the combining of Indian manufactures and materials with French design motifs as demonstrated by the floral beadwork of this new art style.

The coherent merger of French and Indian lifeways is most strikingly brought home in John Crawford's essay on the métis language spoken at Turtle Mountain, North Dakota. Michif, as he describes it, appears to be basically Cree-Ojibwa in structure but with a sizeable French vocabulary, particularly in nouns. I have heard of areas where the opposite process has taken place, that is, where the language is French in structure but Ojibwa in content. The language spoken by a large part of the population on the Garden River Ojibwa reserve near Sault Ste. Marie, Ontario, is such an example. Sault Ste. Marie, as Jacqueline Peterson and others have pointed out, witnessed the growth of a métis population very early, although métis consciousness did not develop there as it did on the western prairies.

Métis linguistics is only in its infancy and deserves considerable encouragement.[1] But we also need to look carefully for the cultural symbols of métis identity. When in 1975 I visited the festival at Batoche, Saskatchewan, memorializing the national heroes of 1885, it seemed clear that Red River jigging and certain manners of dress, such as the wearing of the traditional métis sash, were visible signs of métis identity. Moreover, the very presence of Batoche as a place and the important events which occurred there must certainly be viewed as both historical and cultural reminders of the distinctiveness of the métis as a people.

If we are committed to examining the métis peoples, a sociogeographic "map" combining both historical and anthropological perspectives may prove useful in making sense of what would seem to be an extremely complex tangle of relatively discrete métis communities stretching across northern North America. Drawn simply to provoke discussion and thought, such a typology might include the following subareas.

1 The majority of the métis population still lives in what I would term the "classic" métis regions. These are métis populations descended from the old Red River people, who still live on the northern plains but not on Indian reserves or reservations. This type of métis community is found in southern Manitoba and the Pembina area of North Dakota, central Saskatchewan with a few communities in the southern section of the province, east-central Alberta, and northern Montana. These areas represent a kind of "retreat" of the métis westward across the northern plains. Historical dynamics, cultural expression and self-image vary as one moves westward through these communities.

Acculturation to either French or Cree norms is a significant process in the classic northern plains region. Where Quebec French-Canadian settlers have moved into métis communites in this area, métis appear to have become Quebecized and absorbed by the new French-speaking population and, in a few instances, are assuming a lower caste position relative to the newcomers. Acculturation to Cree norms and to the Cree language in parts of Saskatchewan on the part of some métis groups there is also apparent.

2 A second sociogeographic category would include those descendants of the Red River métis who now live in new natural-social environments. Many métis moved into the "bush" of northern Manitoba after the first Riel resistance in 1869. The same process occurred in Saskatchewan after the second resistance in 1885. This movement must have initiated a whole new social and cultural dynamic within these métis groups. Métis families also moved from central Saskatchewan to the North West Territories in the same period. Many of these families now act as intermediaries between whites and Dene (Athapascan Indians) of the area. There are, moreover, clusters of métis families throughout British Columbia which likely represent the westernmost edge of the Red River métis diaspora.

3 A third category encompasses those descendants of the Red River métis who now live on Indian reserves in Canada or on reservations in the United States. On some reservations, as at Turtle Mountain, North Dakota, and on a few reserves in southern Saskatchewan, they are a majority population. On other reservations, métis families are very much in the minority but are socially powerful. The redefinition of the métis as "native" or "Indian" people seems to have been overwhelming in these new social circumstances. Terms such as *mixed-bloods* and *full-bloods* are used today on these reservations, but with the implication that all are one people. Other métis families simply live *near* reserves and reservations and evince other adaptations.

4 Category four would include those local and fairly autonomous groups of mixed-blood peoples which have no social or historical connection with the Red River métis: for example, the group near Jasper, Alberta, described by Trudy Nicks; native mixed communities which formed around forts in northern Alberta; and the Scots-Cree mixed-bloods near Prince Albert, Saskatchewan. Historical and anthropological data on these communities would highlight the dynamics of peoplehood among the métis of the northern plains.

5 We might profitably look at the Great Lakes sector in greater detail. There is some evidence, according to Jacqueline Peterson, of an incipient métis identity in this region prior to the emergence of the Red River métis. Further, mixed-blood families moved from this area west into the River region during the decades when the Red River métis were beginning to express themselves as a people. Others from the Great Lakes region moved onto local Indian reservations and became marginal Indians or, alternatively, tried

to maintain themselves as "French" within the general American population.

6 A sixth area would include native mixed-blood social groups which are still connected to more traditional Indian bands – for example, the French mixed-bloods among the Oglala Sioux at Pine Ridge, South Dakota, and the "halfbreeds" of lower James Bay.

7 Seventh are the new métis migrants to the cities. The modern urban situation is so complex that I will only timidly suggest that we attend to this arena. Yet thousands of métis have moved to prairie cities in recent years; both Winnipeg and Regina now have large Indian-métis ghettos. Oral history projects such as the one now in progress at the Provincial Archives of Manitoba in Winnipeg would be invaluable at this particular time in métis development. I stress time because, as we are all discovering, historical processes are key determinants of both the variation and strength of métis consciousness.

Along with the above points, we also need to consider a recent set of dynamics which is having an effect on métis identity – the legal demands of Canada and the United States. In Canada, the métis recently have been granted a legal status by their inclusion with Indians and Inuit in the aboriginal rights provision in article II of the Constitution Act of 1982. The full ramifications of their new status as an "aboriginal people" are as yet unclear; in Canada, the legal category *métis* remains subject to competing definitions which may include a variety of social types – the descendants of Red River métis, enfranchized former Indians, products of recent intermarriages, and others. Métis who wish to build political solidarity are forced both to negotiate these questions among themselves and cope with externally devised government frameworks, producing massive social difficulties. The question becomes, can a sense of peoplehood be built among such disparate social groups without eroding the identity and solidarity of some of the same groups? In the United States, one must be legally either Indian or white. Métis in Montana are now grappling with that not-so-palatable dichotomy.

Thus, métis social cohesion must struggle against the power of definition of two major North American states. In addition, to the extent that Canadian native and American Indian peoples have been persuaded by the peculiar logic of categories created by whites, métis must distance themselves from the very peoples with whom they may feel the strongest ethnic, social and political affinity in order to preserve a separate métis peoplehood. Whether this will be possible or even desirable remains to be seen.

Whatever the ultimate will of the peoples who would call themselves métis, I wish to congratulate the contributors to this volume and that larger community of scholars who attended the 1981 conference on the métis in North America. Their work has excited me and stimulated my intellectual interest, which is no small accomplishment. If I read correctly the intellectual thrust evidenced in these pages, I want very much to participate further in exploring the origin and development of the métis peoples, their unique cultures, and the place of the métis in the modern world.

Robert K. Thomas

NOTE

1 A valuable new work on métis linguistic patterns at Lac la Biche, Alberta, has just appeared. See Patrick C. Douaud, *Ethnolinguistic Profile of the Canadian Métis* (Ottawa: National Museum of Man Mercury Series, Canadian Ethnology Service Paper no. 99, 1985).

Contributors

TED J. BRASSER Drs., cultural anthropology, Leiden University, the Netherlands. Ethnologist, Museum of Man, National Museum of Canada, Ottawa, Ontario. Recognized authority on métis art. Author of "Métis Artisans" (1975) and numerous articles on the culture of Eastern Algonquian peoples, including "Early Indian-European Contacts" and "Mahican" in the Northeast volume of the *Handbook of North American Indians*, edited by Bruce Trigger (1978).

JENNIFER S.H. BROWN Ph.D., anthropology, University of Chicago. Author of numerous articles on fur trade social history and ethnohistory, and of *Strangers in Blood: Fur Trade Company Families in Indian Country* (1980). Co-organizer of first international Conference on the Métis in North America, September, 1981, Newberry Library, Chicago. Currently associate professor of history, University of Winnipeg, Winnipeg, Manitoba.

JOHN C. CRAWFORD Ph.D., linguistics, University of Michigan. Professor of English linguistics, University of North Dakota, Grand Forks. Author of articles and papers on the métis language, including "Michif: A New Language," in *North Dakota English* (1976) and "Standardization of Orthography in Michif" (1979). Editor of *The Michif Dictionary*, by Patline Laverdure and Ida Rose Allard (1983).

OLIVE P. DICKASON Ph.D., history, University of Ottawa. Associate professor of history, University of Alberta. Author of *Indian Arts in Canada* (1972), *The Myth of the Savage and the Beginning of French Colonialism in the Americas* (1984), and numerous articles on Amerindian relationships. She is currently working on European concepts of Amerindian sovereignty and territoriality.

VERNE DUSENBERRY Ph.D., anthropology, University of Stockholm. Former associate professor of anthropology, University of Montana, director of the Indian Studies Institute of the Glenbow Foundation in Calgary, Alberta, and editor of the Anthropology and Sociology Papers, University of Montana. From 1951 to 1953, he was visiting professor of English at Northern Montana College in Havre, where he began his compilation of data on the little-known people on the Rocky Boy's Reservation. Dr. Dusenberry died in 1966.

R. DAVID EDMUNDS Ph.D., history, University of Oklahoma. Professor of history, Texas Christian University. Recipient of the Parkman Prize (1978) for his book, *The Potawatomis: Keepers of the Fire*. Editor of *American Indian Leaders: Studies in Diversity* (1980) and author of *The Shawnee Prophet* (1983) and *Tecumseh and the Quest for Indian Leadership* (1984). Consultant for the Amon Carter Museum of Western Art (1980) and an advisor to the D'Arcy McNickle Center for the History of the American Indian at the Newberry Library (1982–   ) and the Smithsonian Institution (1984).

JOHN ELGIN FOSTER Ph.D., history, University of Alberta. Associate professor of history, University of Alberta. Author of numerous articles on the Red River métis, including "The Origins of the Mixed-Bloods in the Canadian West," in *Essays in Western History* (1976), and "The Plains Metis" in *Native Peoples: The Canadian Experience*, R. Bruce Morrison and C. Rod Wilson, general editors (forthcoming).

MARCEL GIRAUD Ph.D., University of Paris. Author of the first major work in the field, *Le Métis canadien: son rôle dans l'histoire des provinces de l'Ouest* (1945) which, as a result of a grant from the Canada Council, is to be reissued in 1985 in English translation by the University of Alberta Press. Also author of the four-volume work, *Histoire de la Louisiane française*.

JOHN S. LONG Ed. D. candidate, University of Toronto, Ontario Institute for Studies in Education. Authority on history of missionaries, schooling, treaty-signing, local communities and fur trade families in the James Bay region; teacher, Northern Lights Secondary School, Moosonee, Ontario. Author of articles in *Ontario History, The Canadian Journal of Native Studies, Papers of the 16th Algonquian Conference, Teacher Education,* and of *A Canadian Indian Bibliography 1960–1970*.

TRUDY NICKS Ph.D., anthropology, University of Alberta. Associate curator of ethnology, Royal Ontario Museum. Author of "The Iroquois and the

Fur Trade in Western Canada," *Old Trails and New Directions*, edited by C.M. Judd and A.J. Ray (1980) and "Iroquois Fur Traders and their Descendants in Alberta," *Annual Report of the Métis Association of Alberta* (1980). Her 1980 thesis is entitled "Demographic Anthropology of Native Populations in Western Canada, 1800–1975."

KENNETH MORGAN Associate professor of genetics, University of Alberta.

JACQUELINE PETERSON Ph.D., history, University of Illinois at Chicago. Assistant professor of native American studies and history at Washington State University. Author of five articles on Great Lakes métis, and others on the fur trade and native American women. A former assistant director of the Newberry Library Center for the History of the American Indian. Co-organizer of the first international Conference on the Métis in North America, September 1981, Newberry Library, Chicago. Research associate of the *Atlas of Great Lakes Indian History*, Helen Hornbeck Tanner, general editor (1985). Winner of the 1984 Robert F. Heizer Award in ethnohistory.

IRENE M. SPRY LL.D. *hon. caus.* Professor emeritus of economics, University of Ottawa. A senior specialist on western Canadian history and resource management. Author of numerous articles, including "The Transition from a Nomadic to a Settled Economy in Western Canada, 1856–96," *Transactions of the Royal Society of Canada*, Section II (June 1968) and "Innis, the Fur Trade, and Modern Economic Problems," in *Old Trails and New Directions* edited by C.M. Judd and A.J. Ray (1980). Editor, *The Papers of the Palliser Expedition* (1968) and Peter Erasmus, *Buffalo Days and Nights* (1976).

ROBERT K. THOMAS M.A., anthropology, University of Chicago. Head, American Indian studies, University of Arizona, Tucson, Arizona. A long-recognized authority on American Indian peoples, author of numerous papers and articles on North American Indian tribes. Contributor to Contemporary American Indians volume of the *Handbook of North American Indians*, edited by Vine Deloria (forthcoming).

SYLVIA VAN KIRK Ph.D., history, University of London, England. Associate professor of history and women's studies, University of Toronto. Author of numerous articles on fur trade social history and of *"Many Tender Ties": Women in Fur Trade Society, 1670–1870* (1980). Currently working on the Alexander Ross family and (with Jennifer S.H. Brown) on the papers of Nor'Wester George Nelson, 1802–1823.

Index

Printed in the USA
CPSIA information can be obtained
at www.ICGtesting.com
JSHW012020140824
68134JS00033B/2797